UP SPIRITS

UP SPIRITS

A young tot-drinker's memoir

PETER BROADBENT

CHAPLIN BOOKS

www.chaplinbooks.co.uk

First published as an ebook in 2016 by
Chaplin Books
Gosport PO12 4UN
This edition published 2018
www.chaplinbooks.co.uk

ISBN: 978-1-911105-40-4

CONTENTS

ODE TO THE TOT

In the days of Admiral Nelson
Or it might have been before.
The Navy got its heritage
Its customs and its law.
Now some of these were good things
And some of them were not
But they'll never find how to replace
That daily little tot.
It isn't served haphazard
Like tea or even beer
But with pencil, book and water
And other useless gear.
Jack Dusty and his winger
Perform a sacred rite
They brew a swill called 'two & one'
Over which we have to fight.
With bottle, jug and fanny
We muster at the shrine
'Get into line, you sailors
... that first fanny's mine.'
Then with murmured incantations
Such as 'seven, one, two'
The high priest and his acolyte
Dispense the holy brew.
When the seas are breaking over
And you feel you've had enough
When the chef has dropped his tatties
And his oppo's burnt the duff.
When your locker's full of hogwash
And your hammock's gone to rot
There's nothing that can quite touch it
... your daily little TOT.

FOREWORD

I WANTED to record, from a young man's perspective, that most enjoyable of moments immediately before lunch when all of us who were entitled gathered around the mess table and kept the tradition of tot time and rum-fuelled, lower-deck dialogue alive.

The messdeck tot, for those below the rank of Petty Officer, was known as grog and consisted of one gill (0.142 litres) of neat rum mixed with two gills of clean water. The addition of water prevented us from stock-piling it.

'Up Spirits' was piped at 11:45 every day. In a corner of a messdeck somewhere onboard, someone would respond in the time-honoured fashion ...

'Stand fast the Holy Ghost.'

I was still serving on 31 July 1970 - 'Black Tot Day' - when the Royal Naval tot was officially withdrawn, bringing to an end a tradition dating back more than 300 years.

I joined *HMS Gurkha* when I was twenty years old and this book, interlaced with a good deal of 'tot-time' banter and lamp-swinging, is a reasonably accurate account of her second commission from the dreariness of a Rosyth Dockyard refit in December 1964 through a nine-month stretch in the Persian Gulf visiting Bahrain, Abu Dhabi, Dubai and Muscat before these places became unashamedly wealthy. *HMS Gurkha* was one of the first ships to blockade the port of Beira in March 1966. When she was relieved by *HMS Eskimo*, she was relieved in more than one way. *Eskimo* graciously transferred a crate full of toilet rolls to us at sea when we ran out. In return, we transferred something alcoholic in a brand new Pusser's galvanised bucket that was never returned. I believe that this was the bucket that became the iconic 'Beira Bucket' that is now on display in the Royal Naval Museum, Portsmouth.

We'd been on Beira Patrol because the Government of Rhodesia (now Zimbabwe) had unilaterally declared itself independent; in response the United Nations imposed sanctions and Royal Navy ships were given the task of preventing oil tankers from discharging their cargo at Beira, the nearest port serving land-locked Rhodesia. The blockade was to last nine years.

Beira Patrol was a lacklustre and monotonous affair. To alleviate boredom, HM ships devised a variety of ways to make the time more pleasurable. Sods' operas and inter-ship competitions were very popular, varied and sometimes bloody. The prize of these contests was the Beira Bucket, generally won by the relieving vessel and occasionally hoisted high on the winning ship's yardarm.

HMS Gurkha was one of the last ships to allow a 'run ashore' in Aden. She suffered an engine room fire after leaving the Seychelles en route to Aden, but nevertheless made it back through the Suez Canal to Gibraltar in time to celebrate the night England won the World Cup in July 1966.

This book is based on my own personal memories combined with a good deal of 'lamp-swinging' and story telling. The only real people in the book are Miss Margaret Mary Lamin, Sir William Luce, his daughter Miss Diana Luce, Miss Vicky Vigors - and me. No other characters in the book represent, or are based on, actual second commission crewmembers onboard HMS Gurkha.

My sincere apologies to those in authority onboard HMS Gurkha at the time. My characterisation has been done for amusement and in no way reflects the attitude or professionalism of anybody. My criticism of the Stokers and Communication Branches is also done for laughs and in no way reflects their professionalism. I also apologise to anybody who held decision-making positions at Pudsey Town Hall. I hope that I don't offend anybody. If I do, please accept my apologies: I'll buy you a very small beer ... if you can track me down.

I would like to acknowledge the help of Ian Green, George Runacus, David Smith and Anthony Walker who have allowed me to use some photographs and have reminded me of details of HMS Gurkha's second commission. Thank you all.

I hope that my fellow tot 'imbibers' can still smell and taste that unique blend of six of the world's finest

Caribbean rums ...

I leave you with this:

'You cannot imagine how tough these people were: Royal Navy men were a race apart. They walked differently, they talked differently, they dressed differently, they drank excessively and were built to last. They knew if they got drunk they would be punished ... and they still got drunk.'

Peter Broadbent (P/053653)
Ex Junior Seaman 2nd class
Hondón de Las Nieves, Spain.

PS: Miss Diana Luce met Lieutenant David Hart-Dyke onboard *HMS Gurkha* and they subsequently married. 'Four Weeks in May' (A Captain's Story of War at Sea) published by Atlantic Books, is David Hart-Dyke's story of his time as Captain of *HMS Coventry* during the Falklands Conflict: it's a remarkable book.

1
A Dryad RP2?

I'M THE only person joining *HMS Dryad* this morning and the only person in the Ship's Office queue.

'Name?'

'Broadbent.'

'Rate?'

'Able Seaman.'

The face is different but the attitude of the world-weary Petty Officer sitting on the opposite side of the chest-high counter is exactly the same as the last time I joined the Royal Navy's Radar Plotting establishment at Southwick. He flicks through his card index tray with nicotined fingers before looking up at me with unfriendly eyes.

'You tired, laddie?'

'No, PO.' I stiffen slightly: he's a Scotsman.

'Then don't lean on my counter.'

I straighten up.

He looks at my right arm. 'Are you the Able Seaman Broadbent who repeatedly failed his simple starring exam a couple of years ago?'

'Yes.'

'Yes what?'

'Yes, PO.'

'What simpleton recommended you for an RP2 course, Able Seaman Broadbent?'

'Don't know, PO.'

'So,' he said, waving my index card in front of me. 'What shall we do with you until your course starts?'

'Sullage party?' I suggest: I'd enjoyed a stint dealing with *Dryad*'s rubbish the last time I was here.

'Sullage party ... sullage party.' He scratches the side of his veined nose with his pen. 'A perfect combination perhaps ... you and rubbish. I'll talk to the Buffer.' He drops his pen. 'You're in Ross 8 mess. Report to the Buffer at 08:00 tomorrow morning.' He slaps *Dryad*'s ridiculously complicated joining routine papers on top of the counter. 'Complete those and return them fully stamped by 15:30 today. Next! And don't you lean on my counter, laddie.'

There is nobody behind me.

As I turn to leave, the Petty Officer lights a needle thin, hand-rolled tickler.

HMS Dryad is a familiar place and I take my time getting some of my joining routine stamped and signed at the numerous offices and hideaways. With half of it complete I decide that enough is enough for the time being: having reached the magic age of twenty I'm looking forward to my tot and dinner.

Tot-time at *Dryad* is an anti-social affair. I join an orderly queue under the watchful eye of the Officer-of-the-Day, the duty Regulator and the Master-at-Arms to show my ID card and be ticked off on the 'entitled' list.

It's my first day, my joining routine is only half finished and my name doesn't yet appear on the list.

'Stand over there,' says the Leading Regulator, waving me away before nodding to the bloke behind me. 'Name?' I wait patiently until the queue has gone. The Officer-of-the-Day takes a while to calculate, from my date of birth shown on my ID card, that I am old enough to draw my tot.

'Your joining routine should have been completed before you came for your tot, young man,' says the Master-at-Arms, glaring at me from beneath the peak of his cap.

'Didn't realise that, Master,' I reply as I wrap my 'green coat' tightly around me.

He nods towards a tray on which stands a solitary glass of 'two-in-one'.

I grab it, knock it back, place my empty glass upside-down on a tray near the dining hall door and slope off without a backward glance. The tot was over-diluted and disappointing. I stifle the time-honoured post-tot belch as I join the back of the dinner queue.

The benefit of my tot doesn't kick in until I am partway through choosing the least unappetising of the over-cooked vegetables on offer.

'What are these, chef?' I ask, waving a hand at a tray full of purple-tinged stuff.

'I'm a cook ... not a ferkin detective,' replies the bloke, brandishing a vegetable scoop. He sniffs and wipes his nose on his sleeve. 'Want some or not?'

'Stick 'em.'

'Please your ferkin self.'

*

So begins an enjoyable period working as a member of *HMS Dryad*'s Sullage Party. It's a 'Blue Card job', which means I don't have to do duty watch and I therefore avoid the indignity of having to sleep fully clothed in a Nissan hut as part of *Dryad*'s Emergency Party armed with a badly fitting tin hat, a Pusser's torch and a night stick.

The canteen lady, who hands me my Saturday morning stand-easy tea and cheese roll, asks me if I am still in touch with Wilco.

'No, not recently.'

'She's living with a Chinese bloke apparently ... in Hong Kong.'

'Really?'

'In the latest issue of the NAAFI Magazine someone wrote that she was getting engaged to an Oriental magnate.'

I vividly picture the advertisement that regularly ran in *The Beano* for a powerful magnet. I'm completely confused. 'A what?' I ask.

'An Oriental magnate,' she replies, pulling an equally confused expression. 'Don't ask me, love ... I only pour the teas.' She overfills my cup and wipes up the tea puddle with a grubby cloth.

I pay for my tea and cheese roll. My stomach does something unusual. I've suddenly lost my appetite.

*

Despite the weather being awful, Easter leave is a welcome break. I go to Elland Road on Good Friday and watch a surprisingly efficient Leeds United give Newcastle United a footballing lesson. Johnny Giles, a new signing from Manchester United, is brilliant and scores the game's only goal. The toilets are in the same disgusting condition as they were the season before last. On the plus side, my half-time pie has a little less gristle in it than I remember.

I'm no longer inclined to wear my uniform while on leave: I've realised that a Royal Naval uniform doesn't impress anybody these days, particularly the girls of land-locked West Yorkshire. That oft-used phrase 'the decade of free love' when referring to the 1960s unfortunately doesn't apply to 1965 West Yorkshire: as far as I'm aware Pudsey hasn't signed-up to it.

I ask Mum what an Oriental magnate might be. After a bit of a laugh she explains that it could mean someone from the Orient who has lots of money. I don't know if I'm pleased for Wilco or not. I certainly miss her and I decide that I'm more than a little jealous of the Oriental bloke who is currently enjoying her skills.

*

Last year, onboard *HMS Lincoln* in the Far East, I eventually passed my starring exam and was promoted to Able Seaman. Despite being kept away from anything remotely Radar-related while onboard *Lincoln*, I was

Outside the entrance to Fort Purbrook. A class of experienced Radar Plotters (the exception being the lad second from the right on the back row)

mistakenly recommended for an RP2 course when I left the ship. I don't know who recommended me - probably either someone who doesn't know me or who has made a potentially dangerous clerical error.

One wet and windy afternoon, while slumped in the Laundry after all the day's rubbish has been collected and dumped, I decide that it's time I got to grips with this Radar Plotting stuff. Otherwise I will be branded a complete dead-loss to the Royal Navy's most up-to-date branch.

My RP2 course starts on the second day of June 1964. Our Course Instructor tells us that concentration is the key to Radar Plotting success - concentration and more concentration.

Along with the rest of class RP2/40 I become a regular at the Red Lion and the Golden Lion public houses in Southwick village. Most nights, I stagger up the back drive and sit hung-over in Fort Purbrook's or *Dryad*'s classrooms the following morning trying my best to concentrate.

At the end of June I surprise myself by passing the Fort Purbrook part of the course. I get an official pass mark, but am nearer the bottom of the class than the top.

I will miss the NAAFI steak & kidney pies that were a favourite Stand-easy treat from the Fort's NAAFI canteen. I will also miss the relaxing morning and the end-of-day bus journey to and from *Dryad* along the top of Portsdown Hill.

The remainder of the course is at *HMS Dryad* itself and the possibility of getting roped-in for morning Divisions is a disturbing possibility.

In mid August I surprise the Royal Navy's Radar Plotting branch and, more importantly, their Lords at the Admiralty by passing the RP2 course with a creditable 77 percent. I'm not the top of the class, but nor am I the bottom. I spend the entire evening unpicking my RP3 badges and replacing them with RP2 badges. I'm flabbergasted and more than a little proud of myself ... I think I may have mastered this concentration business.

After returning to the Sullage Party, I realise that being an RP2 doesn't impress my intellectual superiors in the pig-sties. Once fed, they totally ignore me and my new status.

*

It's a dismal day when I am summoned to the Ship's Office. The world-weary Petty Officer sitting behind his chest-high desk looks at me for a moment, scratches the side of his nose with his pen, exhales and sighs. 'Able Seaman Broadbent, you are living, walking, talking proof that miracles do happen ... even at HMS Dryad.'

'Am I, PO?'

'How in heaven's name did you pass the course?'

'Concentration and lots of hard work, PO.'

'I think their Lords at the Admiralty should re-examine the course syllabus.'

'If you say so, PO.'

'Sarcasm is far too sophisticated for you, young man.' He waves a card in front of my face. 'You have a draft.'

I question him by raising an eyebrow.

'HMS Gurkha, Rosyth in December,' he says enthusiastically.

'Thank you, PO.'

'Fortunately a good distance away from the centre of Royal Naval operations on the south coast.'

'Yes, PO. Thanks.'

I saunter back to the Laundry. Rosyth. As if life couldn't get any worse: December north of the ferkin border ... oh no! I make a point of telling the pigs that I have a draft to Scotland. They smile, break wind and retire indoors without a backward glance.

*

Summer leave is a relaxing affair. I have no girlfriend and the football season is finished. I meet up with a couple of my old school friends but we have little in common. I spend some time watching Pudsey Saint Lawrence play cricket but I don't see my mate Sir Len at any of the matches.

Mum takes my forthcoming visit to Scotland with a pinch of salt: she is getting used to my globetrotting.

It is the first time since joining the Navy that I really don't mind going back at the end of my two weeks leave. I'm bored with the limited delights of Pudsey and am looking forward to seeing my messmates again.

At the end of November I assemble with the rest of *HMS Gurkha*'s Radar Plotters for five days Pre Commissioning Training. My recently perfected concentration skills are once again stretched to their limit as I learn all about the new Tribal Class frigates and the new type of radar they have onboard. We are a varied bunch, ranging from a Petty Officer at the top of the RP pyramid to a group of Junior Seamen Radar Plotters fresh out of the basic course at *Dryad* at the base. Along with three other RP2s, I am ranked somewhere in the middle.

Dryad has constructed a copy of a Tribal Class Frigate's Operation Room and we spend hour after hour cooped up in this darkened space while the Senior RP and the occasional Officer show up to assess our performance. *HMS Gurkha* has a sophisticated long-range air search radar that I know nothing about.

Me and a bloke called Mack McCubbin from Scotland are thrown together on more than one occasion and begin to work as a team. Mack qualified as an RP2 five months ago and is pleased to be drafted to Rosyth as he lives in a place called Queensferry which he says is nearby.

In December I return my folded and ironed overalls in a mock ceremony held in Dryad's laundry at the end of my last day on Sullage Party. Everybody wishes me well.

To rub it in, someone plays a dirge on his nose that he thinks sounds like a badly tuned bagpipe.

*

As the train clatters over the Forth Railway Bridge, I glimpse Rosyth through the swirling Scottish mist. It hasn't changed since I was last here on *HMS Bermuda*. If anything, at this time of year it looks less welcoming.

On arrival at *HMS Cochrane*, we Radar Plotters are allocated a murky mess-space below the waterline onboard *HMS Hartland Point,* a manky floating accommodation vessel berthed some distance away. Some of us grab hammock-slinging points, others find places to lay out their hammocks on a dry section of deck. Alongside us is *HMS Girdleness* and the destroyer *HMS Chevron* both used as overflow accommodation ships.

I am grabbed by the shoulder as I'm stuffing my kit into a small, smelly locker under a hull-side bench.

'Well, if it isn't the boy heaving-line thrower! Are you following me around the fleet, you ugly old bastard?'

I turn to face a smiling oppo of mine. 'Hey Sugar, you ugly old bastard.'

'And you, you young bugger. How are you?'

'I was OK ... before I arrived in this ferkin dump.'

Sugar and I were onboard *HMS Bermuda* together and we bumped into each other in Singapore last year. He was one of the Able Seamen who helped me, as a newly promoted Ordinary Seaman, come to terms with the intimidating main Seamen's Mess onboard *Bermadoo*. We clashed at times when a heaving-line thrower was required on the quarterdeck as we both reckon we're brilliant at it.

'You on Gurkha?' he asks.

'Yep, you?'

'Yep. Get changed and we'll have a couple of wets in the Canteen. Do your joining routine tomorrow.'

I nod. 'Is there anybody else ex Bermadoo here?'

'Not as far as I know. They're all probably locked up securely somewhere.' He laughs.

'Yeah, right.'

The Rosyth Dockyard Canteen hasn't changed since I was last here. The snooker tables look a little worse for wear. There are patched areas and dark cigarette burns on the not-so-green baize and the wooden surround is patterned by the circular marks left by thousands of damp pint glasses. The linoleum deck is stickier than I remember. On the plus side, the local 'Heavy' is brilliant.

Sugar buys the first round. He has brought his mate 'Jack' Tarr with him, a gunner from Cumbria.

True to form, Sugar spends some time chatting to the peroxide-blonde lady behind the bar whose party piece is pulling a couple of pints of Heavy at the same time from pumps three feet apart. She has impressive upper arms, well-developed shoulders and a cleavage that is full of Highland promise.

Returning to our table, Sugar spreads his hands palm upwards and smiles. 'The lady behind the bar has invited me home for tea and stickies.'

'Tea and stickies?' I say.

'Metaphorical.'

'Wha?'

'Metaphorically speaking.'

'What's meta ferkin forical when it's at home?' I ask.

Jack leans on his elbows. 'It's when you say something that represents something completely different. He may not actually be going to her place for tea and stickies.'

Sugar nods and winks. 'Correct. I hope to be offered something much more enjoyable.'

'More enjoyable than tea and stickies?' I ask seriously.

Sugar waves a hand at me. 'There speaks a Yorkshireman.'

I've asked a number of times before, but nevertheless I ask again. 'How do you do it, Shugs? You've only been here a quarter of an hour. What have you got that the rest of us haven't?'

'Charisma, young Peter ... charisma,' he smirks. 'And a noticeable bulge in mi trews.'

'But that's your rolled-up hanky,' says Jack.

'You and I know that, Jack,' says a smiling Sugar. 'You and I.'

'What's this about a hanky?' I ask.

'Finish your beer, young 'un. It's your round.'

'What's her name?' asks Jack.

'Sorcha.'

'Sorcha?'

'Apparently it's Gaelic for "bright",' says Sugar. 'I know it's naff, but she says I can call her Bridgette if it makes me feel better.' He wraps his coat around himself. 'I'll let you into a secret, lads.' He bends low and whispers. 'I spent the whole of yesterday evening at the bar chatting up Sorcha. Groundwork, my friends, groundwork. Always worth the time and effort.'

Our mouths hang open as we watch Sugar and Sorcha, each cupping the other's bottom, amble towards the exit door and depart without so much as a backward glance.

*

The following morning Sugar is bleary-eyed as we muster for both watches.

'Good night, was it?' I ask.

'Unbelievable. I think I met my match last night in the suburbs of Dalgety Bay. Either that or I'm out of practice.'

'Where?'

'Dalgety Bay - somewhere to the east of here.'

'Was it everything you hoped it would be?'

Sugar blinked repeatedly. 'Give me a moment.'

'OK.'

'More, young Pete,' mumbles Sugar. 'Much more.'

'Did you call her Bridgette?'

'A number of times ... if memory serves me.'

*

The weather clamped firmly above the Firth of Forth is dreadful and shows little prospect of improvement. The Scots onboard have all opted for second leave so that they can celebrate something distinctly Celtic. A week before Christmas, along with the majority of *Gurkha*'s non-Scottish crew, I depart Rosyth for the more mellow climate south of the border. I leave my ship in the capable hands of those who commemorate something called Hogmanay.

As I travel south through Newcastle and York the weather barely improves. West Yorkshire has its own micro-climate at this time of the year. To emphasise the fact that Yorkshire folk are a sturdy breed, the conditions scream winter. On my arrival in Leeds the white stuff is a foot-and-a-half thick, with more hovering like an intimidating grey blanket above my head. West Yorkshire is preparing to shut itself down: this is how it survives this time of year.

My mother owns a busy off-licence business at 63 Robin Lane in Pudsey; my younger brother Tony lives at home having recently left school. During the Industrial Revolution, Pudsey was reputed to be one of the most polluted areas of the UK due to its position in a valley midway between the two industrial cities of Leeds and Bradford. The valley trapped pollutants and created thick black smogs. This is believed to have led to jokes that pigeons in Pudsey fly backwards in order to keep the soot out of their eyes and that residents put up chicken wire fences to keep the fog out. Despite Pudsey's grimy history it is the place where I grew up and I have a soft spot for it.

I was educated at the superb Greenside Primary school and then at its brilliant grammar school. I learned to swim in the local swimming baths, made some interesting friends and enjoyed a brief physical entanglement with the well-developed girl who lived next door but one.

Pudsey is typical Yorkshire, an area of England known for its deep pockets and short arms. When I arrive, the main subject of conversation is how Pudsey will illuminate and decorate the town centre for the festive period. A front page article in the local paper reports that the town centre illuminations this year will be provided by the Assistant Secretary to the Chief Clerk who has been instructed to leave her office light on in the Town Hall over the Christmas holidays. One of our customers, who works at the Town Hall, is outraged at this display of civic extravagance and says it should be re-examined.

I'm surprised when I take a wander around the darkened Market Place on Christmas Eve and notice a single light from one of the Town Hall windows casting a mellow, yellow glow on the pavement outside. Maybe there is a growing age of recklessness within the corridors of Pudsey's civic offices.

Christmas morning is a low-key affair. The weather has prevented anybody going into Leeds to buy anything, so we pass each other as much money as we can afford. I end up with enough to buy myself the Charlie Buchan's 1965 Soccer Annual. We enjoy a brilliant Christmas lunch of turkey and for the first time I have an entire bottle of Tetley's Family Ale all to myself. The snow stops briefly as Christmas Day draws to a chilly, West Yorkshire close.

I forego the pleasure of the Boxing Day match at Elland Road because the snow has started again and the Sammy Ledgards bus service between Pudsey and Leeds is cancelled. It's just as well as Leeds United can only muster a scrappy 1-1 draw against Blackburn Rovers.

There is a letter in the Boxing Day edition of the local paper from an anonymous Town Hall employee, complaining about the 'frittering away' of taxpayers' money on the Christmas illuminations. He, or she, claims that a similar effect could have been obtained from a 60-watt bulb instead of the 100-watt bulb that was used. The writer hopes that fiscal lessons will be learned before next year's festive period.

My leave expires on the morning of 27th December. Tony and I spend an hour or more clearing the waist-high snow from the front door. I say my goodbyes and hang around the bus stop outside the shop in the hope that Sammy Ledgards can negotiate the sludgy roads as far as Leeds City Railway station. It's important that I get back north of the border so that my Scottish colleagues can go 'haeme' to celebrate Hogmanay.

*

Jack and I are in the habit of going to the payday dance at the Mecca in Dunfermline every other week. Jack, who is an enthusiastic dancer, is the first to latch onto a woman, who dances with him all evening. Sometime later, I manage to have more than one dance with a Scottish girl called Lorna. Initially I have a problem with her Fife accent but I work hard to come to terms with it as Lorna is a good-looking lassie ... and a nurse!

The following night I smother myself in Old Spice toiletries, courtesy of Sugar, and catch the bus into Dunfermline. Lorna and I have arranged to meet in the main bus station. We spend a brilliant evening in a bar where we drink frugally and talk about each other nonstop. She is the eldest daughter of Mr & Mrs McDoone frae Limekilns. By the end of the evening, we know an awful lot about each other and have built the foundations of an Anglo-Scots relationship. She works at the hospital in Kirkcaldy. We kiss each other briefly after I chaperone her the short distance to Dunfermline's bus station to catch her bus home.

During the following month my relationship with Lorna develops along traditional Anglo-Scots lines: seriously non-sexual. It is plainly obvious, even to a relatively inexperienced young Sassenach like me, that the senior members of the McDoone clan don't take kindly to their eldest daughter walkin' oot with a transient English sailor. Lorna's younger sister takes a serious dislike to me.

*

At the beginning of February, *Gurkha*'s refit is visibly coming to an end. The Captain clears lower deck and assembles us in the dining hall as it's raining cats and ferkin dogs everywhere else in Scotland.

We shuffle our freezing feet as an Officer with three gold rings on his arm introduces himself as the Captain.

'Gurkha ship's company stand at ease and relax,' he says. 'I won't keep you from your duties for longer than is absolutely necessary. Firstly may I tell you that you are crew members of one of the Royal Navy's most advanced class of frigates, the Tribal class. As regards our programme, all I can tell you at the moment is that we are due to start day-running out of Rosyth at the end of this month. We will then proceed south for our work-up period at Portland before going to Portsmouth to take part in this year's Navy Days. We are programmed to depart for the Persian Gulf sometime in October, a tour of duty that is scheduled to last eight to nine months. We are due back in Rosyth in August of next year. Before I end I am told that it is traditional for us all to learn *HMS Gurkha*'s war cry ... 'Ayo Gurkhali' which means 'the Gurkhas are here!"

We look at each other.

'Ayo Gurkhali?'

*

On St Valentine's Day we leave the hovel that is *HMS Hartland Point* and are allocated messes onboard a spick and span *HMS Gurkha*. Compared to my previous ships, *Gurkha* is brilliant. She is one of the first Royal Navy frigates to be fully bunked: not a hammock anywhere. We no longer have to collect food from the galley and eat it in the mess as we have a fully equipped dining hall. *HMS Gurkha* is also air-conditioned throughout. Built by Thorneycroft in Southampton and accepted into service three years ago, she is one of the first class of frigates to carry a helicopter. All of *Gurkha*'s bulkhead tallies are embossed plastic; this may not be of much importance to other crew members, but to me this represents a labour-saving leap into the twentieth century. I had spent a good percentage of my time at sea on *HMS Bermuda* polishing brass bulkhead tallies over and over again for no reason other than it kept me busy. I offer up a prayer of thanks to the genius at the Admiralty who agreed to sticky plastic bulkhead tallies.

Gurkha is armed with a single Mark 7 Bofors gun and two 4.5 inch Mark 5 guns salvaged from a Second World War destroyer. She also has a telephone system onboard with handsets in every compartment including messdecks. The disadvantage of this of course, is that people can contact you easily.

According to Clanky Barrowclough, a member of the Stoker's branch I share a table with in the Dockyard Canteen one afternoon, *Gurkha* has an engine arrangement of steam and gas turbine called COSAG. Apparently she is able to cruise on her steam plant and use both systems driving the same shaft for a high-speed boost. The other Tribal class frigates currently in commission are *HMS Ashanti, Eskimo, Mohawk, Nubian, Tartar* and *Zulu*.

I give Lorna a Valentine's card this evening; in return, on the back seat of an empty and distinctly cold double-decker bus, I am rewarded with a lingering kiss. Lorna McDoone is becoming quite good at kissing ... and a first-class slapper of wandering hands.

*

Tuesday 16th February 1965 is my twenty-first birthday. Along with some of my new *Gurkha* messmates, Sugar, 'Burbs' Macintosh, 'Kit' Carson and 'Jack' Tarr, I go ashore on a birthday party pub crawl in Dunfermline. At exactly 22:05 all of us, very drunk and probably obnoxious, refuse to comply with the bizarre Scottish custom of not having any 'drinking up' time. Baton-wielding members of the City Constabulary arrive to bundle us out of the bar, down a long series of steps and into the back of a waiting Black Maria. We are whisked away to a local underground dungeon complex where we are each allocated an individual cell. I am thrown a handful of handkerchief-sized blankets to keep me warm. The unpainted stone walls of my accommodation, deep in the solid stone bowels of Dunfermline, run with condensation and the naked, high wattage light bulb is kept on all night.

In the morning I am woken before sun-up. I think I can hear the clink of cups and the smell of crisply fried bacon but it proves to be my imagination as nothing comes my way. In the charge room at ground level, our names are logged and a head-and-shoulders photograph of each of us it taken. All five of us are then released without charge. Sugar asks if we can have a lift back to the Dockyard.

The response from the spluttering night-shift custody sergeant is ... brief. 'Ferk off all o' yea.'

Seated on a couple of cold stone slab benches in a dank, dripping open-air bus station we exchange experiences of a night none of us can clearly remember. Burbs tells us that he had a couple of full-sized blankets last night and was awakened with a cup of strong, hot tea and a couple of shortbread biscuits this morning.

'Wha?'

'Wha?'

'Whaaaa?'

Faced with such an orchestrated series of grumbling queries, Burbs admits that he is bullshitting about the shortbread biscuits.

'You got tea though?'

'Yeah,' he says, blushing.

'Nothing to do with you being Scottish I suppose,' splutters Sugar.

'Naah,' replies Burbs.

'Of course it was,' says Kit, who lights his third cigarette of the morning.

'I didn't get a morning cuppa,' says Sugar.

'Oh you poor, unfortunate bastard,' says Jack.

Blissfully unaware of my incarceration, Lorna spent the evening at home in the bosom of her family playing a Scottish edition of Monopoly ... with matchsticks.

The following day, Lorna's sister learns of my birthday arrest and informs Mr & Mrs McDoone - who are overjoyed. They are delighted that their daughter's boyfriend has his photograph displayed on the board outside the entrance to St Margaret's public house, alongside pictures of all the other individuals who are barred for life.

Lorna and I make a special trip to Dunfermline to see my photograph. Standing outside the entrance Lorna declares that my picture, bottom row left, is a good likeness.

I notice that Burbs' picture isn't posted.

We find another bar to spend our evening.

*

The following week *HMS Gurkha* slips away from Rosyth Dockyard early in the morning. There is nobody on the jetty to wish us 'God Speed' as it's a particularly damp and dreary Monday morning. It's the start of a two-week period during which *Gurkha* never travels far from the Firth of Forth. Most of our time is spent in calibrating machinery to check that everything is functioning correctly.

I am the Senior RP of one of the four Operations Room teams charged with maintaining an up-to-date surface picture for those on the bridge. As an RP2, I am responsible for communicating with the bridge. I find it a lot easier than I thought it would be.

We have a small hangar down aft. According to those that know about such things, our flight deck is actually the roof of the hangar that can be lowered to stow the helicopter away. Our helicopter is missing.

My mess is on the starboard side and is home to sixteen of us under the watchful eye of Leading Seaman Chats Harris. We have a functioning air conditioning unit on the after bulkhead. I have picked a middle bunk as far away from the noisy mess square as possible. On the port side, separated down *Gurkha*'s centreline, is a mess that is a mirror image of ours and is home to half a dozen members of the Communication Branch and a good number of Seamen. We have three empty bunks.

Chats Harris is only a year and a half older than me. However, while I was gallivanting around the Far East, he had realised the benefits of promotion and knuckled down to study. At the first morning stand-easy Chats assembles everyone in the mess who is entitled to draw their tot in order to establish tot-time rules and the selection of a mess Rum Bosun.

Able Seaman 'Kit' Carson, the oldest Able Seaman in the mess, would traditionally be offered the job of mess Rum Bosun. However, Chats is not keen on the idea.

'How long have you had your set ... beard, Kit?'

'Can't remember exactly, seven and a half years about.'

Chats points at Kit's unkempt beard with the mess pencil. He half closes his eyes and examines the beard closely. 'No offence, Kit, but you probably have within the confines of your facial hair the remains of long forgotten meals ... not to mention sneezes, coughs and God help us ... a variety of sexual encounters.'

'There's been a few of those I can tell ya ... sexual encounters,' says Kit puffing his chest out and smirking.

'Those we can overlook. It's the decaying foodstuffs I'm bothered about,' replies Chats.

'I shower regularly.'

'Do you shampoo ... and correctly rinse the facial hair?' Chats wags the pencil at the offending article.

'Course not. Just rinse it.' Kit looks perplexed.

'I have a rule,' says Chats, inflating his chest. 'Nobody with a set does Rum Bosun in my mess. You're not dangling that abortion anywhere near my tot.'

Kit strokes his beard, knowing that it's traditional that the mess rum Bosun is entitled to 'sippers' of everyone's tot as he dishes it out.

Chats looks around and claps his hands. 'Anybody object to having a clean-shaven Rum Bosun?'

Silence.

Kit stuffs his hands in his pockets, shuffles off to a far corner and slumps himself down facing the bulkhead.

'OK, we need a clean-shaven volunteer for the job of Rum Bosun.'

Instinctively I realise that I'm not experienced enough to volunteer, so I don't. Jack puts his hand up.

'Any objections to Jack being the mess Rum Bosun?'

Silence.

Chats points at Jack. 'Not planning on growing a set are you, Jack?'

'No. Don't worry,' replies a semi-joyful Jack who is on the verge of getting himself the best job in the mess. He can leave work fifteen minutes early to collect the mess's issue of rum ... and get numerous 'sippers' for the privilege.

'I officially declare that Able Seaman Tarr is the official Rum Boson for the mess,' says Chats. 'Congratulations Jack.'

Jack stands, takes a bow and grabs the mess Rum Fanny.

'UP SPIRITS.'

'Stand fast the Holy Ghost,' mumbles Jan.

The first 'tot-time' onboard follows the time-honoured procedure. Jack collects the rum at exactly 11:45. At the head of the mess table the tot glasses are arranged on either side of the mess dishcloth that has been placed flat on the table so that the rum fanny will not slide when *Gurkha* moves. Jack returns to the mess at about 12:00. Using his Rum Bosun's glass, he measures out the individual tots. All the glasses are brand new and virgin clean. In the coming months they, along with the rum fanny itself, will never have their inner surface washed and will gradually develop an amber coating. Conventionally, the Rum Bosun is invited to take 'sippers' from everybody's tot before handing it over. Individual tots are normally downed in one and rarely sipped.

As this is both the time and place where much future business will be conducted, official tot-trading rules are established. Semi-specific values of 'snifters', 'sippers', 'wets', 'gulpers' and 'halfers' are agreed. Rules regarding over indulgence are discussed ... and ignored.

After all the tots have been issued the rum fanny is 'squeezed' to extract every last drop. Depending on how cack-handed the issuing Jack Dusty has been, there is normally some rum left after everybody has had their tot: this is called 'Queen's' and is passed around for everybody to take sippers until all is consumed.

Today the Queen's are plentiful. Jack's final task is to collect all the glasses, wipe the outsides, check for damage and stow them in a locker along with the dishcloth adjacent to the fanny ready for the following day. A sulky Kit says he doesn't want any of the Queen's.

Duly primed, those 'entitled' enjoy a beer chaser and saunter to the Dining Hall for dinner where food is consumed and much rum-fuelled nonsense is discussed.

*

Much to my surprise, at the beginning of March, Petty Officer 'Frothy' Beer, Mack McCubbin and I are sent back to *HMS Dryad* to do something called a Helicopters Controllers course. Frothy is overjoyed as his wife and children are still living in *Dryad*'s married quarters.

2

Me ... a helicopter controller?

THE SAME unsmiling, apathetic Petty Officer is sitting behind the chest-high counter in *Dryad*'s Ship's Office stuffing his copious nasal hairs up his nose with the end of his pen

I cough.

He looks up and points his pen at me. 'Able Seaman Broadbent RP2. Welcome back ... you continue to amaze and baffle me.'

'Pardon, PO?'

'Tell me, do you have friends in high places?'

'No, PO.'

'Did your ex-NAAFI girlfriend have influence with anybody in high places?'

'I doubt it, PO.'

He waves an index card at me. 'We have the doubtful pleasure of welcoming you here to do a Helicopter Controllers course, I take it.'

'I know, PO.' I nod at Mack who is standing behind me. 'We were told before we left Scotland.'

'Your NAAFI girl, according to the buzz, is enjoying herself in Singapore ... or is it Hong Kong ... with a real man.'

'I believe so ... a magnet, I believe.'

'Correct.' He shuffles some papers. 'OK. You and Able Seaman McCubbin will begin your course on Monday at 08:30 in classroom Delta 4. Petty Officer Beer will be your course instructor.'

'Thank you, PO.'

'If you successfully complete this course I'll ... I'll lose the will to live, Broadbent ... and I'll probably eat my cap.'

'I'll try my very best then, PO.'

The mess allocated to those of us doing short courses at *HMS Dryad* is the one furthest away from the Dining Hall. The prefabricated hut is long past its best. The buildings were hurriedly placed here during a Second World War summer with no thought of them remaining beyond autumn. In the November chill, some twenty years later, they are just about tolerable when full of people: when empty, they are freezing. The bathrooms and heads are detached and some distance away outside. The mess fresh-water tank is located high above the mess corrugated iron roof and is un-insulated. When a north wind blows we can't shower or flush the heads.

*

On a cold, grey Monday morning, Petty Officer Beer, Able Seaman Mack McCubbin and I muster in classroom Delta Four.

Being a Helicopter Controller means sitting in front of a radar screen, tracking and communicating with a helicopter while keeping the bridge informed of the helicopter's position and condition. We are responsible for relaying to the helicopter, in clear and concise terms, any operational instructions from the Operations Room Officer and/or the Officer of the Watch on the Bridge. We also keep a watchful eye on the surrounding airspace to identify and report any other aircraft in the area.

In addition to learning all the procedures associated with controlling *Gurkha*'s as yet unseen helicopter, we learn something about the machine itself: the Naval variation of the Westland Wasp. It has a specially designed undercarriage and the ability to 'negative pitch' the main rotor-blades so that it can be safely landed onboard a pitching flight-deck. The tail boom and main rotor blades have been specially designed to fold so that it can be stowed away in our small hangar.

I can understand how useful the Wasp could be for collecting and posting our mail, but I'm surprised to learn that it can also be transformed into a quarrelsome machine with the addition of a couple of live torpedoes. It has seats for three passengers and can carry a stretchered casualty across the rear cabin if required. Apparently, it can cruise at 90 knots for about six hours under North European conditions.

There is a lot of difficult controlling jargon to learn on the course, but I apply my not-yet-forgotten concentration skills and eventually it all makes sense. Both Mack and I sail through the course with a good deal of support from Frothy. Unfortunately, no badge is attached to our newly acquired qualification.

The Petty Officer in the Ship's Office is absent when Mack and I appear to start our leaving routine. The killick who hands us our travel documents tells me that his boss is having difficulty chewing his way through the chinstay of his cap.

While Mack and I prepare to make our way back to Scotland, Frothy wrangles himself an extra week in *Dryad*'s Married Quarters. Rumour has it that his very attractive wife refuses to accompany her husband anywhere north of Waterlooville.

*

Back onboard, running out of Rosyth and east down the Firth of Forth becomes a daily occurrence. As part of the Ops Room Special Sea Dutymen team for our entry and departure down the Firth, I become familiar with the various landmarks along the way. Inchgarvie Island under the russet framework of the Forth Railway Bridge is the first outgoing marker. Travelling east, we pass Cramond Island to the south of us and the small island of Inchmickery with its small T-shaped jetty to the north. Inchkeith Island, with its yellow lighthouse, marks the centre of the Forth between Kirkcaldy and Edinburgh. The Isle of May with its lighthouse and its colony of Shags, signals the end of the Firth of Forth and our entrance into the North Sea.

'Shags eh?' asks one of the young lads in my Ops Room team.

'Don't be so vulgar,' I reply. 'Get on with your plotting.'

'UP SPIRITS.'

Kit has shaved his beard off; he looks strangely different with a pale band of skin where his set used to be.

'Don't recognise you, you clean shaven young man,' says Jack as he doesn't hand him his tot. 'Are you on the 'entitled' list for this mess?'

'It's ferkin me,' says Kit holding out a trembling hand. 'Don't mess me about … give me mi tot.'

Jack looks at Kit's worried face pityingly, takes sippers and hands over his tot.

'How do you feel then … without your set?'

'Naked.'

'Thank God it's only your chin that's exposed then,' says Burbs.

The majority of our days at sea are solitary affairs.

We have no-one to play with and we exercise *Gurkha* all by ourselves. We do regular 'man overboard' rescues with our dummy known throughout the ship as Ordinary Seaman Angus McGillycuddy frae Inverkeithing.

A Chinese laundry crew and a number of Chinese chefs and stewards are transferred to us from one of the other Tribal class frigates that has recently returned from its deployment in the Persian Gulf.

Occasionally, we skip through the Pentland Firth and scuttle along the northern ledge of Scotland where we fire our guns at those places officially designated Ministry of Defence targets. Talmine and Bettyhill are favourite hamlets west of Loch Eriboll that we greet by testing our foghorn whenever we pass, but we never tarry.

Our allies in the RAF take us completely by surprise as we are passing a place called Portskerra. Attacking from overland confuses our long-range air-raid warning team.

'ACTION STATIONS ... ACTION STATIONS. WE ARE UNDER ATTACK BY ENEMY AIRCRAFT FROM OVERLAND TO THE SOUTH. ASSUME DAMAGE CONTROL STATE ONE CONDITION ZULU. DON ANTI FLASH GEAR AND GAS MASK.'

My action station is sitting at the Helicopter Control's spot with Mack McCubbin at my elbow. We don't yet have a Wasp to control so we sit quietly and watch the panic in the Ops Room. Frothy, fresh back from the undoubted delights of *Dryad*'s married quarters, is brilliant: he has an answer to everything that the Ops Room Officer asks of him.

'I've heard that it's our job to defend Great Britain and the RAF's job to deliver our mail,' I tell Mack, who laughs.

'Silence in the corner there,' shouts the Ops Room Officer.

'Bugger, they've noticed us,' says Mack.

*

The Scottish technicians onboard conveniently identify a number of problems that require immediate dockyard attention, so *Gurkha* once again is placed in the hands of Rosyth Dockyard while we take Easter leave.

I spend the first few days of my leave at Limekilns. I don't know how Lorna has arranged it, but I am grudgingly allowed to sleep on the sagging two-seater settee in the lounge for a couple of nights. Each morning Mrs McDoone spends a quarter of an hour or so plumping and re-plumping the settee cushions and spraying them with an English repellent. The younger sister threatens to leave home if I stay for a third night, so I catch a train south to West Yorkshire and my accommodating family.

I soon settle into a Pudsey routine. I go to Elland Road to watch Leeds United, who are FA Cup finalists this year, roundly beat our local rivals Sheffield Wednesday 2-0. We are badly placed in Division One.

I don't have a problem leaving home this time: I'm missing Lorna McDoone but I'm looking forward to *Gurkha* leaving Scotland on her way to England and later to the Middle East.

*

'HANDS TO FLYING STATIONS. FLIGHT DECK CREW MUSTER IN THE HANGAR. FLIGHT DECK FIRE FIGHTING TEAMS CLOSE UP.'

Thankfully, Frothy is already in the Ops Room and is communicating with the Wasp pilot as Mack and I arrive.

'Don't worry lads,' he says, 'I'll get him on the deck

Kate (X-Ray Tango 434)

for you. You go up to the Bridge wings and watch it come in. Give you an idea of what you will be working with.'

It's blowing a Scottish hoollie on the Bridge wings. Mack and I watch as a tiny blue helicopter hovers parallel with our port side. Slowly it moves closer to us and hovers off the hangar before gently disappearing from view. We skip down aft to watch the flight deck crew strap down the helicopter as the pilot switches everything off.

'What are you two doing here?' asks a Chief Petty Officer who appears from nowhere.

'We were sent down from the Ops Room Chief ... to watch the helicopter land,' says Mack.

'We're the Helicopter Controllers, Chief,' I add.

'I don't give a damn where you're from ... or what you are. Clear off.'

'Aye aye, Chief.'

Back in the Ops Room we tell Frothy that we've been bollocked by an unknown Chief Petty Officer. Frothy shrugs his shoulders, says he'll sort it out and tells us to stay behind to meet the pilot.

The pilot, wearing a jump suit covered in badges, is tiny and when he removes his helmet proves to be a bearded individual with a spotty complexion and a boxer's flat nose. Frothy is the first to be formally introduced. Mack and I follow; he is called Lieutenant Morgan. Mack and I christen him 'Pontius', behind his back of course.

'The sign-writer has put her name on the front,' says Pontius.

'Name, sir?' asks Frothy.

'She's now officially called Kate.'

'Why's that, sir?'

'Instructions from on high.'

'Really, sir.'

Mack and I look on in silence.

'She's a nice machine,' says Pontius.

'Is she?' asks a polite Frothy.

The Ops Room Officer invites Pontius to present himself formally to the First Lieutenant.

*

On the first day of May, I discover an English radio station that is broadcasting the FA Cup Final. Unfortunately the Leeds lads are overawed by their first Wembley experience and lose 2-1 to Liverpool.

My relationship with Lorna is on a downward spiral, aided and encouraged by the McDoone clan, who sense that our Anglo-Scottish pairing is flagging. On the few occasions I now go to Lorna's hoose, her parents totally ignore me.

My fears are confirmed the day before we leave Rosyth for the tropical climes of Portsmouth. Lorna decides to end our relationship and call it quits. Reluctantly I agree. At some future time an extremely fortunate individual will enjoy the delights of an unwrapped Lorna McDoone, but regrettably it isn't going to be me.

The following evening a moderate group of family, friends, wives, girlfriends and lovers assemble on the jetty to wave *HMS Gurkha* a proper farewell. *Gurkha*, with its unusually large contingent of Scots, drifts slowly and somewhat reluctantly away from the jetty and the Scottish mainland. I'm not surprised that Lorna isn't among the small send-off party but I am shocked to see the McDoone elders, including the ultra-wizened Granny, standing shoulder to tartaned shoulder on a pile of scaffolding poles at the back of the main group. Grizzly auld Father McDoone is enthusiastically waving a blue-and-white Saltire flag and mouthing pleasantries. It's the first time I've seen all the McDoone clan smile at the same time, obviously bidding me and my ship an enthusiastic Scottish 'fare-thee-well'. Granny McDoone gives us a wavering two-finger salute, loses her balance and falls out of sight among a pile of scaffolding poles.

A tearful Sorcha waves a lace handkerchief at the ship. She doesn't recognise Sugar fully clothed and with his cap on, standing next to me on the forecastle.

'Sorcha looks upset,' I whisper out of the corner of my mouth.

'Yeah,' says Sugar. 'I bought her that hanky as a going away present.'

'You bought her a hanky?'

'Why not?'

'You're a soft old bastard deep down, aren't ya?'

'Suppose I am ... yeah.'

'Yae soft old bastaaarrr.'

'It was only a hanky.'

'Silence in the ranks!' yells someone in authority. 'And keep still.'

Mr & Mrs McDoone are still enthusiastically waving the Scottish flag as we flick our stern at Rosyth and head east doon the Forth.

We are dismissed as *Gurkha* approaches the Forth Railway Bridge. Sugar and I drape ourselves illegally over the Quarterdeck guardrails.

'That woman,' says Sugar, jabbing a finger at the disappearing Rosyth skyline. 'That woman had skills you wouldn't believe.'

We giggle and wander back to the mess as the late evening lights of Rosyth fade in the Firth of Forth gloom.

The weather dramatically improves the moment *Gurkha* turns south. The Scots onboard become a morose and quiet lot. We Englishmen in the mess enthuse about Pompey and the town's many attractions.

*

The pebbled beach of Southsea, Billy Manning's funfair and the Round Tower at the entrance to Portsmouth harbour are welcoming and familiar sights in the clear, early morning Hampshire sunshine.

We berth at the top end of the dockyard overlooking Whale Island with the white chalk cliffs of Portsdown Hill in the distant background. Most of us spend the day ammunitioning the ship and are too exhausted to go ashore: there's always tomorrow.

Both watches are mustered at 04:45 the following morning. A fully ammunitioned *Gurkha* slips unscheduled and unnoticed out of Portsmouth harbour. It is too early for salutes so the sleeping population of Pompey remain undisturbed. Daily Orders are full of TBCs (To Be Confirmed). Those of us who have done a Portland work-up before expect nothing else.

Later in the day the familiar humped outline of Portland appears amid the gloom and fine drizzle of a June afternoon on coastal Dorset. Those gentlemen who are comfortably warm and dry on the Bridge declare that we can't wear our recently acquired foul-weather jackets. We muster in our second-best suits, caps with chinstays down, for *Gurkha*'s first entry into Portland harbour. With our suits drenched and sagging we berth alongside the same wooden jetty that *Bermuda* had almost destroyed four years previously. The electrical substation that had exploded during that visit is nowhere to be seen. Lined up on the jetty alongside a large Army canvas-backed truck are a group of Royal Marines dressed in full combat gear complete with capes: they are carrying rifles. As soon as the gangway is secured they troop onboard, each with a bulging kit bag balanced on their shoulder.

We wait in the rain for the expected, high-ranking visitors to arrive. Eventually a convoy of long black Naval cars arrives and disgorges a stream of elderly Naval officers each carrying an umbrella and a briefcase. We toss our cigarettes over the side. Apparently our visitors are Flag Officer's Sea Training staff and are onboard to assess us.

On the bottom of Daily Orders there is a note formally welcoming our detachment of Royal Marines onboard. They are to be part of the permanent ship's company commanded by a Major Munro. The senior NCO is Sergeant Lecky. The rank and file are to be accommodated in a Royal Marine's mess directly above the main magazine.

From 05:00 the following morning, we are officially into our Portland work-up routine. For the next three days we are exercised continuously. Fire Fighting teams and Damage Control parties are permanently doing something seriously disruptive while the rest of us are closed up at either Action or Defence Stations.

And as soon as we have a quiet ten minutes ...

'ABLE SEAMAN KAYNE AND ABLE SEAMAN BROADBENT REPORT TO MAJOR MUNRO IN THE WARDROOM. ABLE SEAMEN KAYNE AND BROADBENT.'

Sugar tosses his J T Edson paperback onto his bunk. 'Shit, that doesn't sound good.'

I've finished drying myself after a shower and am looking forward to immersing myself in 'The Snake', the latest Mickey Spillane.

'Suppose we had better make our way down the posh end, Pete lad,' says Sugar.

Sugar knocks firmly on the Wardroom pantry door, which is opened by a Leading Steward.

'We've been piped to report to Major Munro.'

The Leading Steward signals for us to wait and closes the pantry door without saying a word.

'Prat,' says Sugar.

'Yeah ... prat.'

Major Munro is a stocky, moon-faced individual with jug ears. His green beret is rolled and stowed under the epaulette of his camouflage uniform. He consults a slip of paper. 'Able Seaman Kayne and Able Seaman Broadbent?'

'Yes, sir.'

'Yes, sir.'

'I have to decide which one of you two stalwarts will be the coxswain of the rigid inflatable for the Dhow Boarding Party.'

Neither of us reacts. We both wait.

'Able Seaman Kayne, you are the more experienced Seaman. Able Seaman Broadbent, you have the experience of being a member of a similar boarding party whilst in the Far East.'

'On HMS Lincoln, yes sir,' I reply. 'Kumpit boarding party.'

'Have either of you had any experience in RIBs before?'

'Sugar emphatically shakes his head. 'No, sir. Not me, sir.'

'Broadbent?'

I decide to stretch the truth.

'A little, sir.'

'Have you operated an outboard engine?'

'Yes, sir.' I compound my deceit.

Major Munro stows his slip of paper in his pocket. 'Able Seaman Kayne, do you have any problems if I select Able Seaman Broadbent as Coxswain ... on account of him having previous RIB experience?'

'None whatsoever, sir,' says Sugar, visibly relaxing.

'That's decided then,' says a half-smiling Major Munro. 'Able Seaman Broadbent - report to Sergeant Lecky after both watches tomorrow morning and he will run through the launching and recovery procedure and issue you with the necessary kit. That's all, dismiss.'

Sugar nods for the both of us. Major Munro closes the door.

'Never volunteer, Pete,' says Sugar as we make our way back to the mess.

'I know. My granddad told me that years ago.'

'And he was right.'

'What does stalwart mean?' I ask.

'It's a growth of some kind.'

'And what's a ferkin Dhow when it's at 'ome?'

'I don't know.'

I scrape my shin on a hatch combing. 'Shit.'

*

The following morning, I report to Sergeant Lecky as instructed.

We shake hands. He is broad-shouldered with close-cropped hair and is in camouflage clothing. He smiles: 'I'm Sergeant Lecky,' he says. 'You can call me Sergeant.'

'Able Seaman Broadbent. You can call me whatever you like ... err, Sergeant.'

'I'll call you Coxswain when you've got your hand on the tiller.'

On the Quarterdeck he introduces me to a couple of black, inflatable rubber boats stowed on the port side. On the back of each is slung a large black outboard motor.

'You've driven one of these before?' he asks. Sergeant Lecky is from the Emerald Isle.

'Yes, Sergeant ... similar.'

'My lads are trained in the launching of these boats. Speed is of the essence. They are put in the water by the radial davit over there.' He points to the single arm davit on the starboard quarter. 'Members of the Dhow Boarding Party will drag the RIB to the accommodation ladder. By the time you get there, the RIB will be secured and ready. You'll be the first down the ladder and you will be responsible for checking and starting the outboard motor ... in neutral ... while the remainder of the Boarding Party and I board. In an emergency we can toss a scrambling net over the side and board the RIB from the quarterdeck. The Boarding Party will consist of five Royal marines in each RIB ...'

I take advantage of a slight pause. 'What's a Dhow then, Sergeant?'

'A boat ... an Arab boat.'

'Thanks, Sergeant.'

'Everything clear so far?'

'Yes, Sergeant.'

'Good. We'll launch our RIB then. You go and wait up by the accommodation ladder.'

'OK, Sergeant.'

A couple of fully kitted Royal Marines are waiting by the accommodation ladder.

'You the driver?' asks a square-shaped bloke with a single chevron on his arm.

'Yep ... Pete.'

I'm Lance Corporal Long ... Dodger.' We shake hands: his right hand is like a well-used, grave-digger's spade.

The RIB arrives. I scramble down the ladder, jump onboard, start the engine and have her ticking over in neutral as the rest of the Boarding Party jumps aboard. One Royal Marine acts as bowman while Sergeant Lecky squats next to me. 'Let's go then, Coxswain.'

I like being called Coxswain. As soon as we cast off, Sergeant Lecky moves people around to trim the boat. One Marine is located in the bows with the spare fuel canister to add some weight and to stop the bows from lifting. Once done, the RIB skims nicely. The guy with the radio strapped to his back establishes communications with Major Munro who is on *Gurkha*'s Bridge.

'Open her up, Coxswain,' instructs Sergeant Lecky.

I look at him for confirmation.

He nods.

I twist the throttle and the response is immediate. There is more twisting room available so I keep twisting until the engine starts to scream. I back off until the engine sounds comfortable and settles to an almost silent grumble. Bouncing across the slick surface of the water proves to be an exhilarating experience. We fly, skimming from wave top to wave top. The power of the single outboard engine is unbelievable.

We spend the next thirty minutes skimming up and down an empty section of water opposite Lulworth Cove until we are all well and truly soaked.

'Slew her round, Coxswain, and make our way back,' says Sergeant Lecky, his face streaming with water.

I throttle back as we approach the accommodation ladder. Despite their drenched condition, the Boarding Party is in high spirits as they disembark.

Sergeant Lecky gives me a Royal Marine waterproof cape that he says will be of more use than the Pusser's foul-weather jacket I'm wearing. It's a symbol of acceptance I think.

'We'll do that again next week no doubt,' says Sergeant Lecky. 'It's your job to make sure the boat has full fuel tanks ... in case of emergencies.'

'OK ... thanks, Sergeant.'

Down the mess I try to explain what it is like to have control of such a powerful outboard engine. 'It was ferkin brilliant,' I say as I remove my soaked number 8's and wrap my towel around me.

Sugar lights a couple of cigarettes and hands one to me. 'Was it that good?'

'Absolutely ferkin brilliant. The power in those outboards - it was almost like flying.'

'Bet it was.'

'And a Dhow is an Arab boat ... apparently.'

'I know that,' says a smiling Sugar. 'Everybody knows that.'

'I didn't.'

*

We spend the following fourteen nights at sea, twelve at Action Stations. We perform over a dozen Jackstay transfers, tow a number of fellow Frigates and a Royal Fleet Auxiliary that is much larger than us. We fire an assortment of ammunition at the designated on-shore firing range and light up a number of sleepy south coast villages with our Starshells. I coxswain the RIB to land Royal Marines on deserted stretches of the Dorset coast to do whatever the Royal Marines do when they are put on terra firma. We exercise fire after fire, floods, equipment failure and we even steer *Gurkha* by some complicated equipment in the Tiller Flat that we are told would be used if and when the wheelhouse is knocked out. I don't know exactly what all the other branches are tasked with ... but everybody, apart from the Chinese Laundry crew, are kept busy.

The Wasp is exercised repeatedly and Mack and I are stuck behind our PPI in the Ops Room for hours on end. We exercise man overboard drills using the Wasp to search for a radar-reflecting Dan Buoy in the middle of the night. We also exercise numerous helicopter torpedo firings and an emergency casualty evacuation at 03:00 one morning. Mack and I are assessed by a member of Flag Officer Sea Training staff who sits in a darkened corner of the Ops Room taking notes. When my Helicopter Control obligations conflict with my coxswain duties, Frothy does my Ops Room stint for me.

Because *Gurkha* is experimenting with ways that the Wasp can assist with civil unrest, Mack and I avoid getting involved in the weekend Riot Control exercise in one of Portland's unused quarries. Most of our messmates enthusiastically join in the exercise and get dressed up in a variety of costumes before being taken to the combat zone. Those of us who have experienced the Portland Riot Control exercises before explain to those who haven't, that Dorset's youth are invited down to act as rioters and they come down in their hundreds. A good punch-up is more or less guaranteed.

We spend the final work-up weekend in harbour. Most of us stay onboard to catch up on our missed sleep.

On Monday morning a rather dishevelled Sugar staggers up the gangway a few minutes before leave expires. He finger-combs his hair and yawns deeply as he collects his station card from the Bosun's Mate.

'Good weekend, Shug?'

'Yeah,' he mumbles as he zig-zags his way forward. Down the mess he arranges people to cover for him and gets his head down.

'UP SPIRITS.'

The rum is measured out. Sugar's tot remains unclaimed.

'Someone go and shake the lazy bastard,' says Chats. 'Tell him he's got two minutes otherwise his tot goes in the Queen's.'

'What time did he get back onboard?' asks Kit.

'Last minute.'

'There must be a ... what is it called? ... a female connection.'

'He's been away for a couple of days, hasn't he?'

'Yeah, he left shortly after getting back from the Riot Control thingy on Saturday.'

There is a respectful silence around the tot table as Sugar, wrapped in his towel with flip-flops on his feet, makes a grab for his tot.

'Put your shirt on, Sugar,' says Chats. 'Tot time rules.'

'Just this once, Chats ... please,' pleads Sugar.

'Only if you tell us what you've been up to,' says Jack who looks to Chats for confirmation.

Chats nods.

Sugar nods to Jack for him to take 'sippers', grabs his glass and knocks it back in one. He closes his eyes, inhales deeply, smothers a belch, places his empty glass on the mess cloth and sits down slowly.

'A weekend at the local monastery then, Shug?' asks Burbs.

'Weymouth caravan park.'

'Gardening?'

'Not exactly. Did anyone see a woman at the Riot Control Exercise wearing full combat gear, a motorcycle helmet and knee-length leather boots?'

'Nope.'

'Naah.'

'No.'

There is a story coming. I sit in anticipation: I have an idea where this is leading.

'Nice lady,' says Sugar. 'Biked it down to Portland from Warminster on Saturday for a good punch-up followed by a few days of recuperation with a good book at a local caravan park.'

'She came to Portland for a ferkin punch-up?' asks Burbs.

'How did she get down here then?'

'On her ferkin motorbike,' explains Sugar. 'Pay attention.'

'So what happened then?' asks a smirking Kit.

'She knocked ten-bells out of a Bootneck in the quarry. Then took me back to her caravan, changed into something slinky and ... well, you can imagine.'

'Yeah?' says a rather puffed-up Kit.

'Is that all you're going to tell us then?' asks Burbs.

Sugar yawns. 'That, gentlemen, is all I have to say on the matter.' He stands, wobbles slightly and heads towards his bunk. 'I am now going to catch up on some sleep - shake me for supper.'

We all look disappointedly at each other, knowing that we've missed out on a stimulating story.

*

We bid a not-so-fond farewell to Portland and head west to Plymouth. Able Seaman Jan Fletcher, who sleeps in the bunk above me, gets all excited as Guz is his hometown and he's been writing to a girl who lives there. His other girlfriend, the freckle-faced lassie frae Inverkeithing, has to take a back seat for the moment.

'Why is Plymouth called Guz?' asks Mack.

'It's because of all the scrumpy guzzling that goes on down Union Street on pay day,' explains Jan.

'That's bollocks that is,' says Kit. 'The real reason is ... let me think.'

'Come on then.'

Kit claps his hands 'Right then. Anybody who has enjoyed the many delights of Bombay or Trinc ... Trincomalee knows that Guz is the Hindi word for a yard ... that's thirty-six inches to you uneducated lot. Jack - who likes to shorten his words - shortened the word dockyard to yard and then he altered it to Guz because it sounds different. Straight up.'

'Don't believe a word of it, says Mack. 'Sounds like typical tot-time bullshit to me.'

'Could have been,' says Kit. 'Can't remember exactly, to be honest.'

'I heard it was something to do with a wartime call sign,' says Mack.

'That's bollocks, that is.'

'So,' says Chats clapping his hands. 'So we don't know then?'

Silence.

We begin the long entry into Plymouth in the dry. By the time we enter the dockyard proper it's absolutely honking it down. Once again, our second-best suits are soaked. Everybody moans about the fact that we aren't allowed to wear the new foul-weather jackets when entering harbour: they could help to keep a small part of our uniform dry.

Jan is the first ashore. He has a strange expectant expression on his face as he strides over the brow smelling of Old Spice aftershave and enveloped in puffing clouds of Brut talcum powder that he borrowed from Sugar.

'Give her one from me,' calls someone.

Jan turns to give the caller a thumbs-up signal, trips over a pile of rubbish, recovers, trips over himself, picks himself up, brushes himself down and skips around the side of a building. It's the first time I've seen Jan move so quickly.

'ABLE SEAMAN KAYNE REPORT TO THE GANGWAY. ABLE SEAMAN KAYNE.'

'He's in t'bathroom,' Ordinary Seaman Cliff Belter shouts at the mess Tannoy.

'Ring the gangway and tell the QM, young Belter,' says Chats, pointing at the mess telephone.

There are Tannoys in the bathroom and a half-showered Sugar, wrapped in his towel, stumbles down the mess ladder as Cliff is still flicking through the ship's telephone directory. He points at Cliff. 'Hop up to the brow and find out what they want will you, Cliff lad?'

Cliff shrugs, drops the directory and shuffles away as Sugar lights a cigarette.

'I'm not duty, am I?' Sugar asks nobody in particular.

'Don't think so,' I say.

A few minutes later Cliff reappears. 'There's a woman called Pamela on t'gangway asking the Officer-of-the-Day if she can see ya, Sugar.'

'Pamela? Don't know a Pamela,' replies Sugar.

We all look at each other.

'Caravan park?' someone asks.

Sugar looks at the deckhead for inspiration. 'Yeah ... yeah she could have been a Pamela.'

'ABLE SEAMAN KAYNE REPORT TO THE GANGWAY IMMEDIATELY: ABLE SEAMAN KAYNE.'

'Shit.' Sugar holds his head in his hands. 'Pete mate, go up to the gangway and tell whoever is up there that I've gone ashore.' He hands me his station card. 'Give that to the Quartermaster to put in the desk for me.'

At the gangway the Officer-of-the-Day is in discussion with a lady screened behind a circular curtain of water cascading from her large black umbrella. She is wearing a transparent pocket raincoat over a short black dress displaying long shapely legs.

I pass Sugar's station card to the Quartermaster. 'Sugar asked me to give you this. He's unofficially ashore,' I whisper.

'No problems' replies the Quartermaster, smirking.

I leave before the Officer-of-the-Day, who is trying to calm the long-legged lady with the umbrella, spots me.

Back down the mess, Sugar is all questions. 'Who was it?'

'Dunno. She was wearing a short black dress ... and she had really long legs ... in shiny black stockings.'

'Mmm.' Sugar strokes his chin.

'It's raining and I couldn't see her face clearly. She had one of those plastic raincoats on ...'

'Did the QM get rid of her?' asks Sugar.

'No ... she was still there when I left.'

'Shit.'

'Was she the one from the caravan park then, Shug?' Cliff asks.

'More than likely,' says Sugar, looking pensive. 'She had a good pair of legs I recall.'

'Can I take her off your hands?' asks Cliff.

'If you want,' says Sugar, waving a hand.

Cliff flies up the ladder.

'Never seen him move so ferkin fast,' says Burbs.

We all sit around the mess table in stunned silence as Sugar grabs his washing stuff and disappears.

A few minutes later a morose-looking Cliff stumbles down the ladder.

'Well?' I ask.

'She's ferkin gone, hasn't she?'

*

At tot-time the following day the Quartermaster who had saved Sugar's skin gratefully downs half of Sugar's tot.

Burbs has been in a strange, uncommunicative mood all morning and after his tot confides to Chats that he is thinking of getting engaged. As the killick of the mess, Chat's advice is generally sought.

Chats ponders the problem for a moment. He takes a deep breath and places a placatory hand on Burbs' shoulder. 'Don't do it, Burbs.'

'Why?' asks Burbs, confused.

'Because at your age ... how old are ya, Burbs?'

'Almost twenty two.'

'You're far too young to get engaged.'

'Why?'

'You've not sewn your wild oats yet, have yer?'

'I have. I sewed a couple of oats in Birmingham a few years ago.'

'Birmingham doesn't count.'

'Doesn't it?'

'No.'

'How about Gosport then?'

'No. That doesn't count either.'

Burbs finishes his tot and stomps away, the problem of his engagement bearing heavily upon him.

Kit places his tot glass on the end of the table, having rolled and tipped it for ten minutes to drain every last drop. 'I've put in a request form to discontinue shaving.'

'Again?'

'Yep.'

'Why's that then, Kit?' I ask

' I feel incomplete without facial hair ... and anyway I think I look better with my set.'

'I beg to differ ... you're an ugly bastard with or without it.'

'Am I?'

'Yep.'

'That does it for me then,' says Kit who shuffles away, crestfallen, to a darkened corner of the mess.

3

Portsmouth Navy Days 1965

THE FOLLOWING day we gain two additional mess members - 'Bagsy' Baker, an Ordinary Seaman gunner fresh out of training who has never been to sea before, and 'Timber' Woods, a Sonar specialist from Portsmouth who failed his Educational Test for Able Seaman and, despite being almost nineteen years old, remains an Ordinary Seaman. They are allocated the two empty bunks in the mess near to the increasingly noisy air conditioning unit.

Jan arrives back from leave on the morning of our scheduled departure. He is cross-examined in the prescribed Naval manner.

'Good couple of days Jan ... get stacks?' asks Burbs.

'Yeah ... loads.'

'Lucky sod.'

We leave Guz in a torrential West Country downpour. During the journey to Portsmouth we are swamped with information about Navy Days: which other ships will be in the dockyard, how many visitors to expect, how to conduct ourselves faced with the British public for an entire weekend.

Mack tells me that he is going down the NAAFI Club when we arrive in Pompey. Sugar overhears and winks knowingly at me.

'Can I come with ya?' asks Bagsy.

'Course you can,' says Mack.

'Pete, you coming?'

'Might do,' I say, keeping my options open.

Having successfully completed our work-up, our entry into Portsmouth is a full-blown ceremonial affair.

Chats says it's the first time he has known a ship fire a five-gun salute to Billy Manning's fun fair at Southsea.

There is a small group of welcoming individuals on top of the Round Tower.

'Atten ...shun! No winking, smiling, twiddling of fingers or shuffling of feet,' says someone in authority. 'Where do you think you are ... on daddy's yacht?'

We fire a single gun salute to the Still & West pub in Old Portsmouth and pipes are made to the many ships we pass.

Our allocated berth is north of South Railway jetty.

As soon as we secure ourselves and rig the brow, all the non-combatants who have wives, girlfriends or bits-on-the-side in Pompey skip ashore. We Seaman, with nothing to rush ashore for, tidy all the upper deck mooring equipment and wash down the gangway area.

Leading Seaman 'Sharky' Ward, our most experienced Ship's Diver, who helped Sugar avoid the long-legged Pamela, is the Quartermaster on duty. I'm just loafing around. We have a brief discussion about diving: I tell him how I had contracted Singapore ear while doing my diving course in Singapore. He isn't as impressed as I hoped he might be.

We both watch in silence as Sugar hands in his

station card and runs over the brow without so much as an over-the-shoulder glance.

'I wonder where he's heading?' I say.

'More than likely the Portsmouth City Museum,' says Sharky with an air of confidence.

'Naah, Sugar in a Museum? That's not Sugar.'

'Never told you about Sally from Sally Port then?' Sharky asks.

'Who?'

'Sally from Sally Port, one of the restorers at the Museum.'

'A restorer?'

'Apparently she's really good at restoring old paintings ... and Sugar's self confidence.'

'Never heard of her,' I admit.

'Sally from Jamaica,' Sharky coughs. 'Sugar's best kept secret. Ask him about her when you next see him.'

'UP SPIRITS.'

Sugar offers me a 'wet'.

I take 'sippers' and hand his tot back to him. He taps me on the shoulder to say thanks.

'Sharky told me about Sally who works at the Museum,' I say.

'Oh yeah.'

'You haven't mentioned her before.'

'I tend to keep the details of my long-term, special ladies to myself,' he says as he downs the remainder of his tot.

'Is that you being gentlemanly, then?'

'Yep.'

'Sharky said that she's a restorer.'

'She certainly is, young Pete, she most certainly is.'

'And that she comes from Jamaica.'

'Born and bred.'

I nod, not understanding anything. 'Any chance of meeting her?'

'Woahha, young Pete. When you're ready - when

you've had a few more years before the mast, mate.'

Navy Days is fast approaching: not everybody wants to be involved. Married men, or those with girlfriends, would much rather spend the weekend ashore than deal with hundreds of complete strangers stomping around their place of work. Consequently, lots of duties are exchanged and much rum is traded. As a single man, and friend, I accept Sugar's Tuesday tot in exchange for doing one of his weekend duties so that he can continue with his restoration programme.

Parked up for Navy Days

On the morning of Navy Days the mess is pleasantly empty; only five of us remain. Resplendent in my second-best uniform, I muster for 'Both Watches' at 07:55 and stand to attention as 'Colours' is sounded throughout the dockyard. Forward of us is berthed *HMS London*, a County Class destroyer. Behind us is the aircraft carrier

HMS Centaur. On the opposite side of the jetty in the basin is *HM Submarine Token* and forward of her are *HMS Pellew* and *HMS Rhyl* berthed side by side. Further aft is a strange looking American warship.

We scuttle around cleaning and tidying the upper deck and along the designated visitors' route. The Wardroom heads are designated as female toilets: the bulkhead mounted 'pistols' are covered with a white-painted canvas dodger. Compartments with equipment considered 'hush-hush' are locked. Lower deck messes are roped off as being out of bounds. Special dispensation is given to family members. Timber's mum, dad and sisters, who live in Stubbington, are coming onboard so our mess is given the once-over: the gash ditched, the bunks made tidy and stowed correctly. All the 'lads' magazines' are secreted away.

By 09:05 the first visitors begin to arrive. Crowds pass us by, heading for the American vessel.

I'm chatting to the Quartermaster on the gangway. A lady with two young girls is standing to one side. Dad is talking to the Officer-of-the-Day.

'Quartermaster, pipe for Ordinary Seaman Woods to report to the gangway,' says the Officer-of-the-Day.

Burbs arrives to tell us that Timber is in the shower. So I offer to escort his family down the mess to wait for him. By the time I get them down the mess, Timber is almost dressed and ready to take his family on a private tour of the ship. I settle down to read some of my latest Mickey Spillane. Mrs Woods is a very attractive lady.

Thankfully *Gurkha* doesn't attract many visitors on Sunday or Bank Holiday Monday. The queues for the American vessel and for *HM Submarine Token* stretch into the distance. We have some visitors who find the queues for other ships too lengthy, but they are mostly grey-haired gentlemen with medals pinned to their chests and cameras strung around their necks.

Our Wasp is part of a Royal Marine display on the

large open space alongside *HMS Victory*. Frothy does all the controlling. Pontius does a good job of hovering while a couple of Marines dangle from Kate's underside on a rope. It's a display enthusiastically enjoyed by the visitors. When the display is finished the Wasp departs for *RNAS Yeovilton*, no doubt so that Pontius can say goodbye to his aeronautical friends.

*

Panic ensues on Tuesday: Jack is late with the rum. All of us waiting around the mess table are concerned that something serious may have happened to him on his way back to the mess.

'Maybe he's been kidnapped.'
'Don't be ferkin stupid.'
'What if he's tripped or fallen over somewhere?'
'And spilt the rum?'
'Don't say that ... think positive.'
'It's possible though isn't it?'
'Suppose so.'
'Could we get a top-up if he spilled any of the rum on his way back to the mess?'
'Don't know. I should ferkin hope so.'
'No, he won't. That trick's been tried before,' Chats states confidently.
'Shouldn't we go up and search for him?'
'Yeah, check that he's OK.'

Jack skips down the ladder. Thankfully the rum fanny looks to be in one piece. Jack also appears intact.

'Where 'ave ...'

Jack sniffs. 'Everybody was late. Officer-of-the-Day had to get someone to help tie his shoe laces, tuck his shirt in and point him in the right direction ... or something.'

Sugar offers me his tot. I drink half and hand the rest back to him. If I'd been a woman, he would have kissed me ... at the very least.

Today we gain a new mess member, a young lad called Paul Waters - known as 'Stormy' - who was promoted to Ordinary Seaman a few days ago when reaching the magic age of seventeen and a half. He is given the only empty bunk; the middle one close to the air conditioning unit and directly below Kit, who has recently been acclaimed as the mess champion 'breaker of wind'.

I take Bagsy and Mack to the NAAFI Club to show them the ropes. Outside there is a large gaggle of young girls.

'They'll bugger off as soon as you sign them in,' I explain.

Nevertheless we stick with tradition and each select a girl to 'sign in'.

Unsurprisingly, Nora's mum is still behind the reception desk. It takes her a while to remember me.

'Stand there a moment, young sir, while I bring you to mind.'

I do as I'm told.

Peter ... Peter, that's it. Your name is Peter,' she says confidently.

'Is it?' I say, smiling.

'It is, yes. What ship you on now, young Peter?' she asks. 'No don't tell me!' She holds up a silencing hand. 'You're onboard Gurkha along with my old friend Sugar.'

'I am, yeah.'

'Fresh out of Rosyth, then?'

'Yep.'

'In for Navy Days then the Middle East for eight months or so.'

'As far as we know, yeah.'

'Abadan for Christmas,' says Nora's mum.

'Where?' asks Bagsy.

'Abadan.'

'Where's that?'

'At the southern end of the Shat El Arab river on the Persian side,' explains Nora's mum.

'Where's the best bar, Pete? I'll get 'em in,' says Mack. Mack's offered to buy a round. I'm too shocked to respond.

'Talk to you later, Peter,' says Nora's mum. 'Don't run off before saying goodbye.'

At the end of the evening, after a significant number of pints, I forget to say goodbye to Nora's mum.

*

There is much trading of rum at tot-time on Wednesday. There is a good amount of Queen's; consequently the only thing I'm good for is getting my head down. I make my excuses, switch the lights off in my corner of the mess and crash out.

A few mornings later a dark green bus arrives and disgorges a group of Gurkhas and lots of bagged equipment. The Officer-of-the-Watch warmly welcomes the British Commanding Officer onboard: apparently they are expected. The Gurkhas make their way over the brow, each carrying a large, strangely shaped bag.

If I'd bothered to read Daily Orders I would know that this is the Gurkha Band we are taking to Jersey. They are to be accommodated mainly in the Dining Hall where there is a large free deck area for camp beds.

'CLOSE UP SPECIAL SEA DUTYMEN. PREPARE FOR LEAVING HARBOUR, HANDS FALL IN ON THE UPPER DECK, DRESS NUMBER 2'S WITH CHIN-STAYS DOWN. HANDS OUT OF THE RIG OF THE DAY CLEAR OFF THE UPPER DECK. CLOSE ALL UPPER DECK SCREEN DOORS AND SCUTTLES. ASSUME DAMAGE CONTROL STATE 2 CONDITION YANKEE BRAVO.'

'Do we have any ferkin scuttles?' asks Bagsy.

'Don't think so,' I reply. 'Haven't really noticed.'

It's a misty morning. The early day sun is a barely focused yellow blotch in a cloudless sky. We decline tugs and manoeuvre ourself into the centre of the harbour in typical *Gurkha* style. We salute everybody and anything. It's our way of saying a ceremonial farewell to the UK for eight months or so. A small number of waving friends and family have gathered on the top of the Round Tower at the harbour entrance.

As we head for the Nab Tower I have a sudden pang: once again I'm leaving my home country for uncharted seas, unfamiliar places. A large part of me is excited because I will experience new things and meet new people. People deal with long-term separation in different ways. Down the mess there is lots of humour and a general air of relaxed enthusiasm for the trip ahead. The older mess members are a little more pensive. Myself? I'm looking forward to tot-time. The Scottish contingent are dealing with departure in their customary fashion, by adopting a dour, long-faced lack of humour.

'Did your mum came down to see you off, Timber?' I ask.

'She was on the Round Tower with Dad.'

'FLYING STATIONS.'

Mack and I don't know who is duty Controller so we both scramble up to the Ops Room. Frothy is already there and in communication with the Wasp that is approaching from the west. Frothy hands me the headset and microphone as the Wasp skims north of Cowes making its final approach.

'Golf Foxtrot Yankee Alpha this is X-Ray Tango 434, over.'

'This is Golf Foxtrot Yankee Alpha, over.' I reply.

'This is X-Ray Tango 434, good morning Able Seaman

Broadbent, misty morning eh? Over.'

'This is Golf Foxtrot Yankee Alpha, roger your last. Ops Room weather is reasonably pleasant, over.'

'This is X-Ray Tango 434. I have some official mail onboard and a box of handmade Oggies from The Yeovilton Women's Institute, over.'

'Very good, over.'

*

Daily orders for the following day start with some disappointing news. Because our programme is dependent on us joining our designated southbound Suez Canal convoy, we will be dropping off the Gurkha band at Jersey and sailing immediately. In the mess we sit in sulky disappointment as Kit had spent the morning telling us what a brilliant run-ashore Jersey is. Lots of sand, plenty of bars and girls. The Channel Islands are going to miss the opportunity of greeting *Gurkha*'s crew.

As we approach St Helier a Gurkha bagpiper takes up position on the top of the bridge and begins to squeeze his instrument. Thankfully the sound is lost on a gentle south-westerly breeze.

We wallow in the gently rolling waters off the harbour and wait for a large Pinnace to secure itself alongside. The Gurkha band is assembled aft of the accommodation ladder with all their equipment and we say a fond farewell to our musical visitors. The last to scramble away is the bridge-top piper.

It is rumoured that we can expect some roughers in the 'Bay of Biscuit'.

Down the mess at tot-time, the general consensus of opinion is that the Frogs designed the Bay of Biscay to be a deterrent to British sea-goers. *Gurkha* will take a line to the west of the main bite of the Bay, so we turn in for the night convinced that our superiors have made a shrewd navigational decision.

Doing battle with unfriendly French waters

It's dark. I'm thrown against the roll bars of my bunk. There is a crash as *Gurkha*'s bow drops onto something solid. I grapple for my cigarettes and lighter that are travelling aft. The mess lights are switched on; they flicker. The mess gash bucket, full of the previous evening's beer cans and slop water, clatters across the deck. Our bow rises, hovers for what seems to be half a minute and then crashes us into a rock-hard milestone that shakes *Gurkha* to her bones. The ship's side rattles. The air in the ventilation trunks whistles. Lights flicker again but stay on. Loose equipment and items of kit from the top of lockers fly in all directions. Everybody is out of their bunk, except for Wheelie who is still fast asleep. *Gurkha* slews to starboard and her stern lifts. The air conditioning unit clatters and the lights go out. The red emergency lighting comes on.

'UPPER DECK SEAMEN MUSTER IN THE CANTEEN FLAT IMMEDIATELY. UPPER DECK SEAMEN.'

'Oh bollocks.'

'I'll second that.'

'Me too.'

We drag Wheelie out of his bunk and stand him up.

'What the ferk?' he asks.

'We've got to muster in the Canteen flat,' we chorus.

'Why?' says Wheelie rubbing his eyes.

'Cos we're doing battle with the Bay of ferkin Biscuit.'

'Biscuit?' asks Wheelie, confused.

We struggle into our completely useless foul-weather jackets and wait for *Gurkha* to settle herself for a moment before scuttling up the mess ladder as she drops.

In the Canteen flat, we are detailed off into teams of three to close all the designated upper deck ventilation inlets. I'm fortunate to be in the group sent to the Quarterdeck where there are only two bulkhead-mounted ventilation grills. We close them quickly; foaming French waters explode over both sides of the Quarterdeck and the deck above. *Gurkha* isn't coping too well: she is designed to withstand the British North Sea, not this French rubbish.

Soaked to the skin we make it back to the Canteen flat where someone has knocked-up a fanny full of thick, sweet kye.

I find a quiet corner of the canteen flat, plonk myself down and slurp a mug of kye.

Jan Fletcher slithers alongside me and gulps from his mug. 'You been to Gib before, Pete?'

'Yeah, few times.'

'Good isn't it? I like Gib.'

'So do I.'

'The Trocadero.'

'The good old Troc, yeah.'

'Give me your mug, I'll go and get us a refill,' he offers.

The following day is slightly less traumatic, although the French territorial waters remain unwelcoming and unpredictable enough for us to rig upper-deck safety lines and to declare the upper deck out of bounds.

Tot-time in such weather is a different affair. Everybody knocks their tot back quickly. We don't offer Jack 'sippers': he's too busy ensuring the rum fanny doesn't move. After my tot I'm prepared to do battle with whatever the 'Bay of Biscuit' can throw at me and my lovely little frigate.

HMS Gurkha flails her stern like a reckless woman as we reach the north-western coast of Spain, signalling the end of our Biscay traverse and the beginning of the calmer, more civilised waters west of the Iberian peninsula.

We spend some time unlashing and checking upper deck equipment. Surprisingly the two RIBs on the quarterdeck are undamaged. The outboard motors had been stowed away somewhere safe.

The Tannoy crackles into life.

'ADMIRAL COLLINGWOOD'S DISPATCH, DATED 21 OCTOBER 1805 TO WILLIAM MARSDEN AT THE ADMIRALTY REGARDING THE VICTORIOUS BATTLE OF TRAFALGAR STATED THAT THE COMBINED FRENCH AND SPANISH FLEET WERE ENGAGED WHEN CAPE TRAFALGAR BORE SOUTH-EAST AT SEVEN LEAGUES. ACCORDING TO MIDSHIPMAN BELLRINGER, WHO KNOWS ABOUT SUCH THINGS, A LEAGUE IS ROUGHLY THREE NAUTICAL MILES WHICH IS THE HORIZON'S DISTANCE AS SEEN BY A PERSON OF AVERAGE HEIGHT STANDING AT SEA LEVEL ...'

'Well bugger me,' says Jan.

'**TOMORROW WE SHALL POSITION OURSELF AS CLOSE AS POSSIBLE TO THE ACTUAL POSITION AND LAY A WREATH. OFFICERS WILL MUSTER ON THE QUARTERDECK, SENIOR RATES ON ZERO ONE DECK AND JUNIOR RATES WHEREVER THEY CAN FIND SPACE. THAT IS ALL. AYO GURKHALI.'**

Next morning, 21 October 1965, shortly before dinner with a golden Iberian sun warming us nicely, *HMS Gurkha* comes to a respectful halt twenty-one nautical miles north-west of Cape Trafalgar. Along with an interested group from our mess, I stand next to a washdeck locker on the port side of 01 deck, and watch in respectful silence as a wreath is ceremonially thrown overboard at the point where the battle of Trafalgar took place one hundred and sixty years ago today. A lot of sailors - British, French and Spanish - lost their lives here and what remains of their watered souls could still be somewhere below us. There is a short period of reflective contemplation around our washdeck locker and throughout the ship.

'**UP SPIRITS.**'

'Weird isn't it? Being at the exact place where the battle of Trafalgar took place,' says Chats as he downs his tot.

'Yeah.'

'Tis, yeah.'

'Why do they call it Trafalgar?' asks Burbs.

'Because there is a place ashore called Cape Trafalgar,' explains Chats.

We have something called Victory soup on the menu at dinnertime. It tastes the same as the previous day's soup ... and the day's before that ... and the thick brown gravy we had the day before that.

Bagsy, Stormy and Timber haven't been to Gibraltar

before and they all sit open-mouthed while those of us with loads of Gib experience relate our individual, exaggerated stories of runs ashore down Main Street. Sugar and I relate the story of the big fight in the Troc in 1961, underlining the fact that one of the 'female' Flamenco dancers was actually an ex-RAF bloke called Norman.

A lot of the younger lads onboard are on the upper-deck as we approach Gib. No matter how many times I see Gibraltar on the horizon, it's always an impressive sight. 'They call this gap into the Mediterranean The Pillars of Hercules,' I say.

'You're a soft young bugger,' says Sugar. 'Where did you get that nugget of information from then?'

'My geography teacher, Mister Parry, told me. Great bloke.'

We berth ourself as near to the town end of the long eastern jetty as we can. We are the only warship in harbour.

Sugar declines an invitation to accompany us to the Trocadero, saying that he already has plans.

Jan stays down the mess. He wants peace and quiet to write a letter to his girl in Inverkeithing. He is a little worried, as he hasn't had a Scottish letter for weeks.

Bagsy, Stormy and I have a few liveners in the Main Street NAAFI Canteen before heading for the Troc.

The Troc has changed a little since I was last here four years ago. The stage has disappeared, the wooden bench tables have been replaced by plastic-topped tables and proper chairs have replaced the benches. Surprisingly, there is unbroken glass in a few of the windows facing the Square. As *Gurkha* is the only HM ship in town, the place is almost empty. A couple of Stokers and a small number of our Royal Marines are sitting at a table close to the heads. There are no women about.

Nothing happens during the next couple of rounds so

we decide on a crawl along some of the other Main Street bars as it's getting dark.

We are all disappointed that there are no girls around. In one of the bars we bump into a flock of Wrens from *HMS Rooke*, the Naval shore Establishment on Gib, but they are much older than us and not that interested in young blades on their way to the Persian Gulf. We watch part of a football match on TV that is Spanish, boring and goalless.

Sugar strolls back onboard the following morning just a few minutes before leave expires.

'THE INFORMATION OFFICER SPEAKING. TO MEET WITH OUR DESIGNATED SUEZ CANAL CONVOY WE WILL BE DEPARTING GIBRALTAR AT 07:30 TOMORROW.'

'Another early morning start. Saving on saluting guns,' says Kit stroking his stubbled chin.

'ANYONE WISHING TO JOIN OUR ROYAL MARINE CONTINGENT FOR THE TRADITIONAL RACE TO THE PEAK MUSTER ON THE JETTY AT 13:30.'

'I would,' I say quietly, 'if I hadn't recently had my tot.'

My contribution to the traditional Royal Naval race to the peak of Gibraltar is sitting on a comfortable wash-deck locker watching our Royal Marine contingent and Midshipman Bellringer representing the Wardroom, line up to start on Sergeant Lecky's whistle.

I watch until the last Marine disappears round the far corner of the jetty where the large dry dock is. I take a deep breath and light a relaxing cigarette before deciding to retire to my bunk for a well-earned afternoon nap.

'CLOSE UP SPECIAL SEA DUTYMEN. BOTH WATCHES OF SEAMEN TO MUSTER. PREPARE FOR

LEAVING HARBOUR PROCEDURE BRAVO. HANDS OUT OF THE RIG OF THE DAY CLEAR OFF THE UPPER DECK.'

The Gibraltar sun is clear and invigoratingly warm. Devoid of ceremony, we leave Gibraltar and head east. It's a clear, balmy evening and a group of us spend some time squatting on the quarterdeck smoking and telling each other ridiculous sea-stories.

'Sugar is surprisingly coy about his run ashore,' says Jan.

'He's always coy,' I say.

4

From Europe to the Middle East

LIVING SO close together, there is nothing remotely private in a Royal Naval messdeck. Later in the day Jan queries a large taped patch of lint on Timber's back as he is getting ready to go to the bathroom. 'What you done to yewer back, mi 'ansum?'

'Tattoo,' mumbles Timber.

'Let's have a look then,' says Mack.

'Naah.'

'Go on.'

'Haven't seen it myself yet,' says Timber.

'Why's that?'

'Aven't got eyes in the back of mi ferkin head, have I?'

'Go on, Timber, let's have a butchers.'

'I'll undo your sticky tape for ya,' offers Mack.

'Go on then, but be gentle with it.'

Both Mack and Burbs take up position at Timber's back. They each take an edge of the sticky tape and at a nod from Mack rip it away.

'Shitaaaah!' exclaims Timber as he doubles up.

'Almost gorrit ... only one mear,' says Mack.

'Take pity lads ... a bit slower this time ... please,' pleads Timber.

Mack nods and once again they rip.

'You bastards!'

The lint falls away to reveal what looks like a bulbous pair of female breasts beneath a single well developed shoulder. 'Crikey Timber, that's awesome.'

'Is it?' asks Timber.

'A great pair of tits,' exclaims Burbs.

Timber turns to face the assembled mess members in the mess square. 'That's what I asked for.'

'Only one shoulder,' says Kit. 'Is that it then, Timber? Is it finished?'

'Naah, there was a power cut, wasn't there? ... he had to stop.'

'She's only got one ferkin shoulder,' says Kit. 'And no face.'

He said he'd do the other shoulder, her face and her legs when we come back.'

'So you're going to have a one shouldered person with a great pair of tits all over your back for the next eight months then?'

'Unless I can get someone else to finish it off for me before then. Can I have a look at it? Has anyone got a mirror?'

'A mirror? Where do you think you are ... in the ferkin Stokers' mess?' says Burbs.

'If you stand over there just to one side of Pete's locker you should be able to see your back in Stormy's locker opposite ... if he takes his manky towel off the door,' explains Kit.

Stormy flicks his towel from the front of his locker, sniffs it and drapes it over the rail of his bunk.

Timber twists and turns and eventually his eyes

open wide. 'They are a great pair aren't they?'

'Sure are.'

'Can I put my towel back now?' asks Stormy.

We trundle eastwards. The weather remains calm with a pleasantly warm southerly breeze coming off North Africa.

When Malta is within range Mack controls the Wasp in to the Naval Base to collect mail. It is our first non-exercise controlling job. Mack and I have equipped our darkened and remote corner of the Ops Room with all our Helicopter Controller bits and pieces. We have details of call signs and the correct voice procedures taped to the back of adjacent equipment.

The Wasp returns with a couple of bags of mail. I receive a couple of letters. One has a Scottish stamp and was posted ten days ago in Limekilns: it's from Lorna who wishes me a safe journey and confirms that we have made the correct 'relationship' decision given the circumstances. It's a Fife-type Dear John - no kisses. My second is from Mum wishing me a pleasant trip and advice on looking after myself in sandy, foreign places.

Opposite me Jan tosses a scrunched-up sheet of pink paper over his shoulder. 'Would you Adam and ferkin Eve it?'

'Wha?' asks Burbs.

Jan recovers his paper and waves it. 'Listen to this. This is from that bird from Inverkeithing ... Brenda.' He looks at his watch. 'Who, up until about two minutes ago, I thought was one of my girlfriends.'

'One of yewer girlfriends?' asks Kit scratching his chin.

'Yeah. The Scottish one.'

'Go on then,' says Burbs.

'Listen to this,' Jan clears his throat and reads from the crumpled pink sheet. 'Jeremy ... that's me,' he pokes his chest. 'Jeremy, you are hereby free to go out with, date, or have unprotected sex with anyone of your choice as from receipt of this letter. Have a safe trip. Don't contact me when you return to Scotland.'

'Bloody hell,' says Burbs. 'Didn't know your name was Jeremy.'

''Tis, yeah.'

'Bit naff isn't it?'

'Suppose so,' says Jan. 'Are there any women in Suez or Aden?' He asks expectantly.

'Loads, but definitely not available,' explains Chats who is the only person in the mess who has been to the Middle East before.

'Shit. How about Bahrain?'

'Same ... no available women. It's a Muslim country,' explains Chats.

'Surely there are women in Muslim countries?'

'There are, but not for the likes of us.'

*

Gurkha makes a slight detour to pass close to the volcanic island of Stromboli. It is rumoured that the Jimmy has a fascination for mountains that spew molten lava.

'THE VOLCANO INFORMATION OFFICER SPEAKING. THE ISLAND OF STROMBOLI, KNOWN AS THE LIGHTHOUSE OF THE MEDITERRANEAN, HAS BEEN IN ALMOST CONTINUOUS ERUPTION FOR THE PAST 2,000 YEARS. EJACULATIONS OCCUR AT INTERVALS RANGING FROM A FEW MINUTES TO HOURS. IN THE EARLY 1900s A FEW THOUSAND PEOPLE INHABITED THE ISLAND, BUT THE POPULATION NOW NUMBERS ONLY A FEW HUNDRED. AYO GURKHALI.'

'Did I hear a Commissioned Royal Naval Officer say "ejaculations"?' asks Kit.

'What's surprising about that?' asks Bagsy.

'Five syllables.'

'What's a syllable?'

'It's what kept you out of the WRNS, darling,' explains a serious-looking Kit.

Bagsy thinks for a second. 'That can't be right.'

A few of us go up top, beers in hand, to witness the Stromboli show. In the dark of night the whole thing appears to be one massive molten mountain, giving off the most brilliant volcanic firework display; spluttering and spewing molten stuff from the top. Downwind it smells sulphurous: there is a thickness to the air that is only relieved by Royal Navy duty-free cigarettes.

'Good eh?' asks Bagsy.

'Yeah, fantastic,' says Wheelie as he leans on the guardrails.

'Don't lean on the guardrails, young 'un,' says Chats.

'Sorry.' He straightens up.

Gurkha does a complete circumnavigation of Stromboli before tracking south heading for the Straits of Messina.

'Did anyone take a photograph of Stromboli?' I ask.

Silence.

I shuffle back to my bunk space mumbling something like 'What's the point of having a camera if you don't ferkin use it?'

Continued silence.

Once through the Straits of Messina we turn east on the last leg of our journey to the northern entry to the Suez Canal and a farewell to Europe.

We are having breakfast when the first serious Tannoy broadcast of the day shatters the silence.

'THE MIDDLE EASTERN LIAISON OFFICER SPEAKING. WE WILL SHORTLY BE ENTERING A PART OF THE WORLD THAT IS PREDOMINANTLY MUSLIM. THOSE OF YOU WHO HAVEN'T BEEN TO THIS PART OF THE WORLD BEFORE WILL NOTICE THE MANY

CULTURAL DIFFERENCES. THOSE WHO HAVE BEEN
TO THE MIDDLE EAST BEFORE SHOULD EXPLAIN ...'

'Come on then, Chats, you've been to the Middle East
before ... explain the differences to us,' someone asks.

Chats waves a dismissive arm.

Silence. Only the crunch of deep fried bread and the
whir of the exhaust fan can be heard. Breakfast is
definitely not the time for conversation at the main
Seamen's dining table.

'THE MIDDLE EASTERN LIAISON OFFICER
SPEAKING AGAIN. YOU WILL NOTICE THAT MUSLIMS
ARE REQUIRED TO PRAY FIVE TIMES EACH DAY.
MOST WILL PRAY IN THE MANY MOSQUES BUT IT IS
NOT UNUSUAL TO SEE MEN PRAYING OUTSIDE IN
THE OPEN AIR. IT IS INCUMBENT ON US, AS VISITORS
TO THIS PART OF THE WORLD, TO RESPECT THE
LOCAL CUSTOMS - PARTICULARLY RELIGIOUS
ACTIVITIES. ALCOHOL IS PROHIBITED AND
DRUNKENNESS IS A SERIOUS OFFENCE. I WOULD
EMPHASISE THAT ISLAMIC FEMALES ARE REQUIRED
BY CUSTOM TO COVER THEMSELVES AND UNDER NO
CIRCUMSTANCES ARE TO BE APPROACHED. IT IS THE
RESPONSIBILITY OF THOSE CREW MEMBERS WHO
HAVE BEEN TO THE MIDDLE EAST BEFORE TO PASS
ON THEIR EXPERIENCES TO THOSE WHO ARE NEW
TO THE AREA. AYO GURKHALI.'

'Ayo Gurkhali,' says someone from a far table.

'What does incumbent mean?' asks Wheelie.

After some consideration Kit narrows his eyes and
nods. 'It's a long, green vegetable ... circular in cross
section.'

'You're a great ferkin help, you are.'

Someone throws a steaming boot in the general
direction of the Canteen Tannoy and misses.

*

There is a strange Middle Eastern smell drifting over us from the land mass to the south as we approach Port Said. Dozens of vessels of differing types swing silently at anchor. It's dark and the twinkling pinpoints of Port Said lights are strangely enticing. We zigzag our way between vessels to our allocated anchoring point and drop anchor with a resounding clatter and an enveloping cloud of rust. As always, the Royal Navy is conscious of being watched by all the other vessels and is determined to show the rest of the assembled fleet just how the professionals perform this relatively simple operation.

Sugar explains. 'Nobody is ferkin interested in us, the rest of the convoy crews are probably all pissed and asleep. It's dark and they don't give a shit how good or bad we are at anchoring. They probably do the same operation with a quarter the number of people, a lot less bullshit and in a fraction of the time.'

Jack and I nod understandingly.

Sitting on the upper deck at midnight, surrounded by a fleet of twinkling ships with a strangely cooling African wind blowing up my shorts is a memorable experience. As Kit, Sugar, Jack and I chain-smoke we try to identify what nationality each ship is; without flags it's an almost impossible task, even after our allocation of beer.

'We had three Russian Intelligence Gathering Ships following Bermuda around all the time,' I say, just to kick-off a discussion of some kind. 'Didn't we, Shug?'

'Looking for anybody with a smidge of intelligence onboard, were they?' says Jack.

'Cheeky sod. It was because we were the Flagship of the Home ferkin Fleet,' states Sugar as he flicks his cigarette end into the eastern part of the Mediterranean.

'Yeah we know all about Bermuda,' says Kit. 'It was

where they threw all the Home Fleet's oddballs.'

'That's not quite true - Pete and me were on the Bermuda,' says Sugar, lighting another cigarette.

'Need I say more,' says Kit opening his arms wide.

The following morning we align ourselves in convoy order and enter the northern section of the Suez Canal. We are sandwiched between a couple of cargo vessels. The one forward of us is a Panama-registered rust bucket and the one astern is larger than us and flying a Russian flag.

'Bet she's a Ruskie,' says a senior member of the Communication branch standing alongside me.

'Yeah, PO - you're probably right.' I never fail to marvel at the observational talents of members of the flag-wagging branch.

Down the mess, Chats gives those of us who have never been to the Middle East before the run-down on what to expect. Apparently the Arab blokes all walk around in full-length robes with turbans on their heads. Women, if you see any, are clothed head to toe in all-enveloping cloaks and some have their heads and faces totally covered. When we hear a bloke singing or shouting from the top of the mosque tower calling people to prayer, everything will stop. Crane drivers will stop working in mid lift and porters will drop whatever they are carrying.

'So all the women are covered then?' asks Sugar.

'Yep.'

'Why?'

'It's a cultural thing.'

'But why?'

'I don't know, do I?'

On the upper deck it's a strange experience to see land so close to us on both sides. To the west are the green fertile fields of northern Egypt and to the east the barren brown desert of the North Sinai desert.

'THE SUEZ CANAL TRANSIT OFFICER SPEAKING. IT WILL TAKE APPROXIMATELY EIGHT HOURS TO NAVIGATE THE NORTHERN SECTION OF THE CANAL. THEN WE WILL ENTER THE BITTER LAKES WHERE THE CONVOY WILL REASSEMBLE FOR THE SECOND SECTION SOUTH TO THE GULF OF SUEZ AND THE RED SEA. THE TOWN ON THE STARBOARD SIDE IS ISMAILIA. AYO GURKHALI .'

We anchor in the Bitter Lakes as the sun is setting and are immediately surrounded by small boats loaded to the gunwales with Egyptian tourist stuff. Every boat has a pile of camel-shaped stools, colourful cloths, boxes of cheap electrical goods and locally made wooden crates and boxes.

'This is the real reason we stop here, to let the local traders earn some of our money,' explains Chats. 'They're known as bum-boats.'

Well after dark, the blokes and young boys in the bum-boats continue to extol the virtues of their wares and various camel-shaped articles are hoisted onboard in exchange for UK money. Heated discussions abound. The bum-boats are never satisfied with the amount of money offered and we are trying to get something for nothing.

The after Accommodation ladder is lowered and a couple of local Egyptians come onboard and are escorted aft as the Accommodation ladder is quickly hoisted. The oldest Egyptian, wearing a filthy brown robe, well scuffed sandals and a tatty red fez, clears a space on the quarterdeck and entertains us for half an hour with magic tricks involving metal rings, lengths of rope and small metal balls. The Officer of the Watch stands and observes the performance from the deck above, arms folded imperiously across his chest.

'They call this type of bloke a 'Gully-Gully' man,' says Chats.

'Why's that then?'

'I don't ferkin know. Maybe because he comes from Gully.'

At the end of the performance the Gully-Gully man and his helper pass a tatty red fez round and we throw our loose change into it.

In the early hours, the bum-boats begin to depart and many of *Gurkha*'s crew search for somewhere to stow their Egyptian 'rabbits'.

The smell of Egypt is different from any other place I have ever visited; it has a hot, dry smell to it, mixed with more than a hint of Middle Eastern bodily waste.

*

It's one of those moments down the mess when everybody is preoccupied with doing their own thing. Some are reading, a few are letter writing, a quartet are playing a very civilised and polite game of Uckers.

'Why are they called "rabbits" – the things we buy abroad?' Stormy asks me.

'I don't know.'

'Must be a reason though, don't you think?'

'Chats, why do we call souvenirs "rabbits"?' I ask.

'Don't you young lads know anything?'

'Naah ... suppose not,' we chorus.

Chats coughs in preparation for an explanation. 'Yonks ago there was an island near Chatham that was overrun with rabbits. Jack would regularly go to the island to kill a rabbit to take home on leave ...'

'Whaaa?'

'Meat was scarce in those days and this was a way of giving the wife some free and nourishing meat,' Chats concludes.

Giggles.

In the afternoon I am seconded to the forecastle part of ship to help raise the anchor. Our convoy appears to be in a state of chaos as all the ships reposition themselves. The smell of a lively, hot Ismailia, drifting south over our starboard quarter is a disturbing experience.

We leave the relative open space of the Bitter Lakes and enter the southern section of the Canal. The land on the west side has changed from green to dry brown: it appears as though we are floating gently through sand - a weird experience. Ahead of us is a strange wide-beamed vessel that looks as though it has been converted to something resembling a passenger ship. It's called *Arabian Enchantment* and is Panama registered. Behind us is a small wooden warship flying a Turkish flag.

Down the mess, four of us have set up the Uckers board and are throwing the dice to decide who will go first, when Bagsy slides down the mess ladder in a state of some excitement. His face is a shiny crimson. 'Lads ... lads, there are naked women on the arse end of the ship in front of us.'

'Naked women?' splutters Burbs.

'Naked women?' ask the remainder of us in chorus.

'Yeah and they're dancing on the back end of the ship in front of us. Some are wearing shorts ... some are wearing only their underwear ... some are ...'

'You said they were naked,' says Sugar.

'They are ... almost,' replies an increasingly flustered Bagsy.

We scramble up the mess ladder. The mess is emptied in less than a minute. The Forward Seamen's mess are the first of a large bunch all craning their necks to get a glimpse of the women on the back end of the *Arabian Enchantment*. Bagsy is right: there are about twenty women doing a choreographed dance routine. They are dressed for the warmth of the Suez Canal, some are wearing shorts, some are in short skirts and T-shirts and two are wearing only their underwear. One in particular, a top-heavy lady is clad in skin-coloured underwear and looks almost naked from a distance.

'THIS IS THE SUEZ CANAL TRANSIT OFFICER. CLEAR THE FORECASTLE. DO YOU HEAR THERE ... CLEAR THE FORECASTLE. AYO ... WHATSIT.'

Reluctantly we all begin to drift away aft. I look up at the bridge: I can see a number of binoculars trained on the after deck of the *Arabian Enchantment* behind the glass screens.

'Make the most of it, lads,' says Chats as we shuffle aft. 'You won't be seeing anything like that again for a good many months.'

Bagsy and I skip up to the deck behind the bridge to watch the dancers practise their closing routine. The lady in the flesh-coloured underwear is of particular interest.

'What could you do with those, eh Pete?'

'I dunno ... I just don't know, Bagsy.'

'All that jumping up and down ... dancing stuff ... she's going to give herself a black eye.'

'A couple of them probably.'

We giggle.

'Fag?'

'Go on then.'

I spend a fitful and disturbed night, and I bet I'm not the only one.

*

The following morning we are out of the Canal. We skip past the ships that are assembled for the northbound convoy. The *Arabian Enchantment* is nowhere to be seen.

'THE RED SEA TRANSIT OFFICER SPEAKING. WE ARE NOW HEADING SOUTH TOWARDS THE RED SEA. TRANSIT OF THE RED SEA AT OUR ECONOMICAL CRUISING SPEED WILL TAKE US APPROXIMATELY FOUR DAYS. YOU WILL NOTICE A SIGNIFICANT

INCREASE IN THE TEMPERATURE AND YOU ARE ADVISED TO AVOID SITTING UNPROTECTED IN THE SUN FOR LONGER THAN TWENTY MINUTES DURING THE AFTERNOON.

YOU ARE REMINDED THAT THE INABILITY TO PERFORM YOUR DUTIES BECAUSE OF OVER EXPOSURE TO THE SUN IS A PUNISHABLE OFFENCE. AYO GURKHALI.'

'Shirts off then, lads,' says Burbs, tossing his into his locker and bounding up the ladder. The rest of us look at each other and decide to expose our bodies to the Red Sea sun ... a little less enthusiastically.

Bagsy hasn't fully recovered from watching the woman in the flesh coloured underwear and decides to crash-out.

We are not permitted to fly the Wasp while crossing the Red Sea, so Mack and I join up with surface plotting team who have plenty to do as there are lots of ships trundling up and down this relatively narrow stretch of water.

'THE ROUTINE OFFICER SPEAKING. AS FROM TOMORROW THE SHIP WILL OPERATE A TROPICAL ROUTINE. WEEKDAY WORKING HOURS WILL BE FROM 07:00 TO 13:00 WITH A STAND-EASY AT 10:30. UP SPIRITS WILL BE AT 12:45. DRESS OF THE DAY IS TROPICAL RIG.'

'Zero seven double bubble!' splutters Mack.

'Yeah, but every afternoon off,' explains Jack.

'So, shorts and sandals then. Put your No 8 trousers into the laundry and stow them away in the back of your locker,' says Chats. 'Shirts off in the mess is OK but always wear a shirt at tot-time and in the dining hall.'

'Why?'

'Normal practice,' says Chats. 'Would you like to be

eating, or drinking your tot, opposite Kit with his hairy chest out?'

'Suppose not ... no.'

A large fanny full of a pale green liquid appears in the dining hall. Alongside it is a notice explaining that it is recommended that we have at least one glass of lime juice every day to prevent the onset of scurvy. Most of us ignore it until Burbs declares, 'It's nice enough to ferkin drink.'

Timber bounds down the mess ladder. 'You'll never guess what I've just been told.'

'What?'

'To keep my back covered while in the Middle East.'

'Why?'

'In case it offends the locals.'

'Who told you that?'

'The Red Sea Transit Officer.'

'We're in the middle of the Red Sea - they'd need some stonkingly good binoculars to see anything from the coast,' quips Burbs.

'Why isn't the Red Sea red?' asks Stormy.

'Go and ask the Red Sea Transit Officer. He'll ferkin know,' says Mack.

*

I'm lounging on a washdeck locker in the port waste with Chats and Wheelie, and we're enjoying the fresh air, smoking, drinking our allotted two cans of evening beer and flicking our dog ends into the Red Sea.

'I had a butchers at the chart earlier,' says Chats. 'We're south of Jeddah and I reckon we're about opposite a place called Jihzan in Saudi Arabia on the eastern side.' He swivels and points towards the slowly setting sun. 'And to the west is the Nubian desert. We should be out of the Red Sea tomorrow I reckon.'

'You ever been to Saudi Arabia?' asks Wheelie.

'Naah. Don't think Royal Naval ships are allowed.'

'Sounds like a strange place,' I say.

'That area over there inland from the coast is known as the Empty Quarter on the chart,' says Chats, pointing east.

'Wonder why it's called the Empty Quarter?' says Wheelie.

'Probably because it's ferkin empty,' says Chats.

*

Today Cliff and Wheelie have been crowned mess Uckers doubles champions after a whitewash of Burbs and Jack who, up until recently, had been unbeaten. The older members of the mess, including me, are more than a little annoyed that two young lads are so lucky at Uckers. The crib champion is Burbs, but he adds up his scores and stacks his cards so quickly we suspect that he cheats. He takes 'one for his ferkin knob' too regularly to be honest.

'What's Aden like then, Chats?' asks Wheelie.

'The pits. Ferkin awful place. Worse now because of the troubles.'

'Not a good run then?'

'Save your money, it's the pits.'

'THE INFORMATION OFFICER SPEAKING. FOR TODAY ONLY I AM THE GEOGRAPHICAL INFORMATION OFFICER. THE SMALL ISLAND TO PORT IS CALLED MAYYUN AND MARKS THE SOUTHERN END OF THE RED SEA. WE SHOULD BE ARRIVING IN THE PORT OF ADEN IN APPROXIMATELY SIX HOURS TIME. A CONTINGENT OF ROYAL MARINES WILL BE FLOWN TO ADEN PRIOR TO ARRIVAL IN ORDER TO SECURE OUR BERTH. AYO GURKHALI .'

'What's a contingent?' someone asks.

'Something a bit smaller than a regiment I reckon,' says Kit, the fountain of all ferkin knowledge.

'Bloody 'ell, we have to send in the Marines to secure the place,' splurts Jan.

'It's the first time I've heard anything like that,' says Chats, looking perplexed.

Both Mack and I respond to a call to go to the Ops Room as, once again, neither of us knows who is duty controller. Frothy is already there: we reckon he lives in the Ops Room.

'The Wasp is going to do a number of trips into Aden fully loaded with our Bootnecks. Apparently the Port authorities have recommended that we provide our own security on and around Aden's Admiralty pier,' explains Frothy.

'What's a Bootneck?' I ask.

'Royal Marine. Something to do with a part of their uniform they used to have in the olden days,' says Frothy.

Gurkha puts her foot down as we turn east. Mack is sent down aft to check on the preparations on the flight deck. I establish communications with the Wasp. Pontius tells me that he is busy organising the Royal Marine contingent. He sounds a little stressed.

Twenty miles short of Aden we launch the Wasp for the first time with three fully equipped Royal Marines onboard, one of whom is Major Munro.

It takes an hour and a half to shuttle a dozen Royal Marines ashore.

'THE PADRE SPEAKING ...'

'Have we got a Padre onboard?' asks Mack, surprised.
'Not as far as I know.'
'Nor me.'
'When the ferk did he come onboard then?' asks Kit.
'Must have been in Gib ... when we weren't looking.'
'Maybe it's the Geographical Information Officer

with his shirt on back to front,' says Burbs.

'THE PADRE SPEAKING ...'

'See, we have got a Padre then,' says Kit.

'... ACCORDING TO THE MUSLIM RELIGION, PICTURES OF THE HUMAN FORM ARE OFFENSIVE. THOSE CREW MEMBERS WITH TATTOOS DEPICTING THE HUMAN FORM ... MALE OR FEMALE ... ARE REQUIRED TO KEEP THEM COVERED WHILE ASHORE IN THE MIDDLE EAST TO BE ON THE SAFE SIDE. AYO' ... WHAT? ... AYO GURKHA.'

'That's you buggered, Timber - you'll have to keep the one-shouldered gal covered up.'
'Yeah, but I'm not likely to go ashore without it covered up, am I?'
'What about swimming?'
'Oh shit, never thought of that.'
'Do you think they'll notice that gal on mi lower leg?' asks Kit. 'She'll be about forty years old by now ... she could be a granny.'
'She's a bit hairy, Kit,' Jan says.
'Only if you go ashore in shorts,' I say.
'I'm not going ashore in long trousers, am I?'
'Go and ask the Padre then ... his door is always open.'
'No bloody fear.'

5

Aden – a definite eye-opener

'ANYBODY KNOW what the temperature is today?' asks Burbs.

'About ninety degrees.'

'Shit, that's hot.'

'That's average for Pudsey.' I say.

'What ... ninety?' asks Chats, wide-eyed.

'Sorry, thought you said nineteen.'

The Wasp is secured on deck and we get our first sight of Aden. In a fold of stark, mountainous land lies a gathering of dark grey buildings. It has the reputation of being a precarious place and it looks forbidding and sinister. There is a low-lying sheet of pale grey smoke covering an elevated section of the town at the base of the highest mountain.

We enter Aden in Procedure Alpha. We are all dressed in whites with shorts, caps with chin-stays down

What's not to like about Aden?

and standing to attention in perfectly straight lines. Kit makes a comical point of flashing his naked Granny at the town. All the correct flags and pennants are flying and a gun salute is fired to someone who warrants it. We wallow within a good heaving line throw of a cracked concrete jetty. Lines of RN and Army Land Rovers flank the length of the jetty. Our contingent of Royal Marines stands equidistant along the short jetty; they are cradling their weapons.

Up close Aden looks to be a colourless place: beyond the large, low lying buildings of the port area appears to be a warren of single storey, flat-roofed, slate grey structures.

Sugar throws the first heaving line and it snakes beautifully through the still, humid Aden air and lands on the bonnet of an Army Land Rover, shocking the three dozing occupants. It snakes through the line of static Royal Marines and back into the water.

'Come on Royal, see if you can catch the string next time,' yells Sugar.

A couple of Royal Marines give us a two-finger salute as we all watch Sugar recover and recoil his heaving line. Sugar's second throw arches well over the line of Royal Marines. One places a large shiny boot on the line. Then, with the help of blokes from the RN Land Rovers, we are berthed.

'THE MIDDLE EAST LIAISON OFFICER SPEAKING. THE PORT OF ADEN IS CURRENTLY AN AREA OF INTER-TRIBAL TENSIONS. WHILST LEAVE WILL BE GRANTED, THE SHIP'S COMPANY ARE WARNED NOT TO GO ASHORE ALONE. HMS SHEBA AND RAF KHORMAKSA HAVE CANTEENS WHERE ALCOHOLIC BEVERAGES CAN BE PURCHASED. THERE IS A PERMANENT BRITISH MILITARY PRESENCE ON THE GROUND IN ADEN IN THE FORM OF THE 24th INFANTRY BRIGADE AND THE 1st BATTALION ARGYLL AND SUTHERLAND HIGHLANDERS. ARMY TRANSPORT TO AND FROM MILITARY BASES WILL BE AVAILABLE. THE SHIP'S COMPANY ARE WARNED TO BE AWARE OF ANYBODY AND EVERYBODY. TROUBLE ASHORE COULD RESULT IN SHORE LEAVE BEING CANCELLED. ALL SHIP'S DIVERS MUSTER OUTSIDE THE DIVE STORE. DIVING OFFICER REPORT TO THE BRIDGE. AYO GURK ...   GURK ... HALI .'

Jan says, 'shit.'

'You a ship's diver then?' I ask.

'Sure am. Now's the time to earn my money. I bet this is a bottom search.'

'Searching for what exactly?' asks Wheelie.

'Magnetic mines ... or anything.'

'Probably normal routine in Aden these days,'

explains Chats.

Kit claps his hands. 'Who's for a run ashore then?'

Silence.

There isn't a rush to get changed into run-ashore gear. Aden's reputation is already weighing heavily upon us and a degree of self-protection is kicking in.

Down the mess a typed paper is placed alongside tomorrow's Daily Orders. It explains the official Aden situation:

'Aden has been part of the British Empire since 1839. In 1963 the National Liberation Front started an unprovoked armed revolt against the British. The NLF are followers of Colonel Nasser, the President of Egypt, who apparently inspires the whole of the Arab world. He wants to unite all the Arab countries to expel the western colonial powers from the Middle East.'

I volunteer to ditch the gash before evening rounds. I want to set foot on Arabian soil. On the jetty I empty my gash bucket, light a fag and look around me. The place smells of hot dust and sewage. The Royal Marines remain equally spaced along the jetty. The Diving Officer and a couple of the ship's divers are standing on the side of the jetty looking after the divers who are somewhere underwater. A couple of Army Land Rovers have been parked at the end of the jetty in a position that prevents people and vehicles getting close to us.

Bagsy and Burbs decide to go ashore together. *Gurkha* is Bagsy's first ship and Gibraltar was the first time he had set foot outside England. Burbs is happy to be asked to look after Bagsy.

'We'll go to Sheba, see what the NAAFI has to offer,' says Burbs "You sure that there will be no women around?' he asks Chats.

'They're around, but I doubt if you'll see 'em.'

'Nobody else want to come with us?'

Silence.

'Got letters to write,' says Jack.

'Yeah, letters to write,' confirms Timber.

Down the mess the evening is spent in quiet contemplation interspersed with flurries of activity such as getting the Uckers board out, putting it away and getting the Crib board out.

Most of us have turned in and are reading when Bagsy and Burbs return. Bagsy slips down the mess ladder and ends up splayed out on the deck at the bottom of the ladder. It's a sure sign that he has sniffed something similar to the barmaid's apron.

'What's Aden like, then?' asks someone who hasn't yet learned that you don't engage drunken mess members in conversation.

Bagsy wipes himself down and rubs his backside. 'Not bad at all, was it Burbs?'

Burbs trips over the gash bucket. 'Not that bad.'

'You go to Sheba then?'

'Naah. We went to that RAF place ... Kormak something, because their transport was more comfortable.'

'Khormaksa?'

'Yeah that's it.'

'Any good?'

'Not bad. Good beer and a couple of really attractive NAAFI girls.'

'They weren't. They were abso ... absolutely dogs,' says Bagsy, burping as he struggles to take a shoe off.

'And there were some WRAFS there.'

'How many?' I ask.

'Dunno.' Burbs slings his clothes on the deck and lies on his bunk. 'Talk about it in the mow ... morning.'

Bagsy's shoe comes off unexpectedly and he falls backwards, banging his head on Wheelie's bunk.

Wheelie opens one eye. 'Get turned in you drunken sod.'

'Goin' for a piss first,' says Burbs, and he trips up the mess ladder and away.

*

It's no surprise that it's Sugar who cross-examines Burbs about the WRAFS at *RAF Khormaksa* as we queue for breakfast.

'How many WRAFS were there then? What are they like? Did you talk to them? How old are they?'

'They were just sat at a table in the corner,' replies Burbs. He is looking bleary-eyed.

'How many?'

'Bout half a dozen.'

'How close were you?'

'A couple of tables away.'

'And you didn't introduce yourself?'

'No.'

'Bloody hell, Burbs.'

'I'm thinking of getting engaged you know, Shug.'

'So what?' Sugar notices Bagsy enter the Dining Hall. 'Bagsy! Bagsy! Over here, young 'un. Tell me all about these WRAFS.'

'WE HAVE RECEIVED A SIGNAL INSTRUCTING US TO PROCEED TO SEA TOMORROW, A DAY EARLIER THAN SCHEDULED. CHIEF BOSUN'S MATE, DIVING OFFICER AND THE ENGINEERING OFFICER REPORT TO THE BRIDGE.'

Sugar wraps a grease-laden sausage inside a slice of white bread and takes a bite. 'That's that then, lads. It's today or never for a run ashore this afternoon.'

Timber, Wheelie and I pluck up our joint courage and change into 6As to go ashore for a couple of hours. Sugar and Chats join us.

There is a single Royal Marine at the bottom of the

brow. We ignore the Army and Navy transport and stroll down the deserted length of our jetty towards town. Sugar hops in to the *RAF Khormaksa* Land Rover.

'See you then, Shug,' says Chats.

'See ya.'

It is the first time I have seen blokes dressed in robes and wearing colourful headgear. Round the corner from our jetty there is a group of men. In four lines they are performing something choreographed: bowing and kneeling in response to someone standing alone at the front.

'Prayers,' says Chats. 'Give them a wide berth.'

'No women?' asks Wheelie.

'Can't see any.'

Children, also wearing white robes, run around as though they are enjoying themselves. On the far side of the praying group is a gaggle of grey, bearded men squatting in a circle smoking from a contraption in the centre. It smells strange. The smokers look at us with far-away, blood-veined eyes.

We look around - there is nothing welcoming, only lines of grey windowless blocks, a few battered old trucks, rusting cars and lots of be-robed blokes just lounging about. Only the scampering boy children make a noise.

'First impressions are not good,' I say.

'What shall we do then?' asks Timber.

We all look at Chats for guidance.

'Don't stop - turn round and keep walking,' says Chats.

'But what are we going to do?' asks Wheelie.

'Back to the jetty and grab transport to the Navy or the RAF place?' I suggest.

'Yeah, that sounds like a good idea,' says Wheelie.

'I'm going back onboard then,' says Chats. 'If you're going to Sheba, I'll leave you to it.'

The guy sitting in the driver's seat of the RN Land

Rover is dozing. I slap the roof to wake him. 'Can you take us to Sheba, mate?' I ask.

He blinks his eyes. 'Sure can, pal ... hop in.'

As he drives down the jetty he yawns continually.

'What's Sheba like then?' asks Timber.

'Shit,' replies the driver stifling another yawn.

'Got a bar?' I ask.

'Yep.'

'What's it like?'

'Shit,' he yawns. 'Shit and double shit.'

'How long you been here then?' asks Wheelie.

'Eleven months, three weeks and one day. Leaving this shit-hole in exactly six days time.'

'Any women at Sheba?' asks Timber.

'Couple of the wives drop in sometimes for a swim in the pool and drinks in the afternoon. But only the real piss-heads frequent the bar in the evening.'

'You got a pool then?' asks Wheelie, suddenly animated.

The driver stifles a yawn as he stops in the centre of a narrow dirt lane to let a bloke pushing a cart piled high with plastic containers pass. 'If you can call it a pool. It's a cordoned-off area of the sea. There are a couple of chairs and a few tables and one of those umbrella things. Nobody uses it these days because there are holes in the shark nets.'

'Ferkin shark nets?' I say.

'Yeah to keep the sharks away.'

'But you said there were big holes in them.'

'Naah ... I only said holes ... I didn't mention the size.'

'How do you know there are holes in the nets then?' I ask.

'The locals raise the nets every morning and collect the fish caught in them.'

'Why?'

'To ferkin eat of course.'

*

HMS Sheba is an uninspiring place with armed sentries at the entrance. An elderly NAAFI man serves behind the bar and there are a couple of blokes sitting in the corner playing dominoes.

The pool area outside is a horseshoe-shaped section of sea, at the seaward end of which is a line of plastic orange buoys.

'Suppose those buoys are on the shark nets,' says Wheelie.

'Yeah, suppose so.'

'Fancy a swim then?' asks Timber as he places our six cans of ice-cold beer in the centre of a table.

'Would do if I'd brought my cossie,' I say.

'You wouldn't, would ya?' asks Wheelie.

'No, course not. What's the use of shark nets when they've got ferkin great holes in them?'

'Right.'

'Didn't you get any glasses, Timber?' I ask.

'They haven't got any.' He fishes in his pocket and tosses a can opener on the table. 'Got a can opener though.'

Back in the mess we compare *HMS Sheba* to the facilities on offer at *RAF Khormaksa* according to Bagsy and Burbs. *HMS Sheba* loses on all counts.

'DUTY WATCH OF SEAMEN MUSTER ON THE QUARTERDECK, PREPARE TO SINGLE UP. MAJOR MUNRO REPORT TO THE BRIDGE. BOTH WATCHES OF SEAMEN WILL MUSTER ON THEIR PARTS OF SHIP AT 07:35. AYO GURKHALI.'

'Definitely buggered up now they're getting the top Bootneck out of his stinking pit.'

The ship's divers are the last people onboard as we

single-up ready to leave.

I gaze uncaringly as Aden drifts into the distance and *Gurkha* points herself south. We don't fire any salutes as it's too early. It looks like it's going to be another scorching hot day. It will be nice however to get a refreshing breeze across the deck again.

It's my turn in the Ops Room. Apparently one of our Chinese laundry crew has been left ashore. The Wasp, with a couple of armed Royal Marines onboard, is to return to Aden to recover him.

I'm controlling the Wasp on what is officially termed a 'mercy mission'. Frothy hangs around until he is satisfied that I have the trip under control. I land the Wasp on the end of our recently vacated jetty and with the help of a couple of blokes from the Argyll & Southerland Highlanders our Chinese laundry man is safely bundled onboard along with a couple of bags of mail.

Down the mess Burbs asks Jan: 'What's the ship's bottom like then?'

'Manky and covered in long lengths of straggly weed.'

'Like a stoker's backside then?'

'More attractive,' explains Jan with a serious expression.

'UP SPIRITS.'

The messdeck telephone rings. Jan snakes an arm out and picks up the receiver. 'University of Seamanship, Professor Fletcher Principle Lecturer of Scuttles speaking.' His smile suddenly changes to one of serious concern. 'Sorry sir, just trying to inject a slice of humour into proceedings.' Jan nods. 'Yes sir, it's tot-time.'

Chats mouths 'who is it?' as he takes his tot from Jack.

Jan shakes his head while listening to whoever is on the other end of the phone. He nods acceptance. 'Will do, sir. Thank you for calling the University of Seamanship.' He quickly replaces the receiver.

Chats downs his tot in one. 'Who was it and what did he want?'

'Pete, you've been summoned by Jimmy. Report to the Wardroom. Don't know why.'

'Bollocks. Wonder what that's all about?' I drain my glass.

Jan shrugs his shoulders.

Chats smiles.

I grab my cap and shuffle up the mess ladder. I must have done something wrong.

I knock on the Wardroom door. Eventually it's opened by an unsmiling Steward. 'I've been told to report to the First Lieutenant. My name is Able Seaman Broadbent.'

'Wait.' He closes the door.

'Prat,' I say to the closed Wardroom door.

I kick my heels for almost five minutes until the door is opened by the Jimmy. 'No need for your hat, Broadbent.'

I take my hat off: at least I'm not in the shit then.

'Fancy a game of cricket in Bahrain?' he asks.

'Not really, sir.'

'Not really? Why on earth not?'

'I don't think I would cope well with the heat, sir.'

'What ... a young fit lad like yourself?'

'Yes, sir.'

'Truth is, Able Seaman Broadbent, we're struggling to put a team together. I have it on good authority that you are a player and that you knew Sir Len Hutton.'

'That's a bit of an exaggeration, sir. I sat next to Len at a few local cricket matches ...'

'That's good enough.' The Jimmy nods and points at my chest.

'I didn't know who he was at the time, sir.'

'No matter. Can I pencil you in as twelfth man?'

'No thank you, sir. I have a delicate ankle and wouldn't be much use.'

'How delicate?'

'It's difficult to walk very far without a rest, sir.'

'How far?'

'About twenty yards, sir ... on a good day.'

'Is this an excuse for not playing, Able Seaman Broadbent?'

'No, sir.'

'Is that the truth?'

'Yes, sir.'

'Dismissed,. Jimmy waves an arm at me and closes the door.

'Prat,' I say to the Wardroom door and turn away. I'm glad I got myself out of that one. Only mad dogs and Englishmen would want to play cricket in this heat.

Down the mess Chats asks me what Jimmy wanted.

'He wanted to know if I would play cricket in Bahrain.'

'And what did you say?'

'I told him where to stick his cricket bat, didn't I?' I lied.

Jan slaps my shoulder. 'Good man.'

*

The following morning I'm with Sergeant Lecky on the quarterdeck working out where to fit a small additional fuel tank into both of the RIBs.

'What are we doing Dhow Patrols for, Sergeant? What are we looking for?'

'Contraband. Guns, ammunition, dirty postcards. Anything that would be considered illegal, illicit, unlawful, prohibited, banned or forbidden.'

'Dirty postcards?'

'Dirty, filthy Egyptian postcards.' He taps the side of his nose with his forefinger.

Both Sergeant Lecky and I have a laugh.

I try the same joke down the mess at tot-time but it

doesn't raise a snigger.

We follow the South Arabian coast for the next couple of days.

I get the opportunity to run the RIB at full speed up and around a trundling *Gurkha* whenever Major Munro can arrange it. We are operationally primed as we trundle our way opposite an area of Oman that is reportedly a notorious hang-out of smugglers. Fortunately we come across nothing worthy of an intercept and *Gurkha* gradually works its way north, with the grey mountainous coast of north Oman on our port side. Once through the Straits of Hormuz, we are into the Persian Gulf proper.

'CLEAR LOWER DECK FOR ENTERING HARBOUR PROCEDURE ALPHA. CLOSE ALL UPPER DECK SCREEN DOORS. HANDS OUT OF THE RIG OF THE DAY CLEAR OFF THE UPPER DECK. WE SHALL BE ENTERING BAHRAIN AT 09:00. WE HAVE BEEN ALLOCATED A BERTH MIDWAY DOWN THE MINA SULMAN JETTY. ABLE SEAMAN CARSON REPORT TO THE REGULATING OFFICE. AYO GURKHALI .'

Kit rolls out of his bunk. 'Bollocks ... what now?'

There is nothing that looks to be higher than one storey on the Bahrain skyline. We fall out as we approach a long, slim jetty crowded with vessels of all types on both sides. We head for a small gap astern of another Tribal Class frigate.

A welcoming group of seamen from *HMS Nubian* take our heaving lines and berthing ropes. They help us rig our two gangways and are the first people to come onboard. *Nubian* is being relieved by us and is due to leave for the UK tomorrow. Chats knows the killick in charge of the berthing party and invites him down the mess at tot-time.

'UP SPIRITS. MAIL IS NOW READY FOR COLLECTION.'

I watch as Timber sniffs a letter before opening it.
'That from your mum?' I ask.
'Think so, yeah.'
'Does she put perfume on your letters or something?'
'Sometimes,' replies Timber, looking embarrassed.
'Blimey.'

The Mina Sulman jetty, Bahrain

Down the mess the killick from *Nubian* answers all our questions about Bahrain. Apparently the closest watering hole is the junior rates canteen at *HMS Jufair*, but it's hard to find. The only other place to get a drink is *RAF Muharraq*, but access to this facility is by invitation only as it is rumoured that there are female WRAFS there. There is a small swimming pool within *Jufair* that is kept reasonably clean. The capital of Bahrain is Manama but unless we are interested in medieval Arab architecture and the tang of a non-existent sewerage system, it has nothing to recommend it. We also learn that there is a minesweeping squadron based here consisting of a couple of minesweepers, *HMS Chawton* and *HMS Beachampton*. Our sister ship *HMS Eskimo* is also based here but at the moment she is out on Dhow Patrol.

Chats looks on in amazement as his soon-to-be ex-mate from *HMS Nubian* drinks every drop of his tot: Sandy Bottoms is not what he had been offered.

I place a protective hand over my tot.

Kit slides down the mess ladder. 'You'll never ferkin guess what,' he announces, opening his arms wide and smiling.

'What?' asks Chats, briefly diverting his mournful eyes from his empty tot glass.

'Gentleman, you are lookin' at a genuine Bedouin ship's Land Rover driver.'

'Naah?'

'Told ya that having a driving licence would have its advantages.'

'When was that then?'

'I dunno. Anyway I've got a ferkin Land Rover ... or I will have when *Nubian* pisses off.'

The killick from *Nubian* holds up a silencing hand. 'Tomorrow mate ... we'll be leaving for home at sparrows' fart in the morning.'

'Sparrows' fart?' I ask.

'Early,' explains Chats.

'Make sure you leave us with a full tank of fuel then,' says Kit, smiling. 'And the ferkin keys.'

The killick from *Nubian* bids us farewell. 'Suppose I'd better go and do some work,' he says. 'Thanks for the tot, Chats mate ... see you back in the UK sometime.' And he skips up the ladder and away like a bloke who's just seen-off his mate's tot.

Chats stares at the ladder in bemused silence. There is a glint of a tear forming in the corner of his eye. 'Not if I see you first … you thieving bastard,' yells Chats at the empty ladder.

Jack passes a quarter-full glass of Queen's to Chats. 'Down that, mate.'

Chats looks at Jack with tearful eyes. His expression asks for confirmation.

Jack nods.

Chats looks at all of us sat around the table.

As though choreographed, we all nod in agreement.

Chats drapes an arm around Jack's shoulder and gives it a manly squeeze. 'Cheers fellers.' He downs the Queen's. 'Thanks a lot, fellers.'

'THE PAY OFFICER SPEAKING. MONEY CHANGING WILL TAKE PLACE IN THE PAY OFFICE BETWEEN 13:30 AND 14:30. UNTIL THE END OF THIS YEAR THE PERSIAN GULF RUPEE IS LEGAL TENDER ASHORE. THIS IS PEGGED TO THE INDIAN RUPEE AT A RATE OF THIRTEEN AND A THIRD TO ONE POUND STERLING. AT THE END OF THE YEAR THE PERSIAN GULF RUPEE WILL BE REPLACED BY THE BAHRAINI DINAR EACH MADE UP OF ONE HUNDRED FILS. MORE INFORMATION AS IT BECOMES AVAILABLE.'

The following morning, those of us working on the upper deck offer the traditional verbal farewell that is normally exchanged between ships on their way back to the UK and those that are not. As *HMS Nubian* drifts away from the jetty she responds with a series of lengthy ceremonial blasts on her horn and some unauthorised rings of her ship's bell. Those on our bridge offer a smart, choreographed salute. We, from the lower deck, raise a couple of fingers as a parting gesture.

A PTI from *Jufair*, dressed in the tight-fitting shorts

and singlet of his profession, bounds down our mess at tot-time brandishing a paper list of sporting possibilities. Chats drinks his tot before inviting him to take a seat.

There is little enthusiasm for playing sports of any kind at the moment. Despite our mess air conditioner clanking away for 24 hours each day it makes absolutely no difference to the outside temperature that is well over ninety degrees by dinner time.

'We've already had to cancel a game of cricket as you can't raise a team,' says the PTI in the strange high-pitched tone of his branch.

Chats points a finger at me. 'That was Pete's fault.'

The PTI swivels round. 'Who's Pete?'

'I am,' I admit, tapping my chest.

The PTI squints at me. 'Why?'

'Didn't ferkin want to play,' I say. 'The Jimmy was organising it.'

'I can see that Gurkha is not a sporty ship,' squeaks the PTI.

'Not today ... no,' says Chats.

The PTI bounds up our mess ladder without saying another word.

'He'll get an even worse reaction down the Stokers' mess,' declares Chats.

'Bootnecks might play with him though,' says Kit.

'Maybe.'

Chats and I make our way to the gangway to relieve the Quartermaster and Bosun's Mate so they can have their tot. We watch as *Jufair*'s PTI sprints away down the jetty, skirting expertly around the various skips and piles of rubbish.

'They're a special and irrepressible breed, PTIs, aren't they?' asks Chats.

'Sure are,' I say, although I'm not one hundred percent sure what irrepressible means.

There isn't a cloud in the sky, there's no wind and the temperature is uncomfortable. I hear a strange call from somewhere in the distance.

'Prayer call,' says Chats. 'Lunchtime ... dinner-time prayers. Did you really tell the Jimmy where to stick his cricket?'

'Told him I'd sprained my ankle.'

'Chicken.'

*

'UP SPIRITS.'

'It smells strangely different today lads,' says Jack as he places the rum fanny gingerly on the not-so-clean dishing-up cloth at the end of the mess table.

As is customary, Jack takes sippers of the first tot that is for Chats ... and retches. 'Shit ... ferkin shit.'

Someone from the opposite mess shouts, 'Have you tasted the rum yet?'

Chats sniffs his tot and takes a sip. 'Something wrong with this.'

Sugar holds a hand out. 'Let's have a taste.'

'Piss off. You think I came in on the last banana boat?'

'A tot is a tot,' says Kit and downs his in one. He pulls a face, belches and holds his stomach. 'Aarrrgh ... that was ferkin awful.'

'THE OFFICER OF THE DAY SPEAKING. ALL MESSES ARE TO RETURN THEIR RUM ISSUE. LOCAL BOWSER WATER HAS MISTAKENLY BEEN USED. A REPLACEMENT ISSUE WILL BE MADE.'

'Ferk me,' says Sugar. Let's have mi tot then, Jack. You can say I'd already drunk mine.

'Yeah I'll have a crack at mine as well,' says Jan.

'It's ferkin awful,' declares Jack. 'And you're assuming that we'll get a full re-issue without them measuring what I take back.'

'Tot me,' says Jan.

'Me too,' adds Sugar.

We all have a taste. Sugar and Jan both down theirs in one, then declare it undrinkable.

According to the duty Jack Dusty, responsible for organising the rum issue today, the whole thing was one horrendous cock-up. Responsibility is laid fairly and squarely on the rather sloping shoulders of the second Officer-of-the-Day, a young Sub Lieutenant who joined us in Aden.

Dinner on an empty stomach isn't the same. But the re-issue of rum is a full issue with lots of 'Queen's'.

Kit is duty Land Rover driver and with a couple of tots inside him is keen to get behind the wheel. Somehow he convinces the Officer-of-the-Day that he should do a special, unauthorised trip.

He drives a little way down the jetty to where Mack, Bagsy and I are hiding behind some shoulder-high crates.

'You know where the canteen is, Kit?'

'Haven't got a clue.'

'Do you mean that they bastards on Nubian didn't give you a map ... or a clue or anything?' asks Mack.

'Nope.'

Once off the jetty we are onto a roadless expanse of sand. Kit follows tyre tracks and after ten minutes stops outside a construction of bamboo and wire netting.

'Hop out, young 'un ... see what this is,' Kit says to Bagsy.

Bagsy does exactly as he is told and ambles over to a gap in the bamboo, peers inside and saunters back.

'What is it then?' I ask.

'I think it's a swimming pool,' says Bagsy.

'Is there a bar?'

'Naah, nothing but a big hole in the ground full of water.'

'Clean?'

'Reasonably, yeah.'

'Any women?' asks Kit.

'Didn't see any,' says Bagsy.

We spend the next quarter of an hour aimlessly driving around. Eventually an eagle-eyed Mack spots a building on the horizon with a number of blue Land Rovers parked outside. 'Over there, Kit,' he says.

Inside, it's a typical forces Canteen, but devoid of any NAAFI embellishments. Standing at the bar are a couple of lads. One of them is in uniform with his cap on the bar. 'You get lost then?' he asks us, smiling.

Kit shrugs his shoulders. 'We stopped to assess the sporting facilities.'

The bloke serving behind the bar leans over, resting on his elbows. 'Sorry, lads ,but the beer situation is serious: we've only got a few crates and are limiting everybody to two cans until we receive our next delivery.'

'Naah?'

'Sure as I'm ferkin stood here with my arm around a drooling nymphomaniac ... sorry.'

'What's a nympho ... whatsit?' asks Bagsy.

'A lover of men,' explains Kit.

'Eh?'

'Forget it.'

The temperature is more than a little uncomfortable. The ceiling fans are rotating slowly. There is an air-conditioning unit on the wall by the main entrance door but it's not switched on.

'It's hot isn't it, mate?' Kit asks the bloke behind the bar.

'Tis, yeah.'

'Air conditioner not working?'

'It works yeah. But it's a choice between cold beer and cold air. We can't run the freezer and the air conditioner at the same time.'

We take six cans and find chairs around a chipped and filthy table where the sun doesn't shine.

'Shit hole,' I declare.

'Sure is.'

Two blokes from the sweepers join us. 'What do you reckon to the facilities then?'

'Shit.'

'Welcome to Bahrain.'

'Is there anywhere else that we can get a decent wet?'

'RAF Muharraq - other ranks bar. But it's not easy getting in: they run a 'by invitation only' system because there are WRAFS there.'

'What about Manama?' asks Kit.

'Depends what you want. If you want to smoke something obnoxious from a hubbly-bubbly or drink crappy Arab coffee then it's fine but if you want music, bars and girls then it could be a million miles away.'

'Right then.'

'If you follow the track down towards the white storage tank you'll see the Jufair gate. Follow the single dusty road until you hit tarmac and you'll be in the outskirts of Manama.'

Manama proves to be an uninteresting place to my 21-year-old Yorkshire eyes. We park on the seafront and walk the length of a dusty road alongside which dozens of Dhows are berthed. The smell of fish is overpowering. The Dhows are a crumbling heap.

'Dump,' exclaims Kit.

'Yeah,' confirms Mack.

'Back onboard?' asks Kit.

'Why not.'

Back in the mess there is a lower-deck discussion on the merits of Bahrain. We are getting absolutely nowhere until Chats joins us. 'Bahrain's a relatively relaxed Muslim country,' he tells us. 'However, they don't advertise the fact. The only form of entertainment outside of the Naval base as far as I can remember is the weekly camel racing.

'They race camels?' asks Wheelie.

'It's the most popular sport in Bahrain. Every Friday they strap young boy jockeys on the back ... smaller the better ...'

'I've got a camel joke,' interrupts Burbs.

'Oh yeah?'

'Go on then,' says a resigned-looking Chats.

Burbs rubs his hands together. 'A young camel was asking his Mum questions. "Why do we have three large toes on our feet?" he asks. "So we don't sink while walking on the soft sands of the desert," his mother replies. "Why do we have long eyelashes?" was the youngster's next question. "To stop the sand of the desert storms getting in our eyes," was his Mum's immediate reply. "Why do we have a large hump on our back?" the young camel asks. "So we can cross the many miles of hot desert without needing water," she explains. The young camel looks directly into his Mum's eyes and says, "what are we doing in Birmingham zoo then?"'

Bagsy and I laugh, but the rest moan in the way that messdecks do when told a joke they think they've heard before.

The following morning I take a stroll up the jetty after ditching some gash in the shoreside gash bins. A Stoker I know is doing the same thing. He points to a group of Arabs squatting on the edge of the jetty down aft. 'You'll never ferkin Adam-and-Eve what's going on down there.'

'What?'

'That's where our shit tank overflow discharges into the Gulf. There isn't a facility to take our sewage off the ship.'

'Isn't there?'

'The shit attracts small fish known locally as shit fish.'

'OK.'

'And those blokes are catching 'em.'

'What for?'

'To eat.'

'Naah!'

'Yeah. Come on, have a butchers.'

We walk over and quietly, without disturbing the fishermen, watch as loads and loads of small, brown-skinned fish are netted and placed in plastic bags on the jetty.

'If they only knew,' I say.

'They do.'

Back down the mess I tell everybody about the shit fish.

'Heard about the locusts?' says Chats.

'Nope.'

'They're considered a delicacy here. They sell them in the market. They have them on sticks.'

'Naah.'

'Slimy yellow insides. Arabs love 'em.'

'Naah.'

'When the swarms pass through, everybody comes out with their nets ... and some drive around to catch them in the car radiator grills.'

'You're pulling my plonker.'

*

Kit yells down the mess ladder: 'If anyone wants a lift to the Jufair pool I've got permission to do a shuttle this afternoon.'

'Anyone up for it?' asks Jack as he begins to dish out the rum.

'I'm writing to mi sister,' says Bagsy.

'Why?' I ask.

'To tell her not to write to me again.'

'Why?'

'Because she's a stupid schoolgirl who wants me to write to some of her mates.'

'What's wrong with that?'

'They're all twelve years old.'

About six of us agree to go for a swim and we organise a lift with Kit.

Enjoying ourselves at Jufair pool

A small, very dark-skinned young man welcomes us to the Jufair pool with open arms and a wide smile. We are the only ones there and spend a very pleasant couple of hours playing in the water or sitting on the side staring into space. Someone has a camera.

*

The messdeck rumour that we will be spending Christmas in a place called Abadan in Persia is being discussed.

'I could have told you that when we were in Pompey,' I say. 'Nora's Mum at the NAAFI Club told me.'

'Why didn't you ferkin tell us then?' asks Jan.

'Because I didn't ferkin believe her, did I?'

'How does she know these things?' asks Jan.

'Dunno.'

Nobody in our mess has been to Persia before. The Navigator's Yeoman tells us that Abadan is at the top of the Persian Gulf about thirty miles up a river called the Shatt al Arab.

'Can't be any worse than here,' says Wheelie.

'Can't it?'

'Hope the name Shatt isn't an omen,' Kit says.

'There's a list on the noticeboard for Grippo's in Abadan. Apparently there are lots of Brits and American ex-pats there,' says Chats.

On the afternoon of Friday 23rd December 1965 we depart the fascinations of Bahrain with joyous hearts. We wave a fond farewell to *HMS Eskimo*, who arrived a few hours ago and is staying alongside the Mina Sulman jetty for the festive season.

We miss the midday mail delivery and Mack has the job of directing the Wasp into Manama to collect what will no doubt be our last mail delivery for a few weeks.

'THE INFORMATION OFFICER SPEAKING. WE ARE NOW HEADING NORTH TO ABADAN WHERE WE SHALL ARRIVE EARLY TOMORROW MORNING. ABADAN HAS THE WORLD'S LARGEST OIL REFINERY: LOCALLY THERE ARE A VARIETY OF SMOKING RESTRICTIONS IN FORCE. MORE INFORMATION AS IT BECOMES AVAILABLE. AYO GURKHALI .'

6

The Youngbloods of Abadan

IT'S ALWAYS an enjoyable experience to arrive at a place you've never been before. I roll out of my bunk in anticipation of my first visit to Persia.

First impressions mean a lot and Abadan scores very low on the eye-catching scale. Behind a thin line of vegetation the entire horizon is dominated by the unsightly outline of refinery equipment. Large, visible pipes snake out from the shore to tankers moored on the river. The air is heavy with an overpowering smell of oil: I can taste it.

There is nothing attractive or alluring about Abadan and we all decide to stay onboard, until ...

'THE INFORMATION OFFICER SPEAKING. THE EXPAT COMMUNITY OF ABADAN HAVE INVITED ALL MEMBERS OF THE SHIP'S COMPANY TO THE GOLESTAN CLUB AT 18:30 THIS EVENING. THE LOCAL

COMMUNITY HAVE A REPUTATION OF GENEROUS HOSPITALITY TO THE CREWS OF VISITING HM SHIPS, PARTICULARLY AT CHRISTMAS TIME. THERE IS A FREE PINT OF BEER AT THE BAR COURTESY OF THE SHIP'S TOMBOLA FUND. TRANSPORT WILL LEAVE THE BOTTOM OF THE GANGWAY AT 18:15.'

Golaston Club, Abadan

Mack gets all excited. 'A free pint ... a free pint he said. It's Crimbo Eve after all.'

'Spoken like a true Scot,' replies Jack.

Mack, Burbs and myself are on the jetty showered,

after-shaved and hair combed waiting for the Grippo bus that is not on time. We are part of a group of about thirty. The buzz of a free pint at the ex-pat Club has done the trick.

Eventually the bus arrives ... and it's crap. The seat upholstery is torn, the windows are covered in a grey-brown sludge and the uncarpeted floor is strewn with empty water bottles and screwed-up paper napkins.

From the outside, the Golestan Club looks average 1950s classic. The number of ex-pats inside outnumber us significantly. Instinctively we stumble to the bar where we are given a bottle of Budweiser beer courtesy of the local community and a pint of ice-cold beer courtesy of *Gurkha*'s Tombola fund.

No sooner have we found a spare table and sat ourselves down than I see Sugar gesturing wildly at me.

He is vibrating with excitement. 'Pete lad, I've just met a couple of Yanks who have two daughters ... they've invited me and a friend for an evening meal at their place. What do you reckon ... are you up for it?'

'I'm with Mack & Burbs.'

'Two daughters ... two daughters ... female, feminine daughters, Pete,' says Sugar, slapping me encouragingly on my shoulder. 'Americans.'

'What are they like?'

'Dunno, haven't see them ... but two daughters, Pete ... two of 'em.'

It's difficult to deny an excited Sugar. 'Go on then,' I say.

He drapes an arm around my shoulder and guides me away. I turn and wave to Burbs and Mack.

'Let me get my drinks, Shug.'

I scurry back to the table where both my pint and my bottle sit undisturbed. 'Sorry, lads, Sugar wants help with a couple of girls ... apparently.'

Mack looks at his watch. 'It's ferkin unbelievable, we've been in Persia for thirty five ferkin minutes and

Sugar's fixed up already. How the ferk does he do it?'

'Don't ask me, mate,' I reply as I collect my pint and leave the bottle. I wink a farewell.

Sugar escorts me to a corner of the bar where a very large couple welcome Sugar like a long-lost friend: 'There yar, Sugar Man,' says the bloke. 'Thought you'd lost your good self for a moment there.'

Sugar holds his arms wide, hesitates and smiles. 'Sorry, I've already forgotten your names. This is Pete from Pudsey England.'

The bloke holds a monstrous hand out in my direction, 'Hello there Pete from Pudsey England. My name is Claybourne Youngblood from Baton Rouge, State Capital of Louisiana, United States of America.' He turns to the enormous woman standing alongside. 'This beautiful Southern belle of mine is Magnolia Youngblood, my wife of twenty-seven fruitful years. Call us Clay and Nolia for short.'

'Clay and Nolia,' I repeat as I place my bottle on an adjacent table. 'Nice to meet you.'

'And it's a real privilege to meet you, Peter' says Magnolia. 'We have our two girls with us who are presently in the powder room making themselves gorgeous.'

Sugar gives me an unnoticed jab in the ribs.

'We'll be honoured if you would accept our invitation to dinner this evening, gentlemen,' says Clay.

'Thank you,' says Sugar.

'Yes, thank you,' I say.

'There they are!' exclaims Magnolia as she stretches an arm upwards and waves. 'Haylooo gals ... over here.'

Magnolia's upper arms wobble alarmingly.

Both Sugar and I are dwarfed by the first of the Youngblood gals to arrive. She cuts a powerful, no-nonsense figure, is overly made-up with hair that could stuff an eiderdown, and has extraordinarily extended ear-lobes from which dangle earrings the size of beer mats. She strokes her stubby nose, takes a deep breath and self-consciously introduces herself. 'Hello I'm Shelby Youngblood from Baton Rouge, Louisiana,' she says offering her beringed hand to Sugar first.

He smiles his perfect smile. 'Nice to meet you, I'm Able Seaman Kane, known throughout the Royal Navy as Sugar. Man of the world.'

Shelby blinks. 'I'm the younger daughter and a long-term committed Christian.'

'Hi.' I hold my hand out. 'I'm Peter from Pudsey, I have a Bronze Medallion ... and I'm committed to travel and new experiences.'

Shelby nods at each word.

Sugar stands open-mouthed as the arrival of Shelby's slightly smaller sister.

'And you are?' she asks pointedly.

Sugar coughs and holds out a hand. 'Ken Kayne ... known throughout Her Majesty's Royal Navy as Sugar.'

'Sugar?'

'Sugar Kayne.'

'Of course. My name is Statten. I gave up a well-paid position in Baton Rouge, Louisiana to look after my parents while they are resident in this shit hole.'

Magnolia giggles.

Claybourne snorts.

'Statten?' I ask.

'Same as the New York Island but with an extra consonant in the centre there.'

Statten Youngblood has the edge over her sister in the looks department. She has a perfectly formed nose, reasonably sized ear lobes and is wearing a gapingly low-cut top.

Clay and Shelby ram Nolia's quivering rear-end into the passenger seat of a military-looking vehicle that is the Youngblood family's transport. The robust suspension system barely whimpers as the combined weight of the Youngblood family settles. Sugar and I squeeze onto the bench seat at the back alongside a heavily breathing Statten.

It's a quarter of an hour's drive to the detached property the Youngblood family call home. The front entrance is a heavy armoured door.

'We're within the red area of the facility so we all have special fireproof entrance ways,' explains Clay as he muscles the door open and allows us to pass. The doorway is barely wide enough for Nolia to squeeze through sideways.

Inside is a dining table set for eight. A small, smiling Filipino lady stands motionless at the head of the table.

'Only six for dinner, Carolina,' says Nolia.

Shelby re-aligns the eating irons and plates.

'You sit yourself down there, Sugar.' Statten points at the chair directly opposite her own. 'That will be perfect.'

Sugar does as he's told and I take the seat next to him. We both shoot a look into the shadowy depths of Statten's cavernous cleavage.

'We can't smoke outside, gentlemen, so if you smoke you're welcome to do so,' says Clay.

Carolina excuses herself as she removes plates in front of me. I say: 'Kamusta.'

Carolina smiles. 'Mabuti.'

Clay swivels to face me. 'You speak their lingo, Pete?' He looks surprised.

'Only a greeting. I was in the Philippines in 63.'

'We are ready for starters Carolina,' says Nolia looking at her watch.

Carolina nods and skips away.

Sugar and I offer our cigarettes round. We explain what duty-free cigarettes are.

Statten is the first to light up.

The starters arrive. Before I get the chance to pick up my knife and fork Clay clasps his hands in prayer and starts to say something that sounds suspiciously like grace. Both Sugar and I are taken by surprise. Everybody continues to smoke while Clay communes with the Almighty. Sugar and I take advantage of tightly closed eyes and admire the cleavage opposite. We all finish our cigarettes long before Clay's discourse ends. Sugar and I get a series of mentions partway through.

'Amen.'

'Amen.'

'Amen.'

'Amen to that.'

Sugar and I cough respectfully.

Clay takes one of our cigarettes and lights it with a shaking hand.

Nolia blows her nose on her paper napkin.

The main course is brilliant. Clay proudly explains that the steaks are flown in directly from Texas each week. We finish with pecan pie, which tastes better than it sounds.

A bottle of bourbon, named after a bloke called Jim, is passed around: Clay and Nolia take sensible amounts. Shelby waves the bottle away and Statten fills her glass almost to the brim.

'Tell me about your home town, Peter,' says Clay.

'Small town called Pudsey between the cities of Leeds and Bradford in the north of England ... Yorkshire.'

'And do you have electricity in Pud ... err.'

'Pudsey.'

'Yeah, in Pud ... sey.'

'Of course.' Out of the corner of my eye I notice Statten wiping something from her upper region.

'And paved streets?' asks Nolia. 'Do you have paved streets?'

'Yes,' I reply, tearing my eyes from a quivering Statten Youngblood.

Statten empties her glass, burps gently into her napkin and snakes a hand across the table to Sugar. 'Come on Sugar ... I'll show you around our house.'

Shelby looks at the ceiling, smiles and sighs.

111

'Our room is off limits,' says Clay.

'As always,' mutters Statten as she ushers a shocked-looking Sugar through a door in the far corner of the room.

'More bourbon, Pete?'

'Not for me, thanks.'

'If you would like to join us, we are showing the new James Bond film in our cinema tomorrow. We could reserve a few seats for Sugar and your good self if you are both interested,' says Nolia.

'That' very nice of you - I'll check on the duty roster back onboard.'

'Do you have telephones onboard?' asks Clay.

'Yes.'

He hands me a business card. 'Call me tomorrow if you and Sugar want to see the latest James Bond film ... James is a Limey you know.'

'I know.'

Shelby looks confused. 'What did ya call him, Daddy?'

'Who?'

'James Bond.'

'A Limey.'

'What's a Limey?'

'An English person ... err individual from ... England.' He looks at me apologetically.

'Why Limey?' asks Shelby looking from her Dad to me, and back again.

'It goes back hundreds of years when men of the Royal Navy were issued with lime juice to prevent scurvy,' I explain.

'Scurvy ... what's that?' asks Shelby.

Clay looks at me.

I shrug my shoulders. 'Dunno really.'

'But it's a disease right?' asks Shelby.

'Yep,' I say.

'Lime juice eh?' says Shelby looking at her watch.

I accept a can of beer and field a few more questions

about modern-day England. I realise that our hosts know very little about my homeland and are surprised that we enjoy most of the trappings of modern life. Both Clay and Nolia think that England is a quaint little place where we travel in carriages, wear horse-hair wigs and lack modern bathroom facilities.

Two cigarettes later, a smirking Statten re-appears hand-in-hand with a tousle-haired Sugar. I notice that her top isn't completely tucked into the waistband of her skirt.

Sugar stumbles slightly as he flops into his chair. 'It's a lovely house you have here.'

'Thank you.' Clay looks at Nolia and pulls a knowing face.

'The boys should be on their way,' she says, looking at her watch. 'Only forty-five minutes to our zonal curfew.'

We say our thanks to Clay, Nolia and their daughters for a pleasant evening. Nolia and the girls decide to stay at home to enjoy a serious smoke-in.

The journey back to *Gurkha* is done in almost total silence. We say our goodbyes to Clay at the bottom of the gangway. There are a number of other crew members being dropped off by their hosts: obviously the Abadan curfew has to be strictly observed.

I manage to keep silent until we are over the brow and we have collected our Station Cards. 'How much of the house did you see then, Shug?' I ask as we negotiate the mess ladder. 'Her top wasn't tucked in when she came back downstairs and she looked a bit flushed.'

'Her room ... only her room. Shit, Pete, I've had some experiences in my time ... but Statten Youngblood was a bolt from the ferkin blue. She knew exactly what she wanted and had about ten minutes to get it.'

'Yeah?'

'She put me in an arm-lock and threw me on her bed. She whipped her top off, hoisted her skirt, rearranged her pants, threw one leg either side of me ... and took advantage of me in the most enthusiastic fashion. And her language ... her ferkin language, Pete. I've never heard such filth since I last visited the Stokers' mess at tot-time.'

'Naah?'

'Really.'

'So it was her that ... err did it to you, then?'

'Straddled me, Pete lad. It's not the first time ... but it was definitely the first time it was done so swiftly ... I can tell ya.'

'Non-consensual sex then.'

'Oh, not exactly ... I wouldn't go that far, Pete. I didn't say no. It was quite erotic in a strange sort of way. As soon as she had satisfied herself she slapped my face, gave me a slobbery kiss, zipped me up and marched me back downstairs.'

'Zip you up? You mean you still had your kecks on?'

'She didn't waste time, didn't Statten Youngblood. Believe me, young Pete, she wasn't in the mood to let a zip get in her way.'

' I don't know how you do it Shug.'

'This time, young Pete ... this time I just lay there, did exactly what I was told ... and thought of mother England.'

'You poor, unfortunate sod.'

I'm duty the following day and Sugar refuses point blank to telephone the Youngbloods. More than half of *Gurkha*'s crew are ashore; the rest of us enjoy a brilliant Christmas Day dinner, traditionally served to us by Senior Rates and a couple of Officers who have remained onboard.

The Christmas Day tot and a festive amount of 'Queen's' ensures that we all spend the afternoon and the best part of the evening horizontal.

*

The Tannoy clicks into life early on Boxing Day morning, waking up the entire mess.

'DUTY PART OF THE WATCH AND EMERGENCY PARTY MUSTER ON THE QUARTERDECK. THE OFFICER-OF-THE-DAY IS REQUESTED TO REPORT TO THE GANGWAY IMMEDIATELY. THIS IS NOT AN EXERCISE ... I REPEAT THIS IS NOT AN EXERCISE. AYO GURK ...'

It takes me a while to remember that I'm still duty. 'Shit ... it's only four thirty.'

'And it's ferkin Boxing Day,' says someone. 'It's a bank holiday back home.'

I scramble into my shirt, shorts and sandals and stroll aft to the quarterdeck.

By the time I arrive, the duty Petty Officer has most of the duty watch mustered in two reasonably straight lines. 'Nice of you to grace us with your presence, Able Seaman Broadbent,' he says sarcastically.

'Not a problem,' I say under my breath. I attach myself to the end of the rear rank. I look around: Abadan is ever so dark.

'Listen up there,' the Duty Petty Officer says as he buckles a white webbing belt around his middle. 'There is a potential incident on the gangway.'

The Officer-of-the-Day looks over the guardrails of the hangar top and calls down to us. 'Send the two largest men you have to the gangway, Petty Officer. We have an aggressive American female at the bottom of the brow with a rifle.'

I bend my knees but I'm not quick enough - I'm one of the two tallest, so I'm selected. Standing on the jetty facing the bottom of the gangway is Shelby Youngblood cradling an automatic rifle with a pair of brass bullet bandoliers strapped across her chest. She is wearing a camouflage combat shirt, shorts, a wide-brimmed hat and knee-length leather boots. Her pair of large, brass hooped earrings look out of place. She spots me. 'Hi there, Peter from Pud ... sey.'

I nod. 'Hello there ... err.'

'Do you know this ... this err woman?' the Officer-of-the-Day asks.

'I had an evening meal with her family a couple of days ago, sir.'

The Officer-of-the-Day turns to Shelby, holding his hand up. 'Don't take another step closer, madam ... stay exactly where you are.'

'I only want to invite some of your crew for a shoot ... a cull,' says a smiling Shelby.

'A cull?' splutters the Officer-of-the-Day.

Shelby adjusts one of her bandoliers. 'A Boxing Day tradition according to our British ... English neighbours.' She takes a long, inflating breath and waves her weapon high above her head.

Opposite the gangway, some distance away, is a large, black pick-up full of armed men and women. Statten, dressed in camouflage gear like her sister, stands up in the back of the truck and raises her rifle skywards. 'Is Sugar available?'

The Officer-of-the-Day looks quizzically at me.

'Shug ... err Able Seaman Kayne shagged ... err had a sexual interlude a couple of days ago with the lady who is standing up in the back of that vehicle, sir,' I whisper to the Officer-of-the-Day.

'He didn't? How does he manage it?'

'I don't know, sir.'

The Officer-of-the-Day spins around to face the Quartermaster. 'Get Able Seaman Kayne up here at the double.'

'It's four forty-five sir. An hour and a quarter before Charlie,' says the Duty Petty Officer.

'Do it, Quartermaster,' whispers the Officer-of-the-Day. 'Do as I say.'

The Quartermaster grabs the microphone ...

'ABLE SEAMAN KAYNE REPORT TO THE GANGWAY IMMEDIATELY.'

'At the double,' the Officer-of-the-Day adds. 'Pipe at the double.'

'AT THE DOUBLE ... ABLE SEAMAN KAYNE REPORT TO THE GANGWAY IMMEDIATELY ... AT THE DOUBLE.'

'Do you know anything about this cull, Able Seaman Broadbent?' asks the Officer-of-the-Day, looking increasingly irritated.

'No, sir.'

'You, madam.' He jabs a finger at Shelby. 'Drop your weapon, remove your ammunition and slowly make your way over the gangway.'

'No way, Bubba ... I'm staying right here, fully armed, until I have offered my invitation ... officially.'

'Tell me,' says the Officer-of-the-Day. 'An invitation given to me is considered official.'

Shelby smiles, readjusts one of her bandoliers and places her rifle on her shoulder. 'It's a Boxing Day tradition that we cull some of the stray dog packs that terrorise the town. We do this twice a year to keep the canine population under control. The more guns we have, the better.'

'We can't issue guns can we, Petty Officer?' asks the Officer-of-the-Day, confused.

'No, sir.'

'Thank you for your invitation, madam, but we cannot issue firearms to members of our crew for such a reason.'

'We have spare weapons,' says Shelby, pointing at the pick-up.

'Under no circumstances, madam, are we prepared to allow any of our crew to take part in a dog cull. Thank you for the invitation ... regretfully refused. The English ... British are a well known nation of dog lovers.'

Shelby snorts, chops off a sloppy salute, turns and

heads back towards the pick-up.

A dishevelled Sugar shuffles through the screen door.

'Sugar babe!' yells Statten from the back of the pick-up. She stands, does a marshmallow shimmy and fires a fusillade of shots into the air.

Shelby doesn't flinch as she scrambles over the tailgate.

'Shit,' says the Officer-of-the-Day as he ducks.

'Shit indeed,' says Sugar.

'She called me "Bubba". Do you know exactly what that means?' the Officer-of-the-Day asks the Duty Petty Officer.

'I think it's an American term of endearment, sir.'

Shelby stands proudly in the back of the pick-up. The two Youngblood girls stand back to back, yell something very American and fire a choreographed volley of shots into the air.

The Officer-of-the-Day cowers behind a guardrail.

Sugar, the Duty Petty Officer and I look on in disbelief as the pick-up, with Clay at the wheel and Nolia in the passenger seat, drives slowly down the jetty.

The two Youngblood girls stumble onto their well-upholstered backsides as the pick-up turns a corner and disappears.

'Able Seaman Kayne,' says the Officer-of-the-Day, looking flustered. 'Did you have a sexual episode with that Annie Oakley woman in the back of that vehicle?'

'No sir,' replies a confident Sugar.

I keep a straight face.

'I have it on good authority that you did, Able Seaman Kayne.'

'You have been misinformed, sir,' says a puffed up Sugar. 'I did however enjoy a sexual encounter with the young lady in her boudoir ... but definitely not in the back of that vehicle. I have certain standar ...'

'That's what I meant ... and you ruddy well know it.'

'Sorry, sir?'

Sugar and I exchange smiles.

'She called me Bubba. Is it really an American term of endearment?' asks the Officer-of-the-Day.

'I'm not completely sure, sir,' I say.

'I don't think it means anything significant, sir,' adds Sugar.

'Get out of my sight both of you.'

'Do I take it that the emergency is over then, sir?' asks the Duty Petty Officer.

'Yes Petty Officer,' says the Officer-of-the-Day, wiping his forehead with a scrunched-up handkerchief.

'Can I stand down the duty part of the watch and the Emergency Party then, sir?'

'Yes, PO ... carry on please.'

'Aye aye, sir.'

'Boudoir eh?' I ask Sugar.

*

The following day, before colours, we are unhitched from the jetty and make our way south down the Shatt-al-Arab. The jetty is bare; there is nobody to wave us off.

We re-enter the Gulf.

It's early evening by the time we spot Bahrain; the lights along the Mina Sulman jetty are a necklace of speckled yellow as we slowly approach.

Once berthed, a couple of guys from *Eskimo* poke their heads down the mess hatch to ask if anybody would like to play knock-out darts at the *Jufair* Canteen. Nobody stirs.

Kit drives some of our Junior Officers to a meeting somewhere in town.

The next day the sky is yet again cloudlessly blue, there is little breeze and the day has all the characteristics of being yet another hot and uncomfortable bastard.

Stories of Abadan hospitality abound, but nobody

can come up with anything that can 'black cat' Sugar.

'UP SPIRITS.'

'Tell me honestly, Shug - do you ever have safe sex?' asks Chats with a serious expression.

'If you mean do I check that daddy, hubby or the boyfriend is not liable to interrupt us ... of course I do,' replies Sugar as he gives Jack the go-ahead to take sippers of his tot.

'That's not what I meant,' Chats, smiling.

'I know exactly what you mean,' says Sugar, taking the remainder of his tot from Jack: he drains his glass and suppresses the traditional burp.

'Have you ever thought that you may have spermed some children in your time?'

'Yep.'

'And?'

Sugar takes a deep breath. 'I'm proud to be an exporter of Englishness.'

'What?'

'As an Englishman, I consider it my responsibility to perk up the gene pool ... worldwide. Spread a bit of Englishness.'

'You mean Britishness,' says Mack.

'No ... Englishness,' replies Sugar. 'It's a part of our heritage - we English are well known for perkin' up the gene pool.'

Chats waves his arms and leans back in his chair, resigned to the fact that Sugar actually believes what he is saying.

'That could be the title of a song,' says Burbs.

'Wha?' asks Chats.

'Perkin' up the gene pool.'

'THE PAY OFFICER SPEAKING. ANYONE WITH PERSIAN GULF RUPEES WHO WISHES TO CHANGE THEM INTO THE NEW BAHRAINI DINARS CAN DO SO AT THE PAY OFFICE BETWEEN 13:30 AND 14:30. YOU

ARE REMINDED THAT LOCAL TRADESMEN ARE NOW WITHIN THEIR RIGHTS TO REFUSE PAYMENT IN PERSIAN GULF RUPEES.'

The week between Christmas and New Year's Eve is an odd one. There's no Father Christmas in the Persian Gulf as far as I am aware, there is no sign of anything resembling a Christmas tree, no snow and nobody to buy me Christmas presents.

Timber, Stormy and Wheelie return onboard with desert boots. Timber struts up and down the mess with a silly smile on his face.

'Let's have a look at yours then,' Chats says to Stormy.

Stormy hand his boots over. Chats examines them closely inside and out and gives one of them a manly twist.

'Careful,' says Stormy.

'They're different. How much were they?'

'Can't remember,' replies Stormy.

'Paid for 'em with English money,' says Wheelie. 'Couple of quid a pair. I won last week's Tombola you know ... thought I'd splash out to celebrate.'

'You won last week's Tombola and you never told us?' asks Chats. 'It's tradition, young Waters, to buy everybody a beer when you scoop the Tombola.'

'It was only two pounds three shillings and sixpence.'

'The amount isn't important, Stormy lad ... it's traditional.'

Stormy nods, takes his desert boot and sidles over to his bunk.

New Year's Eve is the night for celebrating the end of one year on station and the beginning of next year on the same ferkin station ... and we do it with crew members of *HMS Eskimo* at *HMS Jufair*'s canteen.

To avoid walking all the way back to the ship in the early hours of 1966, we try to keep Kit reasonably sober and away from the Pusser's rum that someone from *Gurkha*'s Supply Department has got hold of and is selling in full tot measures. He is limiting us to one tot each, and for most of us that's enough. Of course there are those who circumvent the 'one man one tot' rule and quickly fall foul of it.

The bloke behind the bar has figured out how we can have semi-cold beer for the evening at this time of the year when the night-time temperature is reasonably British. He can rotate one central deckhead fan on slow and keep the smaller of his two freezers on at half-cock without tripping the electrics.

The *Eskimo* crowd are the first to break into song: 'Oggie, Oggie, Oggie.'

It develops into a competition between the two ships to see who can sing the loudest and who knows the most verses to 'This Old Hat Of Mine' and 'This Two Funnel Bastard'. Kit decides that he wants to do a table-top dance but we drag him down and keep guard over him in a darkened corner until the supply of rum is finished.

From a darkened *Eskimo* corner the refrains of a popular song drift ...

> I fed caviar to my girl friend
> She was virgin tried and true
> Now this virgin needs no urgin'
> There is nothing she won't do.

From the opposite corner *Gurkha* responds ...

> She says she is not a whore,
> But she bangs like a shithouse door.
> She married an Italian,

With balls like a stallion.
She divorced the Italian,
And married the stallion.

'I've got a joke,' says Burbs during a brief lull.

'Yeah, let's have it.'

'Go on then,' shout some of the more inebriated *Eskimo* contingent.

Burbs coughs to clear his throat. 'Three couples want to join their local church. An elderly couple in their 70s, a middle-aged couple and a pair of young newlyweds. At the meeting with the vicar, they are told that they will only be allowed to join if they can abstain from sex for four weeks ...'

Cat-calls, boos and other derogatory outbursts from the assembled throng.

Burbs waits for the interruptions to subside. 'All three couples are asked to come back in a month and report. Four weeks later they all meet up with the vicar and are asked how they had got on. The elderly couple say that they had no problem whatsoever. The middle-aged couple say that the first three weeks were fine, the last week was a struggle - but they just managed it. The vicar congratulated them and welcomed them into the church. He then turned to the newlyweds. "And how did you get on?" he asks. "Well," says the husband, "the first two weeks were not too bad, the third week was very difficult, but the fourth week was impossible. It was okay until we decided to do some decorating. My wife reached up to a high shelf for a tin of paint and dropped it. As she bent over to pick it up I was overcome with lust and we had sex there and then." "You realise that because of your actions you won't be welcome in this church?" says the vicar. The husband nods. "We're also banned from Woolworth's for life," replies his wife.'

Much laughter. It is the type of joke that tickles the fancy of everyone after half a dozen cans and a tot or two.

A bloke from *Eskimo* stands on the top of the table. 'I've got a joke.'

He sounds a touch Welsh.

'Go on then, Taff,' someone shouts.

'Right then,' says Taff as he scrambles onto a table-top with his frothing can clutched firmly in his hand. 'A family of holidaymakers are driving through Wales. As they are approaching Llanfairpwllgwyngyllgogery-chwyrndrob-wllantysiliogogogoch ...'

Cat calls and whistles from the *Gurkha* contingent.

Taff takes a slurp from his can and re-composes himself. 'A family of holidaymakers are driving through Wales. As they are approaching that place in Wales with a really long name, they start arguing about the correct pronunciation of the town's name. They argue back and forth until they decide to stop for lunch. As they sit down at a table Dad asks the waitress, "Before we order, could you please ... hic ... settle an argument for us? Would you please pronounce where we are... very, very slowly please?"

The girl leans over the counter and says, "Wim ... Pee ... Bur ... Ger ... Bar."

The *Eskimo* contingent double over with laughter. We *Gurkha* lads give Taff a very short round of applause ... but nothing more.

A half empty can arcs over from the *Eskimo* side, hits the central fan and is flicked over in the direction of the bar; beer splatters everywhere.

The barman ducks. 'Watch mi ferkin fan,' he yells.

The barrage of cans, ashtrays and glasses from the *Gurkha* side quickly overwhelms the *Eskimo* side who funnel out through the main door that is at their end of the bar.

Most of the *Gurkhas* follow the *Eskimo* crowd outside and there is an almighty scuffle with badly thrown punches that mostly miss their mark, and lots of inebriated falling over, slipping, farting, shoving and tripping up. All accompanied by lots and lots of swearing as sand is kicked into an enveloping cloud.

The barman switches the lights off and locks the main door. 'That's it, you can all trundle back to your ships. Happy new year.'

All scuffling stops.

We look at each other, wish each other a happy new year and fall into our opponents' arms ... as only members of Her Majesty's Royal Navy can.

Sugar and I drag Wheelie, Burbs, Jan and Stormy round the corner to where Mack has got Kit in a half-nelson. 'If you can't drive, Kit, give me the ferkin keys,' says Sugar.

'I'm OK,' says Kit. 'Thanks to you lot. Gerrin mi motor ... or on the roof.'

Stormy and I are the slowest and we have to scramble onto the roof rack. It proves to be the best place as there is lots of elbowing, farting and spewing inside the Land Rover as Kit drives slowly and deliberately down the Mina Sulman jetty. He manages to get the Land Rover and his passengers back to ship without hitting anything. I don't remember staggering up the gangway, getting my station card or turning-in.

*

'HANDS CLEAR OFF| THE UPPER DECK. CEREMONIAL SIDE PARTY MUSTER AT THE AFTER GANGWAY AFTER COLOURS. THE POLITICAL RESIDENT FOR THE PERSIAN GULF, SIR WILLIAM LUCE WILL BE BOARDING SHORTLY.'

'I'm not ceremonial side party am I, Chats?' asks Bagsy.

'No.'

'Am I?' asks Wheelie.

'No you're not. Why don't you youngsters know

what's going on?'

'I only need one more number to win a full house on Tombola,' says Stormy.

Everybody ignores him, particularly those of us who no longer buy tickets because we never win anything.

According to Daily Orders we are under sailing orders. Unusually, there are a number of rather strange restrictions placed on us. The bridge top and the forward mast area are out of bounds except for emergency repairs or maintenance. The Officers' Cabin flat is out of bounds until further notice.

This doesn't make sense.

The ceremonial side party is summoned immediately following colours while the rest of us are enjoying breakfast.

As we are stacking our trays, Alex Buchan, a dour Scottish Radio Operator from Peterhead, comes over.

'Have I got some news for you, Sugar!'

Sugar slides his tray on top of the pile. 'Go on,' he says.

'We have two women onboard.'

'I know,' says Sugar. 'They're both alive and well and living in your mess - I wouldn't broadcast if I was you ... it's still illegal in this man's Navy.'

'I mean two real, proper women. Sir William Luce's daughter Diana and his social secretary ... called Victoria.'

'Honest?'

At that moment a couple of the ceremonial side party, dressed in full No 6s, enter the dining hall.

Sugar becomes quite animated. 'What's this I hear about two women onboard?' he shouts.

The two side party members toss their caps onto an empty table: 'Two women - one either side of Bill Luce.'

'Yeah ... well, what are they like?'

'Lovely, Sugar ... absolutely gorgeous.'

'Why wasn't I informed sooner?'

SERGEANT LECKY REPORT TO THE WARDROOM IMMEDIATELY. SERGEANT LECKY.'

Sugar raises his nose towards the deckhead. 'If you inhale deeply you can smell women ... women onboard,' he says.

'Piss off, Shug.'

*

'THE ANTHROPOLOGICAL STROKE INFORMATION OFFICER SPEAKING. THE ISLAND OFF OUR PORT BOW IS DAS ISLAND BELONGING TO ABU DHABI. IT IS A FEEDING GROUND FOR TURTLES AND AN IMPORTANT LANDFALL FOR MIGRANT SEABIRDS. THERE ARE TRACES OF ANCIENT INHABITANTS ON DAS ISLAND AND SOME PIECES OF ISLAMIC POTTERY HAVE RECENTLY BEEN FOUND. THE ISLAND IS ALSO USED AS A PLACE OF REFUGE DURING STORMS BY FISHERMEN AND PEARL DIVERS. AYO GURKHALI.'

'Well fancy that,' says someone from the back of the mess.

'Nothing wrong with a bit of culture,' states Chats.

'What's does anthropo ... whatever mean?' someone asks.

Silence.

'Shall we go up top and have a look then?' inquires Stormy. 'Bit of bronzie bronzie.'

'Naah, you go, Stormy. Have a butchers, then come back down and tell us all about it,' says Jan.

'OK then,' says Stormy who slips his flip-flops on, removes his shirt and bounds up the mess ladder.

'THE INFORMATION OFFICER SPEAKING. WE ARE DUE TO ANCHOR OFF THE PORT OF ABU DHABI AT 13:15. TO TRANSFER SIR WILLIAM LUCE THE

POLITICAL RESIDENT FOR THE PERSIAN GULF ASHORE. AS OUR VISIT WILL BE SHORT, NO SHORE LEAVE WILL BE GRANTED.'

'What's Abu whatsit like for a run ashore then, Chats?' asks Timber.

'Crap,' says Chats without looking up from his book.

'Not missing much then?'

'Definitely not ... no.'

Stormy slides down the mess ladder.

'What's the Washing Powder Island like then, young Stormy?' asks Jan.

'Crap. It's ... err ... only an island. No buildings, no turtles and no observed women.'

'Thought it might be,' says Chats, nodding.

*

'FLYING STATIONS.'

It's my turn. In the Ops Room Frothy is in radio communication with Pontius. I take over and run through Pontius' pre-flight checks.

Frothy sidles over to a perch alongside me. 'We don't yet know how we are going to transfer Sir William Luce ashore,' he says, 'by chopper or by water. We've asked the Abu Dhabi authorities if they can collect him in something more suitable than our whaler or the RIB. If they can't and can clear a landing area, the Wasp is the favoured method.'

After a lengthy wait we are told that the Wasp will be taking Billy into Abu Dhabi. We are told that green flares south of the main shoreside mosque will be lit to identify the landing zone.

'Golf Foxtrot Yankee Alpha this is X-Ray Tango 434, over.'

'This is Golf Foxtrot Yankee Alpha, over.'

'This is X-Ray Tango 434, passenger onboard. Ready for takeoff, over.'

'This is Golf Foxtrot Yankee Alpha, Roger. Abu Dhabi bears zero nine five, over.'

'This is X-Ray Tango 434. Believe it or not Ops Room I have Abu Dhabi visual, range approximately one thousand yards, over.'

'This is Golf Foxtrot Yankee Alpha, roger. We are informed that green flares will mark your landing area alongside the main shoreside mosque, over.'

'This is X-Ray Tango 434, roger. Am airborne heading zero eight seven magnetic. I have green flares visual, over.'

'This is Golf Foxtrot Yankee Alpha, roger out.'

Pontius reports a safe landing and that his passenger has been whisked away in an official vehicle.

I log the time.

'This is X-Ray Tango 434, there's a lot of ferkin sand here,' says Pontius. 'I'm coming back. I'll give her a good blow out on my way - get rid of some of the Abu Dhabi dust, over.'

I look quizzically at Frothy. He shrugs his shoulders.

'This is Golf Foxtrot Yankee Alpha, roger out.'

Once the Wasp is safely back onboard we stand down from Flying Stations and wait for instructions.

'UP SPIRITS.'

'Does anyone know where Billy's female entourage are sleeping?' asks Jan as he takes his tot from Jack.

'Yeah. They've each been issued with a Pusser's hammock and a slinging point in the capstan flat,' says Kit.

Everybody pretends to laugh.

'Apparently,' says Chats with a serious face, 'they're both sleeping in the Jimmy's cabin and Jimmy is using the Skipper's harbour cabin.'

'They'd have more fun up this end in the capstan flat,' states Jan.

Abu Dhabi in its 1960s heyday

'Got a joke,' says Burbs.

'Go on then,' says Kit from within his tot glass.

'A three year old boy is examining his testicles while taking a bath. "Mum," he asks, "are these my brains?" Mum replies "not yet."'

'Is that it? I don't ferkin get that,' says Stormy, who is passing the tot-table.

'You will ... eventually,' says Burbs.

'Think about it, Stormy lad,' explains Chats.

. 'We rigged a canvas dodger around that piece of deck forward of the bridge this morning,' says Cliff.

'Why?'

'Ferk knows, but something's going on. The Buffer's had a bit of a panic on.'

'You won't believe what they're using that bit of deck in front of the bridge for!' says an out-of-breath Communicator from the opposite mess.

'Wha?'

'Women ... two of 'em.'

'Explain yourself, my good man,' says Jack as he hands Burbs his tot.

The Communicator takes sippers from Burbs' tot. 'Thanks, mate. The two ladies in bikinis are on the bridge preparing themselves to go out onto that piece of deck in front of the bridge to have a sunbathe,' he says so quickly he almost stumbles over his words. 'When I came off watch they were covering each other in lotion.'

'Two women dressed in bikinis sunbathing on our ship?' asks Burbs, wide-eyed.

'Covering themselves with lotion!' exclaims Kit.

Sugar slides down the mess ladder: 'You'll never guess what I've just seen.'

'Two women in bikinis sunbathing on that bit of deck in front of the bridge,' says Jack. 'All lotioned up.'

'How the ferk ...?'

'Our friend from the port side mess just told us.'

Burbs opens a can of beer and the contents fizz all over the table. 'You haven't been up the mast again have you, Shug?' he says.

'Who me?' asks Sugar as Jack hands him his tot. 'I was doing bridge look-out.'

'Of course you were, mate.'

'I don't suppose anybody has a pair of binoculars in their locker?' asks Sugar.

No replies.

'Or a telescope?'

It's getting dark by the time we fly the Wasp back into town to pick Billy up.

'THE INFORMATION OFFICER SPEAKING. WE SHALL REMAIN AT ANCHOR OFF ABU DHABI OVERNIGHT. SPECIAL SEA DUTYMEN AND THE FORECASTLE PART OF SHIP WILL CLOSE UP AT 07:30 TOMORROW. ETA DUBAI 12:30.'

From the sea, Dubai is as uninspiring as Abu Dhabi: sand coloured and featureless. As we anchor a mile or so off shore, not far from a rusting cargo vessel, a rather swish-looking barge comes alongside and Sir Bill, resplendent in his official going-ashore gear complete with feathered headgear and sword, is ceremonially piped down the starboard accommodation ladder and whisked away.

A couple of hours later the barge re-appears, with Sir Bill. Those on the bridge are in a flat spin, unprepared for Sir Bill's unexpected return. Cups of partly consumed coffee are hastily abandoned, triangular cucumber sandwiches quickly stuffed into pockets. The Quartermaster is told to signal the barge to lay off until the official welcoming party is correctly mustered.

Perched partway up the main mast, Sugar and I are admiring the two bikini-clad ladies sunbathing on that piece of deck forward of the bridge.

'Wonder which one is Bill's daughter?' asks Sugar.

'The one nearest the sun I reckon.'

'Obviously,' replies Sugar, smiling.

Within minutes of Sir Bill's return *Gurkha* ups anchor and steams north.

7

'I'll write to Moorehouse's'

CHATS TAPS the mess table. 'How many of you have girlfriends at home?' he asks.

'Whaa?'

How many of you have girlfriends at home?'

Jan raises his hand.

'You still writing to the kipper-eater from Inverkeithing then?'

'Course not,' says Jan, sulkily. 'She gave me permission to have unprotected sex with anything and anybody that moved, didn't she?'

'So she did.'

'I'm still writing to the girl in Guz though,' says Jan.

'Anybody else writing to girlfriends?'

Burbs raises his hand. 'I thought I had one ... but she hasn't written to me for ages.'

Sugar is rolling his tot glass between his hands.

'You must be writing to a girl or two, Shug?' asks Kit.

'Don't do letter writing,' says Sugar.

Burbs owes me 'gulpers' which I graciously accept.

'How many of you currently have a wife ... or ex-wife?' inquires Chats.

Nobody moves.

'Only me then,' says Chats. 'Well, we have long periods at sea during the next six months or so and the runs ashore won't provide many opportunities to meet members of the opposite sex. So, in order to maintain messdeck morale I propose that we put our heads together and find some ladies to write to and get them to send photographs to us. What do you reckon ... could be fun, couldn't it?'

'Sounds like a good idea,' says Kit.

'Yeah ... why not?' says Burbs.

'Count me in,' says Mack.

'Bloody good idea,' blurts Kit.

'Great idea,' I add.

'You can't do it, Kit ... you've got a new beard,' says Mack.

'Shows I'm a real man ... long gone are my bum-fluff days, mate.'

Before we all drift off to the dining hall I have somehow volunteered to write to the Moorhouse Jam factory in Beeston, Leeds. I used to live close by and remember that it employed hundreds of girls. It was my tot combined with the 'gulper' from Burbs that did the volunteering for me. After loads of tot-fuelled advice from everybody else it was unanimously agreed that I should write a snivelling letter to the Moorhouse factory, explaining that we are a lonely, good-looking bunch of sailors who are 'roughing it' in the heat of the Middle East looking after England's interests and who would like to receive letters from girls back home who are prepared to spend a bit of time keeping a sailor happy. There was plenty of other advice that got laughs ... but I was told to ignore it.

My grandfather's sound advice rings in my ears: 'Never volunteer for anything, Peter'. But it's too late ... my tot said that I'd do it.

'ABLE SEAMAN BROADBENT REPORT TO THE BRIDGE.'

'Wonder what that's about?' I mumble. 'Suppose I'd better saunter up top and find out.'

'They've heard that you're writing to the jam factory,' says someone.

'Maybe they have some advice to offer,' says Kit.

'I wouldn't think so,' I reply.

There is a flurry of activity on the Bridge. The Navigating Officer sees me and beckons me over to where he is poised looking through his binoculars.

'Are you an ambitious young man, Able Seaman Broadbent?' He puts his binoculars down. 'Or are you a lazy, unmotivated Able Seaman who is satisfied and comfortable with his place in the order of things?'

That's a complicated question. 'Never thought about it much, sir.'

'That's what concerns me. Surely you don't want to stay an Able Seaman for the rest of your life, do you?' he asks the glass screen in front of him.

'Never given it much thought, sir.'

'Mmmph,' He flicks a tablet of chewing gum into his mouth. 'We are convening a Leading Seaman's Qualification Board in late February. An opportunity for you to get your foot on the promotion ladder - are you interested or not?'

'I suppose so ... yes, sir.'

'Are you sure?'

'Yes, sir.'

He hands me a blue hardback book. 'You'll need that then.'

'Thank you, sir.'

'I'll pencil you in, Broadbent.'

'Thank you, sir.'

Back in the mess I flick through my new book. It's the 1964 edition of the Admiralty Manual of Seamanship: a good deal thicker than my current edition. From a reasonably modest 290 pages, my 'bible' now fills 494 pages ... almost doubled in size. Obviously seamanship has become significantly more complicated since I left *HMS Ganges*.

Down the mess I ask if anybody else has been roped in to do the Leading Seaman Qualification Board. Mack and Cliff say that they have.

*

The eastern coast of Oman is a bleak and inhospitable looking place - a blackened spine of mountains edged by low-lying, steel-grey coloured dunes. Mile upon hot baked mile of barren nothingness.

From a distance Muscat looks like Dubai on a really unattractive day. It has nothing to recommend it; the entrance to its harbour is flanked by a pair of bare black mountainous piles. As we approach, a tall fort-type structure becomes visible on the top of each of the sheer-faced mountains. As we get closer we can see that the seaward face of the southernmost pile is covered with hundreds of painted ships' names and crests: we later learn that this is known as the 'Sultan's calling card'. Nestled on the narrow strip of visible land between the two sentinels is a low-lying village. To the north is a bare stone and wooden structure where half a dozen Dhows are berthed.

We anchor more than a spitting distance from the shore in the protected waters of the two flanking peaks.

'FLYING STATIONS.'

I could tell instantly - Muscat is going to be a fabulous 'run ashore'

Once again it's my turn to look after Pontius. On my way to the Ops Room I catch a whiff of womanly perfume and glimpse a pair of shapely ankles climbing the short ladder to the bridge. Missed ... just my luck ... bugger!

'THE INFORMATION OFFICER SPEAKING. SAUDI ARABIA AND OMAN HAVE RECENTLY CLASHED OVER OWNERSHIP OF THE BURAIMI OASIS AND A GUERRILLA BAND RECENTLY SABOTAGED THE BRITISH AIR BASE AT SALALAH. IN RECENT YEARS THE DOHAR LIBERATION FRONT HAVE ORCHESTRATED ATTACKS ON OIL COMPANY INSTALLATIONS AND GOVERNMENT POSTS. MANY OF THE DLF ARE TRAINED FORMER SOLDIERS OF THE SULTAN OF OMAN'S ARMED FORCES, OR THE TRUCIAL OMAN SCOUTS.BECAUSE OF THE VOLATILE SITUATION IN OMAN WE ARE UNABLE TO PROMULGATE SHORE-LEAVE DETAILS. AYO ... AYO GURKHALI.'

I get Pontius and Sir Bill safely into the air and point them in the direction of Muscat. The Bridge has organised the helicopter to land on a large open area located on top of the northerly of the two mountain-top forts. An official welcoming party is in attendance.

'Golf Foxtrot Yankee Alpha this is X-Ray Tango 434, over.'

'This is Golf Foxtrot Yankee Alpha, go ahead, over.'

'This is Kate. I have the official welcoming party visual on the northernmost fort. I will do a circuit before landing over.'

'Kate this is Golf Foxtrot Yankee Alpha, roger out.'

A period of silence.

'Mother this is Kate. Suggest we find an alternative landing space. The space is full of rubbish ... I can see some rusty old cannons. There is no way I can land safely. How did anyone think I could land amongst this load of crap, over.'

'Kate this is Golf Foxtrot Yankee Alpha, wait one, over.'

I relay the message to the Officer-of-the-Watch on the bridge who tells me to instruct the helicopter to hover.

'Kate this is mother. The bridge instructs you to hover until a solution is found, over.'

'This is Kate. Hovering in this area is definitely not an option. Many of the official welcoming party are armed. Some have obviously never seen a big flying machine up close before and are already showing signs of irritation, over.'

'Kate this Golf Foxtrot Yankee Alpha, wait one, over.'

I relay the message to the Officer-of-the-Watch on the bridge who tells me to 'wait one'.

'Kate this is mother, I have relayed your message to the bridge who are instructing you to 'wait one' over.'

'Mother this is a rather pissed-off Kate. I am not "waiting one". A member of the official welcoming party has something that looks suspiciously like a ferkin rocket launcher and is becoming increasingly restless. I am departing this location and will hover off your starboard side unless I receive alternative and sensible instructions in the next thirty seconds.'

'Kate this is Golf Foxtrot Yankee Alpha, roger out.'

I relay the message to the Officer-of-the-Watch on the bridge who tells me to 'wait one'.

'FLYING STATIONS. AWAY SEABOATS CREW.'

Frothy relieves me. 'Are you seaboats crew?'

'To be perfectly honest, PO ... today I don't have a ferkin clue.'

'I'll take over. You go down and find out what you are doing with the seaboat.'

'OK, PO. By the way, I don't think that Pontius will be in the best frame of mind. He wasn't too happy about the shoreside landing facilities.'

'OK, thanks.'

Outside the Ops Room I detect the sweet smell of freshly perfumed woman.

I make myself known to the PO in charge of lowering the seaboat. He says that the boat is fully crewed.

Kate hovers off the starboard side of the hangar. There is panic among the flight deck crew as Pontius is making a series non-standard manoeuvres.

'UP SPIRITS.'

I clip my chinagraph pencil in my pocket and shimmy off down the mess. Down the mess Jack arrives with the rum.

'Muscat looks like a bit of a shit-hole,' says Wheelie.

'Anyone been here before?' asks Chats.

Silence. There is a noticeable change in attitude once the tot has worked its magic.

'Suppose it will be an interesting place to have a look around.'

'Yeah.'

'Who's up for a run ashore then?'

'I am.'

'And me.'

'We've got to wait for details.'

'What does promulgate mean?' asks Timber.

'Don't you youngsters know anything?' asks Kit. 'It's a fruit with lots of little pips inside it.'

'Bollocks, that's a ferkin Pompey-granite,' says Jan.

'That's a pomegranate, you idiot,' corrects Chats.

I nod in agreement.

'So who's right then?' asks Timber.

Jan departs to a quiet corner.

'It's a fruit, young Timber,' explains Kit. 'Take my word for it ... I know about such things.'

'THE INFORMATION OFFICER SPEAKING. LEAVE IS GRANTED TO ONE PART OF THE WATCH ONLY AS FROM 14:30. MUSCAT IS A WALLED CITY WITH ONLY ONE GATE THAT IS CLOSED AT SUNSET. THE AREA OUTSIDE OF THE WALL IS CLASSIFIED AS 'OUT OF BOUNDS' AS UNCONTROLLED TRIBAL GANGS ROAM THE COUNTRY. YOU ARE ADVISED TO GO ASHORE IN GROUPS. AS MUSCAT HAS A LIMITED ELECTRICAL SUPPLY. LEAVE WILL EXPIRE AT 17:30 FOR JUNIOR AND SENIOR RATES. THAT IS THIRTY MINUTES BEFORE SUNSET.'

'One of the official Wasp welcoming party had a ferkin rocket launcher,' I say. 'The pilot wasn't too happy.'

'Why?'

'One of the official welcoming party had a ferkin rocket launcher,' I say with some emphasis. 'So they might take Bill ashore by boat.'

'Bless 'im. Has he got his feathery hat on?'

'I dunno. I've been in the Ops Room.'

'OUT BOOMS AND LADDERS. DUTY WATCH OF SEAMEN MUSTER ON THE QUARTERDECK.'

'Shit,' says young Bagsy.

'Don't go running off, Bagsy,' says Kit. 'If you're the first to arrive you'll be boats' crew. Be one of the last to get there ... that's the way to do it.'

'Right then.'

'SIDE PARTY MUSTER BY THE STARBOARD ACCOMMODATION LADDER.'

Wheelie cups his hands and shouts at the Tannoy, 'What about the boats to take us ashore then? And can we go ashore in civvies?'

'DRESS OF THE DAY FOR JUNIOR AND SENIOR RATES GOING ASHORE IS NUMBER 6As'

'Shit.'

'Thank you very ferkin much,' Wheelie says to the Tannoy.

As Burbs, Cliff and I wait by the accommodation ladder with the others going ashore, I watch as Kate is lowered into the hangar. An unsmiling Pontius storms past us on his way to the bridge.

The whaler arrives with Sharky as coxswain.

'Get yourselves seated,' orders Sharky. 'No smoking or farting in my boat. I've done a couple of shuttles already and I haven't seen any skirt ... so I hope you have a really interesting run ashore. Keep your hands and elbows inboard, my friends.'

'Can you drop us near to the red light district please, Sharky?' someone asks.

'That'll be the bit of town that has electricity then?'

'Eh?'

'Sorry, I can only land you near the old coaling jetty, gentlemen,' says Sharky.

'That'll do then.'

The coaling jetty is a rickety wooden structure stretching across a natural cleft in one of the cliff faces. At one end of a stone-built raft is a heap of slate grey coal the size of a modest bungalow.

Me and an unknown Omani

We disembark onto a gravel track that follows the contour of the coast, deviating only where the rock base intrudes. A hundred yards down the track we come upon Muscat's unloading dock area. A procession of barefoot men dressed only in a piece of grubby material wrapped around their middle and a scrap of cloth tied around their head are collecting bags of something from a large, decrepit looking Dhow. They trudge over an unstable bamboo bridge, over the pathway and up a series of steps cut into the cliff face. A couple of overseers, arms officiously folded, stand either side of the snaking column. We stand and watch for a few minutes; this method of unloading goods probably hasn't changed since the Middle Ages. I feel embarrassed and walk away.

Cliff had the foresight to bring his camera so we stop to have our pictures taken with one of the forts as a backdrop.

We pass what we assume to be the city gate, an ornate whitewashed structure set in a cleverly constructed dry-stone wall maybe thirty feet tall. The main doors are slightly open. The flattened sand alleyways separate single storey buildings with small barred windows and robust studded wooden doors that look like they have never been opened. The few people we see are all men dressed in flowing robes and wearing either a white skull cap or a long white scarf wrapped or draped over their heads and around their shoulders.

Muscat's entertainment committee

143

'Ferkin hot eh?' says Cliff.

Burbs stops us. 'Listen.'

We listen but can hear nothing. 'What we listening for?' I ask.

'Nothing ... absolutely ferkin nothing. No cars, no birds, no machinery of any kind. Absolutely bugger all.'

'You're reet,' says Cliff.

'There is a smell though,' I say.

'Yeah but whar is it?' asks Burbs, not expecting an answer.

'Muscat I suppose.'

'Yeah ... Muscat.'

We stroll through a large open area, which we decide must be the main square or market place. A small group of blokes squatting in the shade offered by an overhanging threadbare sheet of brown material, look at us with rheumy eyes. We wave in friendship but don't get a response.

'Wonder how they built those?' asks Burbs looking up at a mountain-top fort.

'Same blokes we saw unloading that Dhow I suppose ... or their great-great-great-grandparents.'

'You're probably reet,' says Cliff.

We find a long slab of stone about the right height for sitting and plonk ourselves down in a strap of shade offered by an adjacent building that has a bit of a tilt to it.

I lean over to one side and I can see *Gurkha* between two vertical rock faces in the distance.

'Looks small, don't she?' asks Cliff.

'Yeah.'

We sit in smoking silence. In harmony with our surroundings, we do absolutely nothing.

We shield our eyes from the lowering sun as it disappears behind one of the mountains. The reflection of the sun in the water lasts for a few short minutes before we are enveloped in almost total dusk. As we retrace our way back through the town square we see the occasional dribble of yellow light in a side street, but nothing significant. The white of the main gate does nothing to illuminate the surrounding area. A group of about a dozen silent men stand under the canopy of the gate and watch us as we approach. The large wooden doors are closed. The shoreside walk back towards the coaling jetty is done in almost total darkness.

The unloaded Dhow has a single light bulb on a rope dangling over the side and swinging close to the glassy flat surface of the water. Three semi-naked squatting blokes are dangling fishing lines in the water. We stop for a short while, bathing in the energising light offered by a low-wattage bulb.

The coaling jetty is ink-black and we find a relatively comfortable piece of rock to sit on and watch an illuminated *Gurkha* in the distance.

Burbs is the first to see the whaler. 'Here she comes.'

Sharky slides the whaler alongside with the practised ease of someone who has done the same manoeuvre many times today. The crew Stoker is waving a Pusser's torch with a yellow beam.

'Get yourselves seated,' orders Sharky. 'We are a bit adrift. No smoking or farting in my boat. I've done more than a dozen shuttles already. Keep your hands and elbows inboard. Did you have a good run?'

'Shit,' says Cliff.

'Ditto,' says Burbs.

'And you, Pete?'

'Don't ask.'

'Get a bit?'

'Piss off.'

Back in the mess we learn that there is no shore leave tomorrow. Apparently the town authorities have said that Friday is a Muscat day of prayer and that we are not allowed ashore.

'So what's it like ashore then?' asks Bagsy.

'Imagine a place with no roads, no women, no

electricity, no shops, no bars and no welcome ... then you've got Muscat on a really welcoming day,' I explain.

'Must be something.'

'If there is we didn't find it,' says Cliff.

Back in the mess Chats claps his hands. 'Jed Constable has organised a fishing master class on the forecastle at 13:00 tomorrow followed by a competition.'

'Oh still my beating heart.' I slap my chest and almost fall off my chair. 'A fishing competition?'

'Yeah, fishing.'

'Have you written that letter to the jam factory yet, Pete?' Kit asks me.

'Not yet.'

'Then extractum ferkin digitum ... and get on with it,' says Kit.

'I will.'

'Is that Latin, Kit?' asks Mack.' That ferkin digitum whatsit?'

Kit puffs up. 'Of course it is. Don't you young 'uns know anything?'

After tot-time and dinner on Friday I drag myself up to the forecastle where I stand transfixed as Jed explains, to the dozen or so crew members who have declared an interest in fishing, what a fishing rod is. The complexities of the circular reel are then explained, at which time a few of the audience slope away. By the time Jed gets around to explaining how to tie a hook to the fishing line I slump onto an adjacent bollard, light a cigarette and completely lose interest.

Later that evening I agree to go ashore tomorrow with Sugar, working on the assumption that if there is anything going on in the Sultanate of Oman then Sugar will sniff it out.

I receive a telephone call from Sergeant Lecky who needs me to coxswain the RIB on Monday to take some of his troop to the south of town where they have permission to do some practice beach landings. There will be food and some illicit beer.

Thanks to the fishing dexterity of one of the Chinese chefs, we have freshly caught swordfish steaks for our evening meal: brilliant.

*

'Try to keep it in your trousers, Sugar,' says Sharky as he drops us at the coaling jetty on Saturday.

Sugar grunts.

I smile. 'As if.'

I don't expect the village women to come bounding out of their houses to greet Sugar ... and they don't. A similar-looking column of coolies are unloading a different Dhow.

Sugar shakes his head in disbelief. 'Unbelievable.'

'The port of Muscat at work,' I say.

'Ferkin unbelievable.'

We watch for a few minutes: I watch an elderly gentleman with large, red-rimmed eyes, grey hair, bare feet and a strip of urine-stained rag wrapped around his middle hoist a large hessian-wrapped bundle onto his bony shoulders. He skips over the bamboo bridge and up the rock-face steps with surprising agility.

We stroll down past the main gate, where a familiar-looking group of men are gathered. The town square is deserted. I see a group of metal-framed tables and some elderly, rusting cannons that are pointing in opposite directions up against a crumbling set of steps that I hadn't noticed before.

'Some place eh?' says Sugar.

'Mmm.'

'Wonder what they do for entertainment?'

'I wonder.'

We sit ourselves down on the same long slabbed stone bench and contemplate our dusty feet.

'Hello, sailor.'

We turn to see two blokes, each dressed in a blue shirt and khaki trousers, with a red-and-white cloth wrapped around their head. They are each packing a side arm.

'Hello,' I say.

'What do you reckon to Muscat then?' asks the taller of the two as he perches himself on an adjacent stone slab. He sounds English.

'Not a lot.' I say.

His mate kicks a stone into the distance and sits alongside us.

'You stationed here?' asks Sugar.

'Trucial Oman Scouts,' says the one who is seated. 'I'm Garry from Birmingham.'

'And I'm Derek - I think I'm from somewhere near Weymouth,' says the standing guy, offering his hand. 'Haven't been back to the UK for so long, I forget.'

We shake hands all round and Sugar and I introduce ourselves. We offer our cigarettes.

'Is that uniform then?' I ask as I point to the red-and-white cloth.

'What ... ghutra? Perfect at keeping the sun off,' says Derek.

'So what do you do here?' asks Sugar.

'Security and the occasional Friday duty,' says Garry.

'Friday duty?' I ask.

'Yeah ... hand removals, finger amputations ... things like that.'

'And the odd firing squad,' adds Derek.

'Yeah, we sometimes do firing squad duty,' says Garry.

'What, you actually shoot people?'

'Of course.'

'And hand removal, what does that entail?'

'Removal of one or both hands.'

'Naah?'

'Every Friday after midday prayers.'

'Naah.'

'True,' says a smirking Garry. 'The bench we're sitting on is one of the places where those waiting for amputations sit.'

I look down.

'There have been some serious bowel movements on that seat I can tell you,' adds Derek, grinning.

I stand up. 'You're ferkin joking?'

'No.'

Sugar jumps to his feet.

'It gets washed down though,' says Derek.

'Shit,' says Sugar.

'Correct. That's why you weren't allowed into town yesterday,' explains Derek.

'Really?' I ask.

Derek nods. There is a short period of silent contemplation.

'You've got Royal Marines onboard?' says Derek.

'We have, yeah,' I confirm.

'Some of our lads are helping with an exercise of some sort on Monday.'

'I'm driving the RIB ... boat,' I say.

'Is there anything to do in Muscat?' asks Sugar, who hands cigarettes around for the second time today - a record.

'Nothing,' says Derek, apologetically.

'Absolutely bugger all,' adds Garry.

'Time to go mate,' Derek says to Garry. 'The local knocking shop will be opening soon.'

'Knocking shop!' Splurts a suddenly animated Sugar.

There is a sudden rush of something through my nether regions.

Derek lays a calming hand on Sugar's shoulder. 'Only joking, mate,' he says. 'The nearest knocking shop is probably about a thousand miles north west of here ... in Europe.'

Sugar and I say our goodbyes and our two Trucial Oman Scouts stride away.

'Amputations and firing squad eh?' I ask Sugar.
'Suppose it keeps them out of trouble.'
'But they're Brits ... English ... both of 'em.'
'Mercenaries.'
'Right then.' I'll look that up in a dictionary later.
'Pity about the knocking shop,' I say.
'I knew they were joking.'
'No you ferkin didn't.'

*

'ANYBODY WITH CLIMBING EXPERIENCE REPORT TO LIEUTENANT BRINKMAN, THE SHIP'S MOUNTAINEERING EXPERT ... ERR ... OFFICER, ON THE BRIDGE. ANYBODY WITH CLIMBING EXPERIENCE.'

'You done any climbing, young Bagsy?' asks Sugar.
'Yeah.'
'Would you call yourself experienced, then?'
'Suppose so - I've been to the Lake District.'
'Then go and find out what it's all about then.'
Someone pokes his head down the mess ladder: 'The girls are sunbathing again ... if any of you "brown hatters" are interested.'
There is a flurry of activity and a rush for the mess ladder.

*

I have one-and-a half tots at dinnertime on Monday, so I'm in the perfect frame of mind to drive the RIB. By the time I arrive on the Quarterdeck my boat is already in the water. Five Royal Marines are mustered in a straight line and Sergeant Lecky is waiting for me.
A couple of the Marines drag the RIB up to the accommodation ladder. I board first, check the fuel

supply is correct and that all the heavy equipment is stowed forward. I look around for the promised beer and food: there isn't any.

Sergeant Lecky unfolds a chart and together we agree on the best route to our destination, which is to seaward of the southern mountain stack, then east between two fingers of rock, across a wide bay and to the landing point on an arched beach area.

'Ahoy there!' bellows a familiar voice from above as the Marines take their seats.

I look up to see Major Munro leaning over the guardrail with a large mug of something in his hand. 'Is everything in hand, Sarn't Lecky?'

'Yes, sir.'

'Fully kitted?'

'Yes, sir.'

'No problems?'

'None, sir.'

'Carry on then, Sarn't.'

'Aye aye, sir.'

So, with the Major's blessing and the symbolic raising of his mug, I slew the RIB away and head south.

I see a group of blokes crawling over the base of the southern mountain but don't get that close. Round the back of the mountain I manage to squeeze the RIB between the two rock fingers and head out across a wide, pleasantly calm bay.

'Something dead ahead, coxswain,' one of the guys up forward shouts.

I look and see a distant line of splashed water. I keep my eye on the area and identify the disturbance as a line of fish jumping out of the water. The closer we get, the larger they appear.

'I think we have a line of dolphins, coxswain,' says Sergeant Lecky peering through a pair of Admiralty pattern binoculars. 'I count eight.'

'Blimey.'

'All in a perfectly straight line and all jumping together,' adds the Sergeant.

I edge the tiller over in the hope that I can avoid them, but they adjust themselves. They are heading straight for us. Unless I do something they will pass on both sides of us ... and I don't know how dolphins will react to a throbbing boat full of uniformed Royal Marines bearing down on them.

'Try and aim between them,' instructs Sergeant Lecky. 'They're playing; they want to fool around with us.'

'Whaa?'

'Aim for a gap - they'll adjust themselves. Dolphins are not stupid.'

'Aren't they? Are you sure?'

'I know about such things, says the Sergeant, smirking. 'It's a well-known fact that they have an IQ superior to that of your average Able Seaman. So aim for a gap.'

'OK then.'

'Everybody anchor themselves,' bellows Sergeant Lecky. 'Able Seaman Broadbent is going for the middle of the line.'

There are a few snorts from those up forward.

'Good luck, Pete,' someone shouts.

Someone breaks wind loudly.

'Silence up for'd there!'

Giggles.

'They're big bastards aren't they?' says someone.

At a distance of about twenty yards our approaching line of soaring dolphins makes a barely visible adjustment to present us with a slightly wider gap between number three and number four: counting from the left.

They disappear. I clamp my tiller firm and straight.

The entire rank re-appears five yards ahead and launches itself skywards. They arch gracefully on either side of us. If I hadn't been tightly holding my outboard with one hand and cupping my boyhood with the other, I could have stretched my arms wide to touch numbers three and four. They re-enter the water aft of us and disappear into our wake ... with barely a splash.

'Ferkin hell,' blurts Sergeant Lecky.

'You can say that again,' I say.

'I only swear twice a day.'

I react like it is an everyday occurrence for us coxswains and continue across the bay, searching the waters ahead for more leaping dolphins. Sergeant Lecky scans the shore with his binoculars. He points. 'There's our target - head for that red-and-white ghutra on a stick. We'll disembark, you can anchor up and take it easy until our exercise is finished, Peter lad.'

'Aye aye, Sergeant.' I wallow off the shore opposite a red-and-white rag tied to the top of a short wooden stick. At a wave from Sergeant Lecky the Royal Marines silently disembark and wade ashore through chest-deep water with their rifles held high above their heads. Suddenly, from behind a dense line of bulbous palm trees, a group of welcoming, unarmed Trucial Oman Scouts appear and applaud our Royal Marines as they emerge dripping from the waters. I throw a small anchor over the side. make sure that it's holding, turn off my engine and relax.

Ashore the Trucial Oman Scouts and the Royal Marines rig a net, strip down to their underwear and have a game of volleyball. As the senior NCO, Sergeant Lecky automatically adopts the position of match referee.

I relax with my legs hooked over the gunwale and my bare feet dangling in the cooling water. The RIB pulls on her anchor line on a gentle ebbing tide.

I'm disturbed by a splash and look around me. About six feet on my port quarter I spot the unmistakeable dorsal fin of a shark running parallel with the coastline where the sea-bed suddenly dips over a darkened ledge. I quickly swing my legs inboard to check that I still have all my feet. I watch as the glistening dark grey monster aims straight out to sea, putting some welcome distance between us. I do a quick calculation: my RIB is about twelve feet long and assuming the dorsal fin is midway down the shark's back ... then that ... that ferkin shark was over fifteen feet long. Oh my God!

I haul on the anchor line. I feel a little less vulnerable in shallower water.

I spend the next hour or so wishing I was safely ashore and not in a rubber boat.

Eventually Sergeant Lecky whistles and waves me in closer.

I wait until all the Marines wade out to the RIB, their rifles and kit held high. Once onboard, they struggle into dry combat trousers and wet boots.

'You'll never believe what I've seen,' I say to Sergeant Lecky.

'What?'

'A ferkin shark that must have been twenty ... maybe twenty-five feet long.'

'You've been out in the sun too long, young man.'

'Honest.'

'You'll be glad to know that we beat the Scouts three rubbers to two.'

'Good.' I haven't a clue what a rubber is.

'Not a word to anyone mind,' says the Sergeant.

'What ... about the shark?'

'About the volleyball. Back to the ship, coxswain.'

Major Munro is waiting for us as I slide us gently alongside the accommodation ladder.

'Good exercise, Sarn't Lecky?'

'Yes sir, very good thank you.'

Down the mess nobody believes me about the shark. I'll trot it out to impress girls whenever I get the opportunity ... sometime in the far distant future.

*

'UP SPIRITS'

Chats ushers me away to a quiet corner of the mess and offers me his tot glass.

'How much?' I lick my lips in anticipation.

'Gulper.'

'Gulper?' It's only the second time I've been offered 'gulpers' and I wasn't one hundred percent sure of the correct protocol.

He nods.

I take what I hope is the equivalent of two 'wets' and hand the glass back to Chats.

He nods. Obviously I've done everything correctly. 'Everybody in the mess is relying on you to spice up their life with letters from the girls in Leeds, young Pete.'

'I'm dealing with it,' I lie.

'Mail closes at 18:30 today. It'll be the last chance to get a letter off for a week or so.'

'OK,' I say: now I have a deadline.

'Yeah, Pete. Get your ferkin finger out,' shouts Kit from a distant corner. 'Extractum ferkin digitum.'

'There he goes again ... speaking Latin,' says Jan.

'I'll do it ... promise.'

Jack comes over swinging his empty tot glass. 'How far you got with the letter then?'

'Haven't started it yet.'

'Come on then. Some of us are getting desperate for letters ... even if they are from Yorkshire lasses. Mail closes at 18:30.'

'I know, Chats just told me. I'll do it, Jack ... promise.'

'Get on with it then.'

Who do I write to? Will it be a man or woman? The opening sentence is crucial. What do I say? What address should I give? How can I pull on the heart-strings without sounding too desperate? I spend the next hour crouched in the corner of the mess scribbling ideas. Once I have pencilled out what I think is a reasonably snivelling letter,

I write it out properly with my best fountain pen. I put my name and address at the top of the letter and address my envelope to the Personnel Officer.

'Is that the letter to the jam factory?' asks Jack, who watches me seal the envelope.

I waft it in the air. 'Yep.'

He holds his hand out. 'Give it to me - I'll post it for ya.' He looks at the address and disappears up the mess ladder.

'What did you write then, Pete?' asks Kit.

'Can't remember exactly,' I look confused and shrug my shoulders.

'Typical Radar Plotter.'

'Did you say that we are a mess full of desperate, good looking blokes who haven't had their end away for over six months?' asks Kit cupping his groin.

'Something along those lines ... but less crude,' I say.

'It's one hundred and eighteen days since we left Pompey,' mumbles Sugar.

'Doesn't time fly ... when you're not getting anything?' says Jack.

*

I find out more about the Leading Seaman Board. Apparently it will take place over two consecutive days. Each day will be broken up into sections during which I will be examined on the varied aspects of Seamanship and the duties of being a Leading Seaman, the lowest grade on the Naval management ladder. The one section that I'm not looking forward to is 'Taking Charge of a Squad of Men'. It doesn't seem that long since I had cowered in the rear rank of class 173 at *HMS Ganges* to learn how to 'Stan Hatta Hease' correctly. Now I'm going to stand in front of a squad of men and teach them how to 'Stan Hatta Hease' correctly, and be examined on how well I do it. I will also have to display my ability to make a squad of men march and manoeuvre in step. I'm confident that I can answer any questions about polishing bulkhead brass tallies: I'm a self-styled expert on that.

Asking those who had been through a Leading Seaman's examination board before is confusing and not very helpful: everybody has different experiences. One thing is for sure - I have to rekindle my enthusiasm for my new copy of the Admiralty Manual of Seamanship Volume 1 ... and get stuck in.

'SPECIAL SEA DUTYMEN WILL CLOSE UP AT 07:00. BOTH WATCHES OF SEAMEN WILL FALL IN FOR LEAVING HARBOUR AT 07:15. SALUTING GUNS CREW CLOSE UP AND AWAIT INSTRUCTIONS. LEADING HANDS AND PRESIDENTS OF MESSES REPORT MESS STATUS TO THE REGULATING OFFICE WITHIN THE NEXT FIFTEEN MINUTES.'

Chats puts me on the spot. 'You got the letter to the girl factory posted?'

'Yep. Jack put it in the box for me before mail closed yesterday.'

'Did you say that we are awfy lonely sailors in the heat of the Middle East with nae female company?' asks Mack.

'Something like that, yeah ... but in English.'

'Who did you address the letter to?' asks Chats.

'The Personnel Officer I think.'

'Do you think they have Officers at Leeds jam factories?'

'Dunno. Couldn't think of anyone else.' I shrug.

'Should have been the Personnel Manager I reckon,' says Chats.

'That's a cock up then,' I admit.

Chats looks around for Jack. 'Did you post Pete's letter, Jack?'

'Sure did.'

At 07:30 the forecastle seamen hoist the anchor. The upper deck seamen fall in as we drift away from the Sultan's 'calling-cards'.

Someone obviously decided not to fire a gun salute; either that or I don't hear it, as we silently depart the Sultanate of Oman without fuss or undue ceremony.

'UP SPIRITS.'

'Well that was a stimulating visit, wasn't it?' states Sugar.

'Reasonable amount of Queen's today,' says Jack.

'Thank goodness for that.'

'We deserve it,' I say.

'Are you one hundred percent sure that the letter to the girly factory was posted on time, Jack?' asks Burbs.

'Sure was,' replies Jack.

Then, we should all offer Pete sippers for his efforts,' announces Chats, handing me his tot. Then he remembers something and takes it back saying, 'You had unusually large "wets" of mine yesterday.'

'Did I? Did I take too much?'

'You most certainly did.'

'What if we don't get any replies?' asks Kit.

'Then we'll drink Pete's tot for a week.'

I don't like that idea much, but I decide to live for the moment and gratefully accept sippers from everyone.

Consequently I spend the afternoon curled up on my bunk, asleep and dribbling over my newly dhobied pillow-case.

I wake in time for the evening meal.

'Welcome to the land of the living, Pete. You can ditch the gash,' says Chats.

I nod OK. I can do with the fresh air.

There is a young Stores Assistant on the Quarterdeck snapping away with his new camera. He snaps me with the mess gash bucket.

'THE INFORMATION OFFICER SPEAKING. WE ARE ABOUT TO ENTER THE STRAITS OF HORMUZ. WE WILL NAVIGATE THE 'KHAWR ASH SHAMM' OR ELPHINSTONE CREEK. THE INLET IS BANKED ON BOTH SIDES BY 3,000 FOOT HIGH CLIFFS. IT IS KNOWN TO BE ONE OF THE HOTTEST PLACES IN THE REGION. THE TEMPERATURE IS CURRENTLY 113º FAHRENHEIT.'

*

Once back alongside the Mina Sulman jetty in Bahrain, Cliff, Mack and I receive details of our forthcoming Examination Board. In exactly two weeks' time we are to be tested on Boat Handling Under Power & Oars, Hoisting & Lowering of Boats, Fire Fighting, Anchor Work, Helmsmanship, Towing, Ship's Husbandry, Replenishment at Sea, Ropework, Awkward Squad, Morse Code and Semaphore. Before the Board we have to produce an eye-splice or a bollard strop in a one-inch diameter wire rope, a back splice in fibre rope and an eye splice in nylon rope: this will require some snivelling around the Buffer and some help from those who know how to splice wire rope.

'What exactly is an Awkward Squad?' I ask Chats.

'A squad of specially selected individuals to test your ability to take charge of a group of men.'

'What's the awkward bit then?'

'They will be instructed to be awkward. Not that it will be difficult, as they'll select those who haven't done much parade ground work.'

This is getting serious. I flick through the index of my Seamanship Manual. There is absolutely nothing about Awkward Squads.

Chats offers to organise a group of men and to give

Cliff, Mack and me some out-of-hours instruction.

Burbs slides down the mess ladder and stands in the mess square to catch his breath. 'The two ladies have just left, along with Bill. He had loads of bags with 'im.'

'Why wasn't I informed?' asks Sugar.

'It all happened so quick, Shug,' says Burbs, looking apologetic. 'I was just passing and anyway ... I didn't think you'd be interested in the number of his bags.'

'That's not what I meant, young Burbs ... and you ferkin know it.'

'Sorry, Shug. Shall I bring them all back ... to do the departure thing again?'

'Very funny, Burbs ... very funny.'

'UP SPIRITS.'

Jack holds up the first tot. 'We have a birthday in the mess.'

'Not another one?' asks Jan.

'Why do we have so many ferkin birthdays?' asks Kit.

'Just the way the ferkin mop flops,' says Jack.

'Whose is it then?' queries Chats, who traditionally is the first to get his tot.

'Pete's.'

'Naah.' Kit turns to face me. 'You had one not that long ago.'

'That was my official one ... this is my actual birth ...'

'ID card then ... proof,' orders Kit.

I slap my ID card on the table. Kit looks at it. 'What day is it today?'

'It's my ferkin birthday,' I say.

'Date?'

'Sixteenth of February.'

'Is it?' says Kit. 'That's OK then.'

I have sufficient 'sippers' to make dinner unimportant. I crawl into my bunk for a ten-minute kip.

I am shaken many hours later by Kit dangling the

ship's Land Rover keys in my ear. 'Come on then, birthday boy. Fancy a trip to the Jufair watering hole for a wet or twelve?'

Kit has to do a couple of trips, as everybody who isn't duty decides to come as it is traditional for the birthday boy to buy the first round. Surprisingly there are people in my mess who have never bought me a drink.

In the *Jufair* canteen the air conditioner, fans and all lights except one are switched off. The barman has recently taken delivery of a couple of crates of Kenyan Tusker beer and the fridge needs all the 'juice' the generator can muster.

Kit has sufficient John Collins to prevent him from driving back.

'I'll drive,' I offer.

'Can ya drive then?' asks Stormy.

'Dunno.'

'We're all walking,' declares Chats.

What is a relaxing ten-minute drive in the Ship's Land Rover proves to be one heck of a long walk that required numerous stops, starts and toilet breaks.

By the time we pull and tug our tired and sand-caked bodies up the brow it is well into the following day.

I have a serious hangover the following morning. It's Sunday.

'How old are ya, Pete?' asks Chats.

'Err, give me a moment.' I check my mental arithmetic. 'Twenty two.'

'Old enough to get out of your bunk by yourself then?'

'Of course.' I give it a go but someone must have strapped me in during the night and I can't move. 'Bastards ... thanks for that.'

8

31-23-32 ... and drop-dead gorgeous!

TODAY I put in my Request Form to be awarded my first good conduct badge.

After breakfast Chats tells me, Cliff and Mack to muster on the jetty.

'I was going for a swim,' says Cliff.

'I've got a wee sore heed,' says Mack.

'And I've got a mouth like the inside of a PTI's plimsoll,' I add.

'Please yourselves. Do any of you have experience at taking charge of a group of men ... awkward men?'

'No.'

'Nope.'

'Naah.'

'Then give me an hour of your valuable time after dinner. I've arranged everything including a squad of men.'

'UP SPIRITS.'

After my tot, I'm ready to tackle a group of awkward individuals.

'So who's going on the jetty to do marching practice then?' asks Kit.

'Me with Mack and Cliff.'

'I might come and come and watch.'

'You silly old bastard,' says Chats. 'At your age you can just about manage to make it back to your bunk after dinner.'

'That's a slur.'

'Everybody for Queen's?' asks Jack as a matter of courtesy.

'Not me ... not today,' I say.

Lots of sarcastic noises and uncalled-for comments.

Panic doesn't really set in until I'm striding over the brow.

A motley group of twelve unhappy looking individuals are lounging on the jetty. The familiar group consists entirely of 'men under punishment': three Stewards, four Seaman, two young, white-faced Stokers, a Communicator and a couple of colour-blind Stores Assistants who have recently been 'weighed off' for trying to nick a cask of rum that turned out to be a cask of vinegar.

'Fall in, three ranks of four. Tallest on the flanks, shortest in the centre,' says Chats. He stands and watches for a couple of minutes while the group scramble around trying to make sense of what they have been asked to do.

Chats stops all movement and organises each member individually. 'You're not as tall as you think you are, Stumpy ... move over. Those of you wearing sandals go back onboard and change into shoes and socks as I asked. Those without caps go back onboard and collect them.'

I take the opportunity to have a cigarette. Mack and

Cliff slump down on the top of a couple of beer kegs.

'When those idiots return, I'll fall them in and then each of you,' Chats nods at each of us in turn, 'will go through the process of teaching them how to "Off Caps". You'll be examined on how you can instruct a squad of men to perform various co-ordinated actions as well as marching. You can all remember how to "Off Caps" can't you?'

We all nod.

With our motley group reassembled, Mack is chosen as the first to take charge.

'Carry on, Able Seaman McCubbin. I'd like you to instruct the squad how to "Off Caps" and give you three cheers.'

Mack looks sheepish. 'Give me three cheers ... me?'

'Yep - three cheers. You can figure out how to do that, can't you?'

'I think so,' says Mack.

'Carry on then.'

Mack turns to face the squad and calls them to attention.

They do it badly.

'That was terrible, Able Seaman McCubbin. Get them to do it again ... give them a bollocking.'

For the next ten minutes or so Mack instructs the squad how to take their caps off and execute a Naval three cheers for him.

He doesn't enjoy it and I'm more than a little nervous as I take over.

'Squad ... Squada ... Stanna ... Hease.'

'More noise, Able Seaman Broadbent,' bellows Chats. 'From the stomach. Open that under-developed chest of yours.'

I cough. 'Squad ... Squada ... Stanna ... Hease.'

'Better,' says Chats.

'Sqwadda ... Sqwadda ... Shun.'

'Now, you can do the "Off Caps" followed by three

cheers for your birthday.'

I perform the whole "Off Caps" sequence and get them to give me three Royal Naval cheers for my birthday. Thankfully I'd watched, and paid attention, to Mack.

'Now then, Able Seaman Broadbent, march your squad of men down the jetty as far as that truck parked alongside the black-hulled vessel on the other side of the jetty. Then about turn them and march them round the back of those two rubbish bins ... and back here.'

'OK.'

'But you stay right here.'

Shit. I take a deep breath. 'Sqwadda ... Sqwadda ... Turn To The Left In Threes, Lefta ... Tin.'

And they do.

'By The Left ... Qwicka ... March.'

And my squad of men start to march away from me.

'Open your chest,' says Chats as my squad of men are nearing the target vessel some distance away. 'Don't leave it too long.'

'Sqwadda ... Sqwadda ... Hay Bart ... Tin.' I scream. And surprisingly they turn about.

Now it's the rubbish bin obstacle. 'Sqwadda ... Righta ... Wheel.'

They overshoot. 'Sqwadda ... Sqwadda ... Halt ... Haybart Tin. Don't ... Belay That ... Sqwadda ... Haybart Tin. Belay My Last ... Sqwadda ... Mark Time.'

One of the squad continues to march off on his own.

'Get him, get 'im,' shouts Chats, pointing at the lone Stores Assistant marching towards the edge of the jetty.

'Where Do You Think You Are Going Lad?' I yell.

The fugitive stops, looks at me with apologetic eyes, about turns himself and scrambles back to his position in the squad, who are still marking time. They are half-hidden from me by the rubbish bins.

'Another five seconds and he would have ended up in the ferkin Gulf,' whispers Chats out of the corner of his mouth.

'He wouldn't have actually marched over the edge of the jetty, would he?' I ask.

'That idiot would ... yeah.'

'Sqwadda ... Sqwadda ... Halt.'

They stand to attention facing the waters of the Gulf.

'Now bring them back.'

I take a deep breath. 'Sqwadda ... Sqwadda ... Hay ... Bart Tin.'

Very sensible,' says Chats.

'Sqwadda ... Sqwadda ... By The Left ... Qwicka March.'

They all emerge from behind the rubbish bins. My squad are now coming towards me. I stop them in front of me and stand them at ease.

Cliff then takes over and does something similar, but lots better than Mack or I.

Down the mess Chats assesses our performance. 'Mack, you need to work on your English pronunciation - the last thing you want is your squad not to understand you. Pete, you need to concentrate - putting your squad into the Gulf is a guaranteed failure. Cliff, you are almost perfect.'

Cliff punches the air and flops onto his bunk in a rather superior fashion.

I present myself at the First Lieutenant's table later in the day to be officially awarded with my first 'good conduct' badge. I don't actually get given a badge. I get something written on my Service Docs and a signed chit from the Regulating Office that I'm told to take to the Stores. In the Stores Office a Petty Officer swivels his chair and hands the chit to a killick Stores Assistant who studies it for a full minute before telling me to come back in 48 hours.

'MAIL IS NOW READY FOR COLLECTION. UP SPIRITS.'

Me and Chats are the only two in the mess.

'Where's Jack?' asks Chats.

'Dunno.'

Chats looks at his watch. 'Not like Jack to be late.'

The phone rings and Chats answers it. 'OK, mate ... no problem. I'll get Pete to do it.'

Chats hands me the rum fanny. 'Jack's busy. You'll have to do Rum Bosun, Pete.'

'Me?'

Chats surveys the empty mess. 'Yeah.'

With the sacred fanny, complete with tight-fitting lid, in hand I make my way to the capstan flat and join the back of a long queue. I haven't a clue how this is organised but by the time it's my turn I've watched and listened to those ahead of me.

I give my mess number and Jed Constable ticks something on a sheet of paper. 'Where's Able Seaman Tarr?'

'Busy,' I reply: the smell of rum is almost overpowering.

The killick Stores Assistant scans a list and repeats my mess number followed by some numbers that mean nothing to me.

The Officer-of-the-Day nods.

I remove the fanny lid and place the fanny on the edge of the wooden barrel, tipped so that the young Jack Dusty, swinging copper measuring jugs, can pour the allocated amount of rum into it. The fanny catches some of the spillage ... but not all of it. The smell of pouring rum is intoxicating.

'Next,' yells Constable.

I make sure my fanny lid is firmly in place and stride away. I'm overly careful when negotiating the mess ladder with a fanny full of rum.

I make it to the mess table with all the rum. I don't get a round of applause or anything. Jack, who is sitting at the head of the table, waves an arm. 'Dish it out, Bosun ... the sippers are all yours.'

I'd watched Jack do the measuring many times but never taken much notice of exactly how it was done. I keep half an eye on Jack as I measure out Chats' tot.

Jack nods and gives me a thumbs-up. I've done it right.

Chats nods. I take a very small sip and hand him his tot.

Tot time is officially under way. I take a sip of everybody's tot, drink mine last and pass around the Queen's. I've done it ... and I feel pleasantly light headed. Fabulous!

Burbs waves a sheet of paper in the air, 'Nother funny from Aunt Peggy - a little bit subtle though.'

'What's subtle mean?' asks Jan.

'Too complicated for you,' says Sugar.

Burbs coughs and reads: 'The Bishop and Mother Superior are discussing the church's attitude to celibacy.'

'What's celibacy?' asks Wheelie.

'I know that. It's definitely a thin green vegetable,' states Kit confidently.

Sugar gives Kit a playful clip round the head. 'Don't listen to him. It means no sex ... forever and ever amen.'

'Shall I start again?' asks Burbs.

'Go on then, Burbs lad,' says Chats. 'Take no notice of these idiots.'

'That'll be difficult,' mumbles Burbs. 'Right then ... the Bishop and Mother Superior are discussing the church's attitude to celibacy. "Do you think they'll ever change the celibacy rules?" asks Mother Superior. "Not during our lifetime," replies the Bishop ... "but maybe in our children's."'

Sugar splutters. It takes a while for the rest of us to get it.

The killick of the opposite mess comes around with his empty tot glass in his hand. 'I've got a problem, lads,' he says. 'I've got a young seaman who is threatening to kill himself.'

'You haven't, have ya?' asks Mack.

'Naah?' says Jan.

'Is he deadly serious?' asks Sugar.

Some of us get it … others don't.

Two days later I get a handful of good conduct stripes: red ones to sew onto my blue uniform jackets, blue ones to sew onto my tropical uniform and a gold one to sew onto my best blue suit jacket. It's one heck of a lot of sewing and takes up a lot of my time that I could have spent doing my splices.

Chats explains to me that they are not actually awarded for good conduct, but as recognition of four years of undetected crime.

*

From an out-of-date English newspaper that has unexpectedly found its way into our Mess, I extract a large picture of a new English model called Twiggy. I am sufficiently impressed with the picture of her in a simple short white dress that I stick it to the ship's side alongside my pillow, covering my photograph of the 1964-65 Leeds United first team. According to the picture's strapline sixteen-year-old Twiggy is short for a top-class model at only five and a half feet tall. She weighs a very feminine eight stone and sports a less than voluptuous 31-23-32 figure. Despite the numbers, I think she's gorgeous.

'DO YOU HEAR THERE, THERE ARE NO SPARE BERTHS ON THE MINA SULMAN JETTY. WE HAVE THEREFORE GIVEN PERMISSION FOR THE DESTROYER USS NEW TO BERTH ALONGSIDE US FOR THE NEXT FOUR DAYS.'

On the upper deck the Buffer scurries around organising loads of large wicker fenders. 'Don't reckon much to the ship-handling skills of our American cousins,' he explains.

Through the mists of the morning gloom I watch as an elderly grey warship slowly approaches.

'Doesn't look very ferkin new to me,' says Kit.

'Naah.'

As *USS New* closes and heaving lines are thrown, we evaluate our new American neighbour. She has old-fashioned lines; she certainly doesn't have the sleekness of *Gurkha*.

The rigging of our neighbour's berthing ropes is performed in almost total silence. Only when the two gangplanks are rigged between the two ships is there any significant exchange of information.

'Welcome to Bahrain,' says Sharky Ward, our Quartermaster for the forenoon watch.

'Nice to be here,' says someone onboard *USS New*.

'How long will you be here?'

'We are programmed to be here for three, maximum four days,' replies a guy wearing sparkly white webbing, buckling his belt.

A couple of *USS New*'s crew carry a polished wooden plinth over our brow and place it alongside our lifebelt on the jetty. It's a highly polished piece of kit topped by a large silvered eagle, its splendidly detailed wings outstretched.

USS New is a few feet longer than us. Her overall colour is a very much darker shade of grey than ours; her decks are dark grey where ours are green. There is a double row of large medal ribbons on the side of her Bridge superstructure. A large wooden desk is positioned at her end of the connecting gangplank; manned by a couple of blokes each with a holstered gun dangling from a thick leather cowboy belt with a horseshoe buckle.

A couple of flags are hoisted high to the yards of her mast.

During the following hour, a number of official

looking gentlemen cross over *Gurkha* to officially welcome *USS New* to Bahrain.

One of a small group of Americans, leaning on their guardrails, ask Jack where the best place to find a beer is.

'Nowhere in town,' Jack replies.

I wonder why Jack doesn't tell them about the *Jufair* Canteen. Then I remember how disruptive the Americans had been at the China Fleet Club in Hong Kong some years ago, and understand why.

USS New smells different and Americans are apparently allowed to lean on their guardrails.

Someone couldn't keep *Jufair* a secret and there is a large crowd of Americans in the Canteen this evening.

Sugar asks one of the Americans passing us on his way to the heads, 'You have any women onboard?'

'We gotta a few who would like to be ... but no actual women, no.'

'Trust you, Shug,' I say.

'Thought I'd check,' he replies. 'I heard a rumour.'

By the end of the evening the beer fridge is struggling. We offer a group of Americans a lift back to the ship. One of them looks as though he wouldn't make it back onboard under his own steam.

Kit organises us and we squeeze six into, and on, the Land Rover which we reckon is about the limit.

We learn on our way back that leave for Americans on the lower deck expires at midnight anywhere outside the United States. Apparently, this is because of something that happened during the Second World War.

Adjacent to the gangplank adjoining the two ships we say our good-nights. Kit, Sugar and I are invited onboard *USS New* for dinner tomorrow.

'After tot-time,' says Kit.

'What exactly is tot-time?' the bloke we now know as Merle, asks.

'Rum issue. We have a ration of rum each day,' explains Kit.

'You get an issue of rum each day?'

'Of course.'

'Well I'll be daw-gonned.'

'It's traditional ... something to do with Nelson.'

'Nelson who?

'Lord Nelson.'

'Yeah ... who? ... oh him.'

'Doesn't matter,' I say suddenly realising that our American cousins don't know what the heck we are talking about.

*

The following day at morning stand-easy ...

'ANYONE WHO KNOWS THE WHEREABOUTS OF THE EAGLE THAT WAS FIXED TO THE TOP OF USS NEW'S DOCKSIDE PLINTH, REPORT TO THE GANGWAY. AYO ...'

'Someone's ferkin nicked the shite-hawk from the top of the American plinth,' exclaims Sugar, grinning.

'Wasn't you lot, was it?' asks Chats. 'You came back with a bunch of our American cousins last night.'

I look at Sugar, who shrugs his shoulder.

Sugar looks at Kit, who shakes his head.

'Not us,' says Kit.

'Was it on the plinth when you came back last night?'

'I don't ferkin know, do I?'

'Did we get invited onboard for something?' asks Sugar.

'Dinner,' says Kit.

'After tot-time,' I explain.

Kit normally secretes himself away in his bunk after his tot and dinner, but today he is keen to accompany us.

Onboard *USS New* all three of us are stopped at the table by a bloke playing with the handgrip of his gun.

172

'We've been invited onboard for lunch,' explains Sugar.

'Welcome. Have ya? Who by?'

'Bloke called Merle.'

'We have a number of Merles aboard.'

'Big bloke, can't hold his beer. We gave him and his mates a lift back to the ship last night.'

'That'll be Seaman Merle Steinway.' He dials a number on a bulkhead telephone and tells us to stand away from the desk.

Merle arrives with another bloke I vaguely remember from last night. 'This is Seaman Buick Eagleburger and I am Seaman Merle Steinway. Welcome onboard *USS New*.' He checks with the armed sentry who has hooked his trigger finger under the butt of his sidearm. 'Please follow me to the dining facility.'

I assumed that all warships would smell the same, but they don't; *USS New* smells significantly different from *Gurkha*. In the dining 'facility' we sit at a corner table and are served. Buick suggests steak for today and orders steak and eggs for us. Without being asked we are brought large schooners of ice cold, frothing Coca-Cola.

'LIEUTENANT ELMER CROWSFEET SPEAKING: THE CREW OF HER MAJESTY'S SHIP GURKHA ARE AWARE OF OUR MISSING EAGLE AND ARE ASSISTING WITH ITS RECOVERY. OTHER VESSELS ON THE MINA SULMAN JETTY HAVE BEEN INFORMED OF THE EAGLE'S DISAPPEARANCE. LIBERTY GUYS TO GLAMORIZE.'

Buick and Merle look quizzically at us.

'The eagle is an important symbol of the United States of America,' says Buick.

'We understand that,' says Sugar.

'And it's silver,' adds Merle.

'Plated silver,' corrects Buick.

'Would you know if anyone onboard *Gurkha* has taken it?'

'Yes ... err yeah, of course,' says Kit. 'We would know ... for sure.'

'But we haven't taken it,' adds Sugar.

Our steaks and eggs arrive and we eat in silence. The steaks are ginormous and the eggs perfectly fried. In the centre of the table is placed a basket of condiments; other than salt and pepper I don't recognise anything.

A large red-faced bloke dressed in blue trousers and a grubby white T-shirt stands silently at the top of our table.

It takes Merle some moments to notice our visitor. When he does he places his fork alongside his plate, wipes his hands on the legs of his trousers and smiles benignly. 'Gentlemen, let me introduce Petty Officer 3rd Class William Zee Louderbeck.'

Without standing I offer my hand, 'Able Seaman Peter En Broadbent.'

William Zee Louderbeck wipes his hands on his trousered backside and firmly shakes my hand. 'Hi there. Welcome aboard USS New. You have just shaken the hand of the man who has shaken the hand of a friend who has shaken the hand of Lyndon Baines Johnson.'

'Have I really?' I ask, somewhat confused.

'Who?' asks Kit.

William Zee offers his hand to Kit. 'Lyndon Baines Johnson, the 36th President of the United States of America following the assassination of President John Ef Kennedy. Whose hand do I have the pleasure of shaking?'

'Able Seaman Kit Carson's.'

'Are you related in any way to the legendary American showman Kit Carson?'

Kit smiles. 'Not to my knowledge. But you have just shaken the hand that has opened the same toilet door that Wee Willy Harris opened in the early 1960s.'

'Pardon me sir?' asks William Zee.

'Doesn't matter.' They shake hands.

William wipes his hands on the front of his trousers. 'Well, Able Seaman Kit Carson, you have just shaken the hand of a man who has shaken the hand of a female family member of Miss Marie Bueno.'

'Who?' asks Sugar.

'Marie Bueno. Winner of the United States Tennis championship and your Wimbledon two years back ... in 1964.'

'Fancy,' says Sugar.

'I'm impressed,' says Kit.

William Zee Louderbeck smiles, waves farewell to our table and struts away.

I look at Merle. 'Did that really happen?'

'Yeah ... unfortunately,' says Buick.

'William Zee is one of the ship's more unplumbed characters,' Merle adds. 'He claims to have a hand-shaking connection to almost everybody in the United States.'

'Including Marilyn Monroe?' asks Kit.

'Including Marilyn,' confirms Buick.

We concentrate on finishing our meal. As soon as we finish, our plates are removed.

'How many crew onboard USS New?' asks Sugar.

'Three hundred and thirty six including Commissioned Officers,' says Buick. 'Onboard HMS Gurkha?'

'Just over two hundred I think,' says Sugar.

'Two hundred and fifty three,' says Kit.

'Why the name "New"?'

'Named after Private First Class John Dee New, who was posthumously awarded the Medal of Honour for selfless conduct during the Battle of Peleliu.'

'The battle of what?' I ask.

'Peleliu. A Pacific Island we fought the Japanese for in World War Two ... and won of course.'

'USS New is a Gearing class destroyer. Top speed

thirty-five knots. And Gurkha's top speed is?' asks Buick.

'Don't know exactly, but probably about the same. But we have a chopper,' says Sugar.

'A chopper?'

'A helicopter.'

'Well I'll be God damned ... you've got a helicopter onboard that little ship of yours?'

'Yeah. Pete here is one of our helicopter controllers.'

All of a sudden I feel important. I nod.

'God damn it,' says Buick.

'Where do you keep your helicopter?' asks Merle.

'In our hangar,' I explain confidently.

'A hangar. You have a helicopter hangar onboard?'

'Yep.'

Merle and Buick shake their heads respectfully.

'You are cordially invited onboard Her Majesty's Ship Gurkha for tot-time tomorrow,' says Kit.

'Tot-time?'

'Our daily issue of rum,' I explain.

'Rum?' asks Merle.

'Not any old rum. Special Royal Navy rum.'

'So we are officially invited?'

'Sure are, tomorrow,' says Kit. 'Come onboard tomorrow.'

'We surely will,' says Buick.

'Surely,' adds Merle.

'William Zee isn't invited.' says Kit. 'I don't think his style of humour would go down well.'

Thereby an Anglo-American accord is established.

*

'UP SPIRITS.'

Next day, Buick and Merle are bang on time and we show them into the mess that has been tidied up a little. Loose clothing has been stowed away, bunks made and stowed, gash buckets emptied and dirty cups and plates stashed away in foot lockers.

Jack appears with the rum and we all move down so that Buick and Merle can sit at the head of the table. Kit explains the tradition of rum and that the consumption of each and every tot should be preceded by the phrase 'The Queen ... God bless her.'

Sugar offers his entire tot to Buick. Reluctantly I then offer mine to Merle.

Jack hands Sugar's tot to Buick. 'What do we say, Buick?'

'The Queen ... God bless her Majesty.'

'Perfect, Buick ... now down in one.'

'Pardon?'

'Drink it without a break. Without stopping.'

And Buick does. He stands up, wobbles slightly, closes his eyes and slowly sits himself down. 'God damn ... that is good ... that really is really, God damn good.'

Merle holds an expectant hand out as Jack offers him my tot. I want him to refuse it.

Unfortunately he accepts it. He sniffs it lovingly and smiles. 'The Queen ... The Queen ... God bless your Queen ... the Majestic.' Then the bastard knocks my entire tot back in one.

Everybody else offers our guests parts of their tot. By the time Jack is dishing out Queen's, Buick and Merle are each slouched across a couple of chairs and are smiling at anything and everything. We open half a crate of beer and offer cans to Buck and Merle.

'All United States warships are com ... completely dry,' slurs Merle.

'Really dry or just officially dry?' asks Chats.

'One hundred percent dry. Banned since pro ...hi ... bish ... prohibition days,' says Merle.

'Long time ago. Hish ...toric,' adds Buick, suddenly loose-lipped.

'Why are you named after a car?' Bagsy asks Buick.

'Daddy had one.'

'A what?'

'A Buick.'

'That makes sense then .'

'You haven't got our eagle, have ya?' asks a wavering Merle.

'Us ... naah,' says Bagsy. 'It's possible that our spanner-wangers could have though.'

'Who?'

From our neighbour we hear ...

'LIEUTENANT ELMER CROWSFEET SPEAKING: THE CREW OF USS NEW ARE WARNED NOT TO ACCEPT HOSPITALITY AT TOT-TIME ONBOARD HMS GURKHA. TOT-TIME ONBOARD ROYAL NAVAL WARSHIPS IS A TRADITION NOT SUITABLE FOR THE CREW OF USS NEW. DISCIPLINARY ACTION WILL BE TAKEN AGAINST ANYONE IGNORING THIS ... ERR ADVICE. LIBERTY GUYS TO ...'

USS New is scheduled to depart at 14:00 the following day for a DIP (Dhow Intercept Patrol). The gangplanks, however, are removed at 11:00 and her departure time brought forward to avoid 'up spirits'.

We help with her berthing ropes. As she slowly drifts away from us we notice that some of their crew are pointing at something on our Bridge wings.

I look up to see a handwritten notice draped over the edge ...

YOUR EAGLE IS IN YOUR
PORT LIFEBOAT
GOD SAVE THE QUEEN

We watch as a gaggle of *USS New*'s crew scramble aboard their port lifeboat. One triumphantly holds the eagle aloft.

From behind and above us a Communicator on the bridge wing shouts 'Look at the port yard-arm of her mast.'

We look and can plainly see the unfurling of a large Royal Naval Battle Ensign on the mast of a US warship.

There is lots of shouting; arm waving and American oaths as a team are detailed to haul the Ensign down. They fall over each other in their haste to grapple the right line. The Battle Ensign is unceremoniously lowered, bundled up and stuffed, unfolded into a flag locker.

On Daily Orders for the following day we are informed of the following message received from *USS New* ...

> 'We thank the officers and crew of *HMS Gurkha*
> for the hospitality shown to us during our short
> visit to Bahrain. We hope that we shall meet
> again whilst on duty in the Persian Gulf, at
> which time we will be happy to return your
> starboard name plate.'

The editor of Daily Orders hopes that *HMS Gurkha* will take the initiative and will now draw a line under this low-level skylarking.

Chats sends Bagsy up top to check that the starboard name plate is missing.

'It's not there,' says Bagsy on his return.

'The thieving bastards.'

*

I choose to do an eye splice in my wire rope and have talked Sugar into helping me. He has spent some time in the rope shop in Portsmouth Dockyard and has lots of advice on how to rig and prepare wires for splicing.

It takes me about ten hours spread over a week to

finish all my splices. Sugar then shows me how to do some tiddly 'serving' which covers the spliced ends and makes them look like a neat, professional job. The rope and nylon test pieces are reasonably easy and I'm pleased with the finished results. I wire nametags to all my pieces and place them in a secure locker in the Buffer's cabooch.

'UP SPIRITS.'

Bagsy, definitely not old enough to draw his tot, stands at the head of the table watching Jack measure out the first half a dozen. 'What's a knee trembler, Jack?' he asks, completely out of the blue.

Jack stops pouring. Along with the rest of us he looks to Sugar for inspiration ... and an explanation.

Sugar slowly places his latest J T Edson face down on the table and holds his hand out. 'Mi tot please, Jack.'

'Jack takes a delicate, respectful sip and hands Sugar his tot.

Sugar downs it in one and belches. He looks Bagsy straight in the eye. 'A knee trembler, young Bagsy, is the performance of a horizontal act in a vertical position.'

'Wha?'

'In Queen's English ... shagging while standing up,' explains Kit.

Bagsy shrugs his shoulders, nods a thank you and scuttles up the mess ladder and away.

'Couldn't have put it more succinctly myself,' says Chats.

'You've probably confused the lad for life, Shug,' says Kit.

'What's succinctly mean then?' someone from the back of the mess asks.

Kit shakes his head. 'It's squidgy, purple vegetable popular with teenage girls in North Borneo, I believe.'

*

My new Admiralty Manual of Seamanship becomes my only reading material. Every night I read and re-read one of the many chapters before going to sleep. I am surprised to discover in the morning that I can remember most of what I've read the previous night.

The day of the Examination Board is drawing close. Mack chickens out, despite his part-of-ship Petty Officer and Chats trying to convince him otherwise. When cross-examined at tot-time Mack confides that he has decided to leave the Navy and become a vicar.

'Whaa?' asks Jack.

'I've had a calling to become a vicar,' repeats Mack.

'What, a telephone call?'

'No,' says Mack, flushing. 'A calling ... a spiritual calling.'

'From who?' asks Jack.

'From the man Himself,' states Mack, looking up at the deckhead.

'Who ... the manager of Plymouth Argyle?' asks Jan.

'Naah ... Him on high.' Mack nods at the deckhead.

'Not Midshipman Bellringer?' blurts Jan.

'Don't be so disrespectful,' says Mack, suddenly turning serious.

'Have you given this change of career your careful consideration?' asks Chats.

'Yep.'

'How long have you had this ... err desire ... err inclination?' asks Jan.

'Couple of weeks.'

'Quite a while then?'

'Yeah.'

'How long will it take you to qualify ... how long to ...'

'Bout five years.'

'But you're a qualified Helicopter Controller, Mack,' I remind him.

'Aye ... for now.'

'And you're a foul-mouthed bastard sometimes.'

'I will resist the temptation from here on in.'

'Whaaa?'

As the rest of the mess know absolutely nothing about the complexities of a religious calling, that's the end of the discussion ... except for ...

'When the big man spoke to you, Mack, what language did he use?' asks Chats.

'Pure English with a Scottish accent of course ... what else? God is, after all, a devout Scot. Deep down we all know that.'

'That's bollocks,' says Jan looking around. 'Isn't it?'

'And you could understand him ... in this Scottish accent?' asks Kit.

'Occhhhh ... of course,' replies Mack from the back of his throat.

*

The day of the examination board dawns. Cliff and I have been well advised and primed by lots of people. Mack wishes us both success and sends us on our way with a secretive and somewhat sloppy, sign of the cross.

Both Cliff and I have our own individual schedule. My first is Ship's Husbandry which is probably the easiest of all the disciplines and something that I know a fair bit about as I've done loads and loads of scrubbing, polishing, painting and cleaning in my time. The Midshipman who examines me knows less about the subject than I do and I sail through my fifteen-minute oral appraisal. I do Anchor Work theory before stand-easy and Replenishment at Sea immediately after. Before lunch the Buffer inspects my splices. He cuts all the 'servings' off my wire eye splice, saying that it is an old dockyard trick to hide a less than perfect splice. Fortunately, thanks to Sugar, my splices are good.

*

We are advised not to drink our tot at dinnertime. I compromise and drink half of mine and give the rest to Mack who has helped me with my revision.

Mack stops me as I head for the mess ladder. He places a gentle hand on my shoulder, 'Go in peace, my child, and good luck for the afternoon sesh.'

'That's very nice of you ... your holiness, thanks.'

'Just practising,' he replies.

After lunch I take charge of the 'Awkward Squad' on the jetty. Surprise, surprise - I am told by an unknown Officer to instruct my squad to give me three cheers. In my humble opinion the three cheers that my squad give me lack a certain something, so I get them to do it again with a little more enthusiasm and co-ordination. Chats had said that a squad bollocking always goes down well with the examining Officer so I 'dish one out'. I cheat on my Morse code examination. Cliff has mastered the dots and dashes, so I make sure that I am paired with him. The way the exam is organised is that each pair takes it in turn to read from a flashing light while his partner, standing with his back to the light, writes down the message as read by the other. I am able to tell Cliff the message in 'dit-dah' mode; consequently I pass with an acceptable message. Hopefully I will never have to read or send Morse in an emergency.

It is one heck of a day and after tea Cliff and I slump onto the bottom bunk nearest to the air conditioner in the mess and take our shoes off.

'How did you do?' I ask.

'OK I think, but mi Awkward Squad wasn't good,' says Cliff.

'Did you have to get them to give the three cheers?'

'Yep, I got them eventually, but they were crap. My voice gave way on me when the squad were halfway down the ferkin jetty. You?'

'Dunno. It's all a blur.'

'Mi splices were champion though,' says Cliff.

'Mine too ... but the Buffer cut all my 'servings' off. What did you think about the Middie who did Ship's Husbandry?'

'Waste of space.'

I'm excused the Boat Handling exam scheduled for the following day. Sergeant Lecky is the examiner and he knows what I'm capable of.

The Fire Fighting session is relatively easy, as is the Ropework examination on the Flagdeck. The Buffer tests me on what I know about Hoisting and Lowering of a seaboat - that takes about five minutes. The remainder of the session turns into a chat about his time at *HMS Ganges* in the mid-1940s. The main difference between *Ganges* circa 1945 and *Ganges* circa 1960 was that when I was there we had a dining hall: in 1945 the boys prepared and ate all their food in the mess.

My final session is all about the duties of a Leading Seaman and is conducted by the Officer who I had lied to about playing cricket. We spend a few minutes discussing the difficulties of managing a messdeck as 'Killick of the Mess', something he knows absolutely nothing about. The following half-hour we discuss the connections between Pudsey, Len Hutton and the Bedser twins. He says that his family are from Harrogate, although he doesn't sound much like a Yorkshireman to me.

*

A couple of days later Cliff and I are summoned to the First Lieutenant's cabin.

'Congratulations, both of you. You have both passed for Leading Seaman with commendable grades. Able Seaman Belter, you excelled at the more academic sections. Able Seaman Broadbent, you had an exceptional grasp of the more practical aspects of Seamanship. All the necessary paperwork will be submitted and your Service Documents notated. All you have to do now is wait for your names to get to the top of the promotional roster.'

'How long could that be, sir?' I ask.

'Can't tell you. Depends on the number of people on the roster and the number of available billets ... it's constantly changing. Details are in the Navy News each month, I believe.'

'Right, sir.'

Outside the cabin Cliff and I smile at each other.

'Congratulations, mate.'

'And congratulations to you, mate.'

'Wonder how long we'll have to wait?'

'Over a year I reckon.'

'Yeah probably.'

'Let's tell the lads, maybe we'll get a wet or two.'

'UP SPIRITS.'

At tot-time Chats asks me for half my tot: apparently this is the traditional way of thanking anyone who has helped you through a Leading Seaman's examination board.

Sugar asks for the other half ... for the same reason.

Reluctantly Cliff and I hand over our tots.

Then we are deluged with gulpers and wets from everybody else's tot. I suppose we both have more than normal as we become rather talkative in the dinner queue.

One of the Communicators in the queue tells us that the UK will decimalise the pound on 15th February 1971.

I work it out on my fingers. 'That's the day before my twenty-seventh birthday,' I say.

'Silly old bugger.'

*

Burbs spots Mack doing a quick sign of the cross before picking up his breakfast knife and fork. 'Never seen you do that before, Mac.'

Mack grunts, not exactly sure what to say.

'Is it because you've got three rashers of bacon?' asks Sugar.

Mack takes a deep breath and scans us all. 'It's actually a sign of thankfulness for my breakfast: the first meal of my day ... breaking my fast.' He coughs. 'Thought I would give it a go ... practising like.'

'So it is because you've got three rashers of ferkin bacon then,' says Sugar.

'I'm giving thanks to God for the gift of food ... sustenance that we are all about to enjoy.'

'I only got two rashers,' says Jack.

'I've already said cheers to the Chef,' I admit.

Mac freezes with a forked sliver of floppy fried egg between plate and mouth. 'Don't trivialise meal times, my children.'

'Right then,' says Chats. 'Shall we have a formal saying of Grace then?'

Mack finishes his mouthful of egg and silently scans us all. 'You serious?'

'Yeah.'

'Sure?' asks Mack as he lays his knife and fork to one side.

'Why not?'

'Go for it, Mack.'

We all put our knives and forks down.

Mack coughs and looks directly at Chats.

Chats taps his fork on the side of his tin mug, stands up and shouts, 'Silence everybody ... just for a moment.'

Everybody in the dining hall falls silent. Even the Chefs look on, their spatulas respectfully empty.

Mack coughs again and makes the sign of the cross. 'For what we are about to receive may we be truly thankful ... for our breakfast. Amen.'

Shocked silence.

Stokers on the adjacent table look at us with open,

slack mouths. One stuffs a fork full of 'train smash' in his starboard ear. Another stabs his nose with a fork.

'Is that it?' asks Sugar.

'That's it,' mumbles Mack.

'So we can get on with breakie now then?' asks Burbs.

'With His ... and my blessing,' says Mack.

'My egg's all runny,' exclaims Kit. 'Will that be his fault?'

'Naah ... that's the Chef's fault.'

'Who rattled your ferkin cage?' says Jack.

'Language ... language. We've just had ferkin Grace.'

'I knew a girl called Grace once,' says Jack.

'Was she religious?'

'God knows,' says Jack.

*

'ABLE SEAMAN BROADBENT REPORT TO THE REGULATING OFFICE.'

Oh shit.

I wait outside the Regulating Office door with my cap in my hand. A summons to this place usually means trouble.

Leading Regulator Jed Constable and Midshipman Bellringer are busy sorting the recently arrived mail.

'You piped for me,' I say.

'Able Seaman Broadbent, as I live and breathe,' mumbles Jed Constable without looking up at me. 'What you been up to?'

'What do ya mean?'

'You've got a pigeonhole full of letters.'

'Really?'

'You've got more mail than the entire Wardroom put together.'

Midshipman Bellringer glares at me.

'Wonder why that is?' I ask.

'Yes, I wonder,' replies Constable.

'Could be that my fan club has eventually figured out where I am,' I explain.

'Your what?'

'Mi fan club.'

Jed slaps a handful of unsorted mail onto the worktop. 'Why should you have a fan club?'

'I'd rather not say ... hookie.'

Jed sniffs and holds me transfixed with his watery, mail-sorting eyes. He motions to Bellringer. 'Pass me the Seamen's mess mail ... sir.' He faces me square on as he hands me a wodge of letters held together by a robust rubber band. 'If I learn that you are taking the piss, Able Seaman Broadbent ... I'll have your guts for garters.'

'Right you are then ... hookie.' I take the mail and stride away. 'Prat,' I say under my breath to the Fire Fighting locker outside the Regulating Office.

Down the mess there are a few letters for Chats and a few for some others. I have a grand total of fourteen ... all postmarked in Yorkshire.

I stroll up and down the mess. 'One for you ... one for you ... one for you.' I give seven letters out to those who want them in our mess and three to the opposite mess. I keep four back to give to the Stokers' mess as I have promised. I'm not in much of a letter-writing mood so I decide not to keep any of the letters for myself.

I watch as those I have given letters open them with expectant expressions on their faces.

There is a lull.

'I've got a ferkin photograph!' yells Mack.

'That's not the kind of language we expect from a prospective man of the ferkin cloth,' says Jan.

'Sorry,' says Mack. 'I am trying not to ... my ... forgive me.'

Laughter.

'And me,' says Bagsy. 'I've gorra a photie.'

'She's got legs,' says Kit.

'How many? asks Jan.

'Mine's called Barbara ... she's from Leeds,' says Jack. 'Works in the Accounts Department and has three sisters and a brother.'

'This one's called Patricia ... looks like the back end of a bus on her photie,' says Bagsy.

Chats explains. 'Beware of those that haven't sent pictures ... they're probably not worth photographing.'

'I've got a 'write back soon'.'

'Mine wants to know if I've got a nice suntan.'

'Patricia wants to meet me when we get back to England.'

'Is she the good looking one?'

'Naah ... unfortunately not.'

'This girl Brenda is pretty good looking,' says Wheelie. 'But she's knocking on a bit.'

'You've got the picture upside down.'

'Have I?'

'Is she any better the right way up?'

'No. She's definitely better upside down.'

'The least you all can do,' says Chats. 'Is to write back to them. They've taken the time to write to you, so the least you can do is reply. Bullshit as much as you like. What's yours called, Pete?'

'Didn't keep one.'

'Why?'

'I wanted to spread them around a bit first.'

In the next lot of mail there are only two letters postmarked Yorkshire. I hand one to Jack, who wants a second one, and one to Wheelie as he wants someone nearer to his mother's age.

9

The great toilet roll shortage

WE LEAVE Bahrain early in the morning, scoot out of the Persian Gulf and trundle south following the coast of Oman. The Navigator's Yeoman has plotted our estimated course on a chart that has been pinned to the main noticeboard, checked and signed by the Navigating Officer. The chart shows the exact point and time we will enter the southern hemisphere. If the dead-reckonings are correct we will cross the equator at about 44ºE on 20th March.

Preparations for *Gurkha*'s 'Crossing-the-Line' ceremony are half-cocked. We find a paddling pool that hasn't been used since it was donated to the ship by an orphanage in North Queensferry early last year. The Buffer's Party have the foresight to rig the pool on the quarterdeck and fill it with seawater to test it. They identify a number of leaks that they fix with patches from a tyre puncture repair kit supplied by the Assistant Supply Officer. We are surprised to learn that the Assistant Supply Officer is a keen cyclist and has a racing bicycle stored in one of the fresh food lockers. He's a well-prepared cyclist and has loads of puncture repair outfits in one of his saddle bags.

I had crossed the equator once before on *HMS Lincoln*, so I hope to be involved in the 'Crossing-the-Line' ceremony as one of the enforcement team. But I am told that the Wasp is going to be used to take a photograph of the ship crossing the line and I will be required in the Ops Room, as Mack hasn't crossed the line before and will be in the queue of those who are to be dunked. Instead of a squad of bears to grapple anyone who had never crossed the line before, Daily Orders decree that all 'crossing the line virgins' should form an orderly queue to be properly initiated. No time was allocated for the manufacture of weapons or for the tailoring of ceremonial robes.

'UP SPIRITS.'

'But there isn't an actual ferkin line,' I explain.

'I heard a rumour ...' says Jan as he gratefully accepts his tot from Jack. 'Your sippers are getting larger incidentally, mate ... I heard a rumour that the chefs had suggested sprinkling flour in the water from the Wasp. As *Gurkha* cleaves the line of white flour a bloke with a camera in the Wasp will take a picture.'

There was a period of contemplative silence as we all absorb this nugget of information.

Burbs downs his tot and belches. 'That's bollocks.'

'Why's that then?' asks Mack.

'Because the downdraught from the Wasp would disperse the flour,' says Burbs.

'Would it?'

'Course it would. Have you ever been near that ferkin

thing when it's taking off or landing?'

'Nope.'

'Well then.'

'It would depend on how high the helicopter was, I should imagine,' says Chats without looking up from his book.

'See,' says Jan, nodding in Chats' direction.

'Suppose,' says Burbs.

'Any Queen's?' I ask.

'Naa ... not much to speak of,' says Jack.

*

The Assistant Supply Officer's puncture repair outfit doesn't work perfectly. The Buffer's Party rig a hose from one of the Quarterdeck fire hydrants and trickle enough water into the pool to maintain a reasonable and safe level.

'CROSSING THE LINE LIAISON OFFICER SPEAKING. FOR INFORMATION WE SHALL BE CROSSING THE LINE DURING STAND-EASY OPPOSITE THE EAST AFRICAN COASTAL TOWN OF KISMAAYO. ALL THOSE WISHING TO BE FORMALLY INITIATED MAKE YOUR WAY TO THE QUARTERDECK. RIG OF THE DAY IS GENTLEMANLY UNDERWEAR ... AS A MINIMUM. AYO GURKHALI.'

'What the ferk does that mean?' someone asks. 'Gentlemanly underwear?'

'Don't ask me.'

'Or me.'

'It means you shouldn't wear your pink, frilly dung-hampers today,' says Mack.

'There speaks a prospective man of the vestments,' says Jan.

'What's a ferkin vestment?'

We all look to Kit.

'I think it's an unpalatable vegetable popular with our Arab friends.'

As the Wasp isn't required and is stowed in the hangar, I am seconded to a team of 'bears' mostly made up of Royal Marines who have crossed the line before. We form an unarmed guard while those who are to be initiated form a line on the Quarterdeck to be dunked.

The Dunking Squad are burly individuals under the command of Sergeant Lecky. King Neptune is played by the Assistant Supply Officer, the ship's cyclist. His Queen, dressed in a flowery top and a short, hitched-up sarong over fishnet tights and high heels, is someone I haven't seen before: she ... he ... looks like he may be from the Supply, Stewards or Writers Department. He definitely doesn't have the legs of a Seaman or a Stoker.

A humorous 'Charge Sheet' of bad decisions is formally read out by Sergeant Lecky. King Neptune accepts the various charges and formally asks the 'Dunking Squad' to begin the initiations. The Captain is ceremonially dunked first, having the advantage of the clean pool water. The First Lieutenant is next, followed by the remainder of the Wardroom. Major Munro is noticeable by his absence. The water becomes more polluted with each dunking.

It doesn't take that long to dunk all those that need to be initiated. Then after some rather boring speeches the whole thing is over and the Buffers Party begin the task of emptying the foul water from the dunking pool and dismantling everything else.

'UP SPIRITS.'

'The World Cup ... the actual cup ... has been nicked while it was on exhibition in London,' says one of the Communicators from the opposite mess. 'Heard it on the World Service this morning.'

'Naah?'

'Bloody nicked?' asks Wheelie.

'Yeah, can't ferkin trust anybody these days, can ya?' says Jack as he passes Chats his tot.

'Bet it was someone foreign.'

'Why?' asks Chats.

'It's something a foreigner would do isn't it?' says Kit as he sniffs his tot.

'Not really, no.'

'So, what will they do if they can't find it?' asks Kit.

'Obvious isn't it?' I say.

'Cancel the World Cup?' asks Mack.

'Naah.'

'Hope not,' says Mack.

'Scotland didn't qualify did they, Mack?' asks Chats.

'Not this time ... no,' says Mack.

'Well then. This is a conversation between those of us who have qualified.'

'That's not very democratic. I can have an opinion ... and be allowed to voice it.'

'Don't get a sad on, Mack,' says Chats. 'Priestly virtues and all that.'

Mack slams his empty glass on the table and walks off towards his bunk.

*

The first day in the southern hemisphere I am brought back to reality ...

'ABLE SEAMAN BROADBENT REPORT TO MAJOR MUNRO IN THE WARDROOM. ABLE SEAMAN BROADBENT.'

Named twice: it must be doubly important.

I knock on the Wardroom door. Eventually a Steward opens the hallowed door a little.

'I've been piped to report to Major Munro.'

'Lucky you. Wait right there a minute.' He closes the door firmly.

'Prat,' I mumble. I kick my heels for a couple of minutes until Major Munro opens the door.

'Able Seaman Broadbent.'

'Yes, sir.'

'The Dhow Boarding Party will be used as the duty seaboat crew while we are in the Mozambique Channel. Report to Sergeant Lecky, who will brief you on your duties for the next few weeks.'

'Right, sir. Where exactly is the Mozambique Chan ...'

He closes the door.

'Prat.'

I track Sergeant Lecky down eventually and am pleased to learn that as seaboat crew while in the Mozambique Channel, I am excused all Ops Room watch-keeping duties. Frothy will cover all my helicopter controlling duties.

'Why are we going to the Mozambique Channel, Sergeant?'

'It's complicated. I believe that someone who knows what is going on is to make a Tannoy broadcast tomorrow lunchtime.'

'UP SPIRITS.'

Jack is passing Jan his tot when the Tannoy crackles into life. Jack jumps and almost spills some.

'That was close, Jack.' says Jan pointing at Jack's quivering glass.

Jack turns to glare at the Tannoy. 'Doesn't he know that it's ferkin tot-time?'

'THE INFORMATION OFFICER SPEAKING ... I KNOW IT'S TOT-TIME. WE ARE STEAMING SOUTH TO JOIN HMS CARYSFORT AND THE AIRCRAFT CARRIER

HMS EAGLE TO PATROL THE AREA OFF THE PORT OF BEIRA. THE REASONS FOR THIS PATROL ARE COMPLEX AND I WILL DO MY BEST TO EXPLAIN ...'

'What the ferk is he on about?' asks Cliff.
'Dunno.'
'Who's going down for dinner?' asks Wheelie.
'Not yet, let's hear what he has to tell us.'
'Who farted?'
Everybody looks at Kit.
Kit waves an arm to disperse stuff.

'THE INFORMATION OFFICER SPEAKING. LAST YEAR THE GOVERNMENT OF RHODESIA UNILATERALLY DECLARED ITSELF INDEPENDENT OF THE UNITED KINGDOM. AS A RESULT, THE UNITED NATIONS ALONG WITH THE COMMONWEALTH AND BRITAIN HAVE IMPOSED ECONOMIC SANCTIONS AGAINST RHODESIA. BRITAIN HAS INSTITUTED A PATROL TO STARVE RHODESIA OF FUEL BY PREVENTING TANKERS FROM DISCHARGING OIL AT THE STORAGE FACILITY AT BEIRA, THE NEAREST PORT SERVING LAND-LOCKED RHODESIA.'

'What's he ferkin on about?' asks Kit as he rolls his tot glass in his hands to release every last drop of rum.

'FOR THOSE OF YOU WHO WOULD LIKE MORE INFORMATION I WILL PUT DETAILS ON THE MAIN NOTICEBOARD. THE BLOCKADE COULD LAST FOR SOME WEEKS.'

'Oh ferkin wonderful. I got that,' says Kit.
'How long will this Patrol last then?' asks Burbs.
'Weren't you ferkin listening? He did say some weeks.'
'That could mean anything,' says Jan.

'I'm seaboat crew for the duration,' I say.

'Gerrim!' says Burbs.

'THE INFORMATION OFFICER SPEAKING. OUR AREA OF PATROL WILL BE WITHIN THE MOZAMBIQUE CHANNEL.'

'Wonder if we'll get a run ashore then?' says Jan.

'Anybody been anywhere near to the Mozambique channel before?' asks Chats. Silence. 'I think an extra can of beer all round is called for.'

*

'AWAY SEABOATS CREW.'

'Ferk it.'

'Go for it, Pete lad.'

I am the first to arrive as the seaboat is being lowered to deck level.

'Somebody get lifejackets,' yells the Buffer. 'You've got to take the Captain and Jimmy over to Eagle.'

We wait patiently while the Captain and the First Lieutenant arrive. Sergeant Lecky is the designated Protection Officer for the trip.

From the perspective of a 27-foot long wooden whaler, *HMS Eagle* is ginormous. Her port aft accommodation ladder is lowered and ropes dangled so that we can easily clag ourself alongside. The Captain and Jimmy are well behaved and say a joint thank you to Sergeant Lecky as they jump expertly onto the bottom platform of *Eagle's* ladder.

We are instructed to return to *Gurkha* and await further instructions. No sooner have I sat down in the mess to enjoy a cup of instant coffee ...

'AWAY SEABOATS CREW.'

'Bollocks.'

'Didn't ask what kept you out of the WRNS, darling,' says Jan.

I flip him a two-finger salute as I scramble up the mess ladder.

The Captain and the First Lieutenant are waiting for us as I put the whaler alongside *Eagle*'s accommodation ladder. After they board and are seated, a smart-suited Steward from *HMS Eagle* hands a couple of bulging plastic bags to Dodger, who is the bowman.

'Bowman, make sure those are given directly to the Petty Officer Steward,' instructs the Jimmy.

Dodger nods. 'Aye aye, sir.'

Back onboard *Gurkha*, having disgorged both of our passengers and hoisted the whaler, we are tightening the gripes when I ask Dodger what was in the bags.

'Bog paper.'

'Wha?'

'Bog paper ... Wardroom arses for the use of.'

'Blimey.'

'Stow all those lifejackets in the washdeck locker will you, Able Seaman Broadbent?' says the Buffer.

This evening we get our marching orders ...

'THE INFORMATION OFFICER SPEAKING. STARTING FROM SUNRISE TOMORROW WE WILL BE PATROLLING A LINE WITHIN THE MOZAMBIQUE CHANNEL STRETCHING FROM THE NORTH OF BEIRA TO A POINT SOUTH OF LOURENCO MARQUES. OUR TASK IS TO IDENTIFY OIL TANKERS AND TO INFORM THEM OF THE LEGITIMATE UNITED NATIONS BLOCKADE. HMS EAGLE IS FLYING RECONNAISSANCE AIRCRAFT AND THE ROYAL AIR FORCE WILL FLY SHACKLETON MARITIME PATROL AIRCRAFT FROM MAJUNGA IN NORTHERN MADAGASCAR ALONG THE LENGTH OF THE CHANNEL. THE ROYAL AIR FORCE ARE ALSO TASKED WITH ENSURING THAT WE GET

FREQUENT DELIVERIES OF MAIL. WE WILL BE ABLE TO SEND PERIODIC MAIL VIA THE GOOD SERVICES OF HMS EAGLE. AYO GURKHALI.'

On tomorrow's Daily Orders there is an explanation of our duty in being one of the first vessels to blockade the port of Beira:

> 'We have the authority to stop and challenge any approaching tankers. This is an internationally recognised challenge and requires merchant ships to answer with name, nationality and destination. We expect that most oil carrying vessels will comply with UN sanctions and turn around. If they refuse, or ignore our request to stop, we are authorised to use force, which includes the firing of our main armament.

*

In early March 1966 we officially begin our period of patrolling the Mozambique Channel. We will be out of sight of land for much of the time apparently.

'THE INFORMATION OFFICER ... SORRY, THE MAIL OFFICER SPEAKING. OUTGOING MAIL WILL BE TRANSFERRED VIA HELICOPTER TO HMS EAGLE TOMORROW. MAIL WILL CLOSE AT 10:00 TOMORROW. WE HAVE CONFIRMATION THAT THE ROYAL AIR FORCE ... GOD BLESS THEM ... WILL BE DROPPING OUR MAIL SOMETIME THIS AFTERNOON. ABLE SEAMAN BROADBENT REPORT TO MAJOR MUNRO IN THE WARDROOM. ABLE SEAMAN BROADBENT.'

'That's you, Pete.'

'It isn't, is it?' I ask as I grab my hat and put a shirt on.

I knock on the Wardroom door. The same Steward as before opens it a little.

'I've been piped to report to Major Munro ... yet again.'

'Lucky you. Stay there a minute.' He closes the door.

'Prat.' I stare at the deck until Major Munro opens the door.

'Ah ... Able Seaman Broadbent.'

'Yes, sir.'

'You have been selected as Mail Boat crew while we are on Patrol. Report to Sergeant Lecky who will brief you on your duties.'

'Aye aye, sir.'

He closes the door.

I take a deep breath. 'Prat.'

I track Sergeant Lecky down. 'What exactly is Mail Boat crew all about, Sergeant?'

'The clue is in the name.'

'Is it? ... Right then.'

'RAF Shackletons will drop our mail in canisters. Our job is to pick them up before they start to leak and spoil all the mail inside.'

'Can that happen?'

'Don't know. I've no idea what the canisters are like.'

'Right then.'

'We are using the RIB because it's quicker to launch and faster than the whaler ... we can collect the canisters quicker.'

Back down the mess, I've finished my tot and am looking forward to the cheese ush on the dinner menu ...

'AWAY MAIL BOAT CREW. AWAY MAIL BOAT CREW.'

'Go and get them letters, Pete lad.'

By the time I've struggled into my plimsolls and scuttled up to the accommodation ladder the RIB is waiting for me.

Dodger and I wait for Sergeant Lecky, who arrives carrying an armful of braided strops.

Midshipman Bellringer arrives with a pair of binoculars draped over his shoulder. He hands the binoculars to Dodger.

'The Shackleton is approaching from the North West and should be here within the next ten minutes,' he says. 'They will try and drop the canisters as close to the ship as is safe. Just lay-off, coxswain, and when the canisters are dropped make your way to pick them up.'

Sergeant Lecky stares questioningly at the Midshipman.

'Carry on, Sergeant,' says Midshipman Bellringer.

'Aye aye ... sir,' Sergeant Lecky replies.

We wallow off *Gurkha*'s starboard quarter for ten minutes or so until Dodger spots the Royal Air Force coming at us out of the sun. 'There she is.'

'Keep your eye out for the canisters,' says Sergeant Lecky.

'There they go.' Dodger points.

We watch as two yellow canisters, each streaming a small parachute, glide gently down. I wham the throttle fully open and head towards what I estimate to be the landing point.

We are within twenty yards or so of the canisters when they splash land.

Up close, the canisters are larger than I expect. It takes a while to get organised but eventually we grapple them both inboard with a combination of well-applied strops, muscle power and Sergeant Lecky's organising skills.

The Shackleton passes overhead and dips its wings at us. May be a respectful salute to the Senior Service.

Within the hour ...

'REASONABLY DRY MAIL IS NOW READY FOR COLLECTION FROM THE REGULATING OFFICE.'

Mail canisters

'Is that another photograph of Patricia from Leeds, Bagsy?' asks Jack.

'No, it's a picture of her pet dog.'

'What's she like now then?' Has she improved since she last wrote?'

'Not much, no.'

'So she's still like the back end of a bus?'

'That's been rear-ended by a cement truck,' adds Bagsy.

'I gorra picture,' says Jack. 'Mine's in the Army.'

'Let's 'ave a butchers then,' says Kit.

'Nice looking eh?' says Jack as he hands the picture over.

Kit purses his lips. 'That's not the real Army, Jack lad.'

'Isn't it?'

'Naah.'

'What is it then?'

'Looks like the Sally Army to me.'

'Wha?'

'The Salvation Army ... God-botherers.'

'She's called Mary.'

'That figures.'

Cliff groans. 'I've gorra picture. She's a bit of a disappointment ... a bit podgy.'

'Let's have a look then,' asks Jan.

Cliff passes the picture over.

'A bit ferkin podgy ... she's a monster.'

'Suppose she is yeah,' admits Cliff. 'I'll ask Pete for another one.'

'I'll give you the next one that comes in,' I say.

'I've got a kiss on mine!' exclaims Timber. 'I've got a kiss from Sandra ... a Yorkshire kiss.'

'Similar to a Liverpool kiss then?' asks Jan.

'Dunno, what's a Liverpool kiss?'

'A head butt.'

'The weather in Leeds is terrible,' explains Stormy. 'Anne says it's raining every day.'

'That's a shame then.'

'I've got a SWALK from Barbara,' says Jack.

'She's desperate then,' says Chats. 'You're not going to send her a photograph are ya?'

'Dunno, why?'

'Because you're no ferkin oil painting, are ya?' explains Wheelie.

I've got one Yorkshire letter left and instead of giving it to Cliff I decide to open it myself. It's postmarked Wakefield and it's from a girl called Margaret. Although she is now working somewhere else in Leeds, she had taken my address from my letter that had been pinned to the Moorhouse factory noticeboard some months ago. It's a nice, well-written letter so, because I haven't got much to occupy myself, I decide to knock-up a quick reply. I tell her that her letter was dropped from the sky by the Royal Air Force in a parachuted canister ... that'll impress her.

*

In an attempt to prevent boredom setting in while on patrol, a number of distractions are devised. An onboard chess competition is instigated and the winner is invited over to *HMS Carysfort* to play their champion.

As we have a helicopter and the edge in seniority over *Carysfort*, we leave our patrol line for a while to transfer a fresh-faced Sub Lieutenant, the recently acclaimed *Gurkha* Chess Champion.

In accordance with Queen's Regulations and Admiralty Instructions of the day, our chess champion is dunked into the turbulent waters between the two ships as we perform our first Transfer-at-Sea since Portland last year.

Needless to say, having no dry clothes to change into, our champion is roundly beaten by a Junior Mechanical Engineer, chess champion of *HMS Carysfort*.

'THE INFORM ... SORRY ... THE ENTERTAINMENTS OFFICER SPEAKING ... OH BOLLOC ...'

'That's the ferkin Information Officer, that is,' blurts Wheelie pointing an accusing finger at the Tannoy.

'FOR THE NEXT THREE OR FOUR WEEKS I AM THE ENTERTAINMENTS OFFICER. ALL RESTRICTIONS ON THE GROWING OF FACIAL HAIR ARE TEMPORARILY LIFTED. AT THE END OF THE PATROL A PRIZE WILL BE PRESENTED TO THE INDIVIDUAL CONSIDERED TO HAVE GROWN THE MOST STRIKING SET. THAT IS ALL. AYO GURKHALI.'

'Does that mean I can stop shaving then?' Jack asks the crackling Tannoy.

'Sounds like it.'

'Nobody could beat the Chief Stoker if he stops shaving. Have you seen the length of the hairs coming down his hooter?' says Kit.

'Much the same as yours, mate.'

'I do trim occasionally,' explains Kit stroking his set.

'What about that strange Writer with the monstrous eyebrow?' says Jan.

'Yeah ... if he stops shaving ...'

'The Chief Stoker has hairs sprouting from behind both of his lug holes,' adds Wheelie.

A note tucked away on page two of Daily Orders informs us that the ship detailed to relieve us has been diverted and our period of patrol has been extended for one more week.

As if this news isn't bad enough ...

'THE SUPPLY OFFICER SPEAKING. AS YOU WILL NO DOUBT BE AWARE, THERE IS A SHORTAGE OF TOILET PAPER ONBOARD. WE CALCULATE THAT BY LUNCHTIME THE DAY AFTER TOMORROW THE SHORTAGE WILL OFFICIALLY BECOME SEVERE, POSING A POSSIBLE DANGER TO THE HEALTH AND WELLBEING OF THE ENTIRE CREW.

WE HAVE EXPLAINED OUR PREDICAMENT TO HMS EAGLE WHO IS LOOKING INTO WAYS SHE CAN ALLEVIATE OUR PROBLEM. IN THE MEANTIME THE SHIP'S COMPANY ARE REQUIRED TO USE THEIR INITIATIVE IN THE USE OF ABSORBENT ALTERNATIVES.

THE WARDROOM HAVE CONCLUDED THAT THE DAILY MIRROR HAS MORE ABSORBENT PROPERTIES THAN OTHER NEWSPAPERS. THE UTILISATION OF DAILY ORDERS OR BACK COPIES OF THE DAILY TELEGRAPH AS TOILET PAPER IS A PUNISHABLE

OFFENCE. CHIEF SHIPWRIGHT REPORT TO THE BRIDGE. AYO GURKHALI.'

*

It's a simple matter for the surface plotting team to identify any vessels heading for Beira. When identified we abandon our patrol line and close the offending vessel at full speed. Within flying range we launch the Wasp. Pontius is instructed to classify the vessel, course and approximate speed along with its name and port of registry. If the vessel is a tanker Pontius will perform an intimidating hover in line with the vessel's Bridge and pull an angry face in order to establish a stern, pig-headed Royal Navy presence.

Once *Gurkha* has the vessel visual, we close to within megaphone/loud hailer range and in perfectly modulated Dartmouth English identify ourselves. We inform the vessel that we are part of an officially sanctioned patrol to prevent loaded tankers from entering the port of Beira in accordance with United Nations Resolution 217. As it is well understood that all sea-going vessels have someone onboard who can converse in Dartmouth English, we wait for a response and for the vessel to alter course and to promise faithfully not to discharge its cargo at Beira or Lourenço Marques. If the promise is not forthcoming a more serious warning is given, stating that we will have no option to open fire if the vessel does not immediately comply. At the same time we rotate our forward turret a number of times and elevate the single barrel. Unbeknown to our target vessel, although the barrel tampon is removed, we certainly don't have the authority or inclination to open fire: the forward turret is not armed.

At this stage of proceedings most approached vessels alter course. If they don't, we adopt a very severe attitude and verbally inform them that we have no option but to implement our ultimate sanction and transmit their details to their Lords at the Admiralty in London. If this doesn't put the fear of Christ up them, we can do little more. The Wasp is recalled and performs a close pass of the vessel's Bridge before departing. We swivel our main armament once again, elevate the gun's barrel, wait and then forcefully retire. Our job, in accordance with our understanding of United Nations Resolution 217, is done.

In early April the Royal Navy's blockade strategy is spectacularly tested. A Greek tanker, the *Joanna V*, is identified and forcefully requested to divert to a port other than Beira or Lourenço Marques. The Master refuses and the *Joanna V* sails on into Beira in breach of Resolution 217.

Once other ship owners learn that *Joanna V* has successfully run the blockade, the door is open for those carrying a suddenly very expensive cargo.

Our patrol period is further extended. Our release date is now sometime early in May.

'THE ENTERTAINMENT OFFICER SPEAKING. A SODS' OPERA WILL TAKE PLACE A WEEK FROM TODAY IN THE JUNIOR RATES DINING HALL. ALL DEPARTMENTS ARE ENCOURAGED TO PRODUCE A FIVE- TO TEN-MINUTE PERFORMANCE. UNNECESSARILY LEWD OR OFFENSIVE MATERIAL IS TO BE AVOIDED ... IF AT ALL POSSIBLE. AYO GURKHALI.'

Within the Seamen's Department we have a number of fledgling musicians who want to mime to a number of Beatles tunes. As nobody else can come up with anything more entertaining, it is agreed that all our efforts would support our very own 'fab four'. The Stokers' Department are very tight-lipped about their performance. The Communicators have decided to do a Tiller Girls routine - that doesn't come as a surprise as the Seamen are convinced that a number of them are closet cross-dressers.

*

'They've found the World Cup,' says Chats.
    'That's wonderful.'
    'Great,' say Mack, looking sullen.
    'That's made my ferkin day,' says Kit.
    'Wrapped in 'The News of the Screws' in a south London garden. Found by someone called Pickles.'
    'Great.'
    'Someone called Pickles?'
    'A dog called Pickles.'
    'A dog?'
    'Yeah.'
    'So the World Cup is back on again?'
    'Yep, suppose so.'
    'Three cheers for a dog called Pickles ... hip-hip.'
    'Don't be so ferkin soft. We're not giving three cheers to a ferkin dog.'
    'Yeah, but it did find the World Cup.'
    'Still not going to hip-hip a ferkin dog.'

*

We all help with rigging the dining hall after dinner on the night of the Sods' Opera. A raised stage is constructed at the forward end and a curtain is rigged behind the stage to shield those taking part.

An extra issue of one free can of beer is authorised for the evening, courtesy of the ship's Tombola Fund.

The Master of Ceremonies is Sergeant Lecky, who successfully deals with some serious Royal Marine barracking from the starboard edge of the audience.

The first act of the evening is a skit on *The Pirates of Penzance* by the Wardroom. They have made an effort with their costumes, but the miming is way off. The makeup is so well applied that it is a while before we identify the Skipper as Frederic. Midshipman Bellringer makes a surprisingly attractive Mabel, the daughter of the Major-General. The finale is so up-lifting that the audience, who haven't had contact with the opposite sex for an unacceptably long time, insist on an encore so that they could once again see Mabel raise her petticoats. Three curtain calls are enough for Midshipman Bellringer, who blushes uncontrollably as he skips off stage ...losing his blonde wig in the process.

The sound system crackles with static while the stage is prepared for our contribution. The suits, wigs and instruments are almost perfect and the music is brilliant. The comically named 'Cockies' mime perfectly to *Help*, *Ticket to Ride* and *A Hard Day's Night* as a finale. The entire audience sing along with all the songs and ask for *Help* to be performed again. Bagsy is a particularly animated Ringo bashing on a couple of upturned buckets that have been cleverly decorated to look like a couple of upturned buckets. The stage is cleared.

To our surprise and total silence from the confused audience, Burbs walks on and with a strangely confident smirk takes centre stage.

He waits for the ripple of uncertain, welcoming applause to subside. 'Thank you.' He holds his hands up. 'Courtesy of my Aunt Peggy, I would like to share with you some of the jokes she has sent me since we left Pompey. I hope that you'll enjoy them.'

Our mess erupts with applause and whoops of delight. None of us realised that Burbs would have the confidence to do this.

Burbs coughs and begins: 'Horatio and Piers, a couple of newly qualified Midshipmen, are walking back to Dartmouth after a night out on the town.'

Whoops of anticipation from everywhere.

Burbs waits for the noise to stop. 'In typical Naval

fashion neither of them has put aside the money to pay for a taxi or even a bus back to barracks. Horatio, who considers himself to be the smartest of the two, suggests that they should pinch a bus from the nearby bus depot. So, they finish their orange juice and head for the nearby depot. Horatio instructs Piers to go in and find the bus while he keeps a look-out.'

There is some uncomfortable shuffling from a couple in the plush seats.

Burbs suppresses a smile directly at the Skipper. 'Piers climbs over the depot wall. Sometime later Horatio, who had learned to tell the time while on course at Dartmouth ...'

Laughter.

'... Some time later Horatio looks at his watch and calculates that Piers had been gone for ages. So he shouts over the wall: "Piers, my good friend, what are you doing? Have you not found the bus yet?" Piers replies that he can't find a Number 16.'

The Skipper holds his head in his hands and stares at the deck.

Burbs coughs. 'Horatio shouts back "No problem, Piers, take a Number 14 instead ... we can walk back to barracks from the roundabout."'

Much laughter and whoops of enjoyment from the assembled audience. It takes a while for those in the Wardroom seats to crack a smile or a smirk: the Gunnery Officer tries to applaud, but his hands fail to make contact with each other.

Burbs takes a bow and waits for the applause to die down completely before continuing. 'A lady walks into a high-class jewellery shop. She browses a while, spots a beautiful diamond bracelet and bends over the glass-topped cabinet to inspect it closer. As she does so, she inadvertently breaks wind.'

A cacophony of raspberries is blown from everywhere.

Burbs places the back of his hand to his mouth and continues in a whisper. 'Very embarrassed, the lady nervously looks around to see if anyone had heard her little mishap. As she turns to her left she sees a salesman approaching. The salesman asks if he can help. Hoping that the salesman had not heard anything, she asks the price of the bracelet.'

Sniggers have already started from our mess. Burbs holds his hand up for silence. The First Lieutenant is staring at Burbs with his mouth agape.

Burbs closes his eyes and look snootily at the deckhead. 'The salesman says, "Madam if you farted when looking at the bracelet, you're going to shit yourself when I tell you the price."'

The place erupts - that is the kind of punch line that we like.

It takes a few minutes for the laughter, coughs and giggles to subside.

'One more?' asks Burbs. 'Ayo Gurkhali.'

Shouts of yeah and much raising of arms ... including some from the cushioned seats.

'A young, recently married and devout Able Seaman 'Smudge' Smith wonders if having sex on the Sabbath is allowed because he is not sure if sex is work or play ...'

The Skipper stares at the deckhead, before taking his head in his hands and bending over to stare at the deck between his feet once again.

Burbs waves a finger at the Captain before continuing. 'So Smudge goes to see the local Padre to ask for an explanation. After flicking through the Bible index the Padre says that after an exhaustive search he is positive that sex is work and is therefore not permitted on the Sabbath.'

Boos from the Royal Marine and Stokers contingent.

Burbs opens his arms. 'Wanting a second opinion, Smudge goes to see the local Bishop. Disappointingly, he receives the same reply: sex is work and therefore not to be performed on the Sabbath. Dejected, but not yet fully convinced, he seeks out the ultimate authority - a man of many hundreds of years of Naval tradition behind him and the ultimate authority on all matters sexual ... he goes to see the Chief Stoker.'

Lots of cheering from the Stokers' seats. Everybody looks at the hunched back of the Captain who is slowly shaking his head. There is wide-eyed apprehension from those on the front seats who all fear for their promotional prospects.

Burbs waits until the laughter subsides. 'I'm joking. He actually goes to see the Skipper ... sorry, the Captain ... who ponders the question, then confidently states that sex is most definitely play. Smudge asks for confirmation explaining that two men of the cloth have told him that sex is classified as work. The Captain leans close to Smudge and whispers "Believe me, Able Seaman Smith, if sex was work, my wife would have the cleaning lady do it."'

Everybody laughs and applauds. Burbs stands centre stage for at least a minute before the audience becomes tired of clapping. The Gunnery Officer, who has given up trying to master hand-clapping, is enthusiastically waving a sheet of paper. Midshipman Bellringer, who has changed out of his 'Mabel' clothes into his uniform shirt and trousers, finds himself a spare chair on the end of the front row.

The Stokers' Department do a ten-minute skit of *The Magic Roundabout* but the sound is terrible and they are clapped off the stage. A quartet of Royal Marines, dressed in civilian clothes, play some brilliant jazz. Some of the audience in the cheap seats at the back are becoming a little bit raucous and are tossing beer cans around when nine Communicators, dressed in basques, nylon stockings, suspenders and high heels, perform a high-kicking Tiller Girl routine to something up-beat played by the Royal Marine quartet. When they bow at the end, it is revealed that one of the Flag-waggers has an unusually attractive cleavage.

Kit, who is sitting close to me, leans over. 'The question is, Pete, how the ferk did they get hold of twelve pairs of nylons, suspenders and the high heeled shoes ... eh?'

'Never thought of that,' says Jan, sitting on my other side.

I keep quiet because it hasn't crossed my mind either.

The penultimate act is a young Stores Assistant seated on the knee of a senior member of his department, doing a ventriloquist act. The older of the two appears to be enjoying himself too much.

The final act of the evening is the Senior Rates mess doing their version of the famous Blood Donor sketch. The Buffer even looks like Tony Hancock on a really bad day. The classic statement, 'A pint? that's almost an arm full' receives an instantaneous round of applause and whistles.

The elderly men receive a polite round of applause as they leave the stage.

For a finale, the 'Cockies' mime to *A Hard Day's Night* while some of the audience mingle with the cast, gallivanting and dancing around the stage and its environs. A drunken Stoker makes a desperate lunge for the Tiller 'girl' with the attractive cleavage, who screams in panic as Stokes grabs a handful of his bared thigh. Midshipman Bellringer looks relieved that he'd changed into his uniform.

The whole thing is brought to a sober close by an unknown Officer who thanks everybody for taking part and the Captain for his support. He closes by saying that we should be relieved within the next ten days by *HMS Eskimo*.

A huge cheer.

*

Daily Orders confirm, beyond reasonable doubt, that today is to be our last day on Beira Patrol: our release day. We are to be relieved by our sister ship *HMS Eskimo*.

'RIG FOR TRANSFER AT SEA STARBOARD SIDE. OUR RELIEF HMS ESKIMO IS THREE MILES ASTERN AND SHE HAS MAIL FOR US.'

'That'll be more from the jam factory then,' says Wheelie, with a hopeful expression.

There is a degree of urgency as we rig everything for transfer. Sugar throws a heaving line which is caught by someone on *Eskimo*'s forecastle.

Eskimo sends over a concrete sinker as a test weight. We give it a *Gurkha* blessing and send it back. *Eskimo* then sends us a couple of bulging, blue nylon bags of mail.

We send the empty traveller back.

Midshipman Bellringer arrives at the transfer point with a galvanised bucket containing two bottles of something wrapped in calico. 'Careful with this gentlemen ... they're our last two bottles. With a bit of luck Eskimo should send us back a couple of boxes of toilet paper.'

'Oh great,' someone says.

We send the brandy over very slowly. Onboard *Eskimo* they unhook the bucket and an Officer wearing immaculately laundered long shorts grabs the bucket and disappears through a screen door.

Eskimo sends over two cardboard boxes of toilet paper.

'How will these be dished out, sir?' asks someone, pointing at the boxes of toilet paper.

'As the nominated Toilet Paper Distribution Officer, I have yet to formulate a plan,' says Midshipman Bellringer as he lifts both cardboard boxes all by himself and strides away.

'That'll be a position he'll be proud to put in his

Midshipman's log then ... Toilet Paper Distribution Officer.'

We don't get our bucket back.

(We didn't know it at the time, but our bucket was to become the iconic 'Beira Bucket', a trophy competed for until the Beira Patrol ended nine years later and which is today on display in the Royal Naval Museum, Portsmouth).

'THE TOILET PAPER DISTRIBUTION OFFICER SPEAKING. WE HAVE RECEIVED TWO BOXES OF TOILET PAPER COURTESY OF HMS ESKIMO. DISTRIBUTION DETAILS WILL BE PROMULGATED SHORTLY. MAIL IS NOW READY FOR COLLECTION.'

Bagsy has two letters from Patricia. He sneaks away to read them in peace.

Chats nods at Bagsy's departing legs up the mess ladder. 'That could be serious,' he says.

'Never,' says Jan. 'Have you seen her photograph? She looks like a ferkin dog.'

'Beauty is in the eye of the beholder, Jan lad,' explains Chats with a smirk.

'That's bollocks, that is.'

'Not necessarily.'

'Bagsy needs ferkin glasses then.'

Cliff tosses his letter onto the table. 'I'm not writing back to this bird.'

'Why's that then, mate?' I ask.

'Well in my last letter I thanked her for her photograph and diplomatically I said that the camera probably made her look a little larger than she actually is.'

'Diplomatically put, Cliff.'

'In here,' he points at the letter. 'She says she's fourteen-and-a-half stone and happy with it. She says that big, wobbly girls have more fun.'

'Blimey mate, that's a bit of a worry.'
'You got any mail, Pete?'
'Naah.'

10
Mombasa ... Erotic relief and free

WITH NOTHING to spend my money on while on Beira Patrol, I've squirreled away a reasonable amount of cash. It's a few days before our scheduled arrival in Mombasa and it's Pay Day again. A Sub Lieutenant with galloping acne, and nothing better to do, faces me. 'Get your hair cut,' he says, staring at my name above my left shirt pocket, 'Broad ... bent.'

'Will do, sir.'

'Good. Make sure you do that, lad.'

'Aye aye ... will do, sir. Thank you, sir.'

I certainly don't intend getting my hair cut. Volcano-face's mistake was not making a note of my name.

I'm disappointed that the Beira LOA is not included in my pay. If I am to believe all the messdeck rumours from those who have been there before, Mombasa is East Africa's version of a good run-ashore. It has all the necessary 'attractions' to satisfy the most demanding of us. Immediately after being paid, the Ship's Office staff set up a counter in the Dining Hall to exchange sterling for East African Shillings.

It's not often I'm in the right place at the right time, but I'm strolling past the main ship's noticeboard as a new notice is pinned up. I have a read.

I slide down the mess ladder, find Mack and ask him if he fancies three days' station leave in an Indian Ocean resort in Kenya called Silversands.

'Why not, sounds good to me.'

Then I ask Wheelie.

'Sounds brilliant to me.'

So we do what is required on the notice and make out our request forms and get our Divisional Officer to sign them before handing them into the Ship's Office.

Five years ago Chats spent a few days at Silversands. 'Unless its changed for the worse,' he says', 'it will still be brilliant. It has its own beach.'

Burbs also puts his request form in.

The following day, along with Wheelie, Mack and Burbs, I am granted three days' station leave at Silversands. Sugar has also been granted three days' station leave, but has decided to spend it somewhere other than Silversands. He is being characteristically tight-lipped about his plans for Mombasa.

'About a week ago Sugar had a letter with a Kenyan stamp on it,' says Kit.

'Shit, I bet he's organised something pleasurable ... and feminine,' I say.

'I'd put all my money on it,' replies Kit, palming his beard aside to a reveal a lecherous smirk.

*

The port of Mombasa is a colourful and vibrant change to the bare blue waters of the Mozambique Channel. We fire a gun salute to someone or other before squeezing ourself between a small Panama registered rock-hopper and a slightly larger, rusting cargo vessel whose name and port-of-registry is written in Arabic. A small team of Kenyan locals do a great job of putting our berthing ropes exactly where we want them. We use all our rattan fenders to protect our ship's side from the ravages of the decaying jetty.

Sugar, resplendent in freshly ironed grey slacks, a freshly laundered short-sleeved shirt and carrying his Pusser's grip, is the first to hand in his Station Card and skip over the brow. Jack and I watch in silence as he opens the passenger door of a waiting car and is whisked away without so much as a backward glance.

'That looks organised,' says Jack.

'Certainly does,' I say.

'Wonder what he's up to?'

'It'll have something to do with the opposite sex ... you can be sure of that.'

'How does he do it?' asks Jack.

'Don't ask me.'

Down the mess we take advice from Chats as to what to pack for our three-day Silversands break. 'Shorts, flip-flops, couple of shirts, washing and shaving stuff, fags, lighter, ID card and money: you won't need much more than that.'

'TRANSPORT FOR THOSE GOING TO SILVERSANDS FOR STATION LEAVE WILL LEAVE THE JETTY IN 30 MINUTES.'

A coach of sorts with 'Silversands' painted on the side rumbles to a halt near to the bottom of the brow.

'That'll be our transport then,' I say.

'With observational qualities like that you've got to be a Wardroom candidate, young Pete,' says the Quartermaster.

Close up, the coach looks as though it could probably

be the oldest and most dilapidated vehicle on the African continent: a confirmed wreck on wheels.

Wheelie and I are the first ones to board and we get one of the only double seats with a cushion: the remainder of the seats are bare springs covered with coir mats. There are two chefs with us, making a grand total of six. The driver, a small boy perched on a pile of cushions, keeps the accelerator pressed with a long-handled sweeping brush while holding a loop of rope wrapped around the top of an elongated gear stick. There are no entrance doors: just an opening. A grey billowing mist envelopes the row of bench seats at the back.

We move away as soon as some of the men-under-punishment finish stowing a pile of foodstuff on the filthy floor immediately behind the driver.

Our journey is a remarkable experience. Other vehicles using the Mombasa roads give the Silversands coach a wide berth. Everybody gives way to us, particularly at junctions and at traffic lights that work occasionally. We shroud the surrounding traffic and pedestrians in clouds of thick, black exhaust fumes. It's a white-knuckle ride.

Half an hour later we chug beneath a sign welcoming us to Silversands. Our young driver screeches to a halt after swerving violently to avoid an inconveniently positioned palm tree.

We scramble for the bus exit, all glad to have survived the journey. A close examination of our driver has him at about twelve years old.

The chefs unload the food. Wheelie, Mack, Burbs and I watch in bemused silence as the coach swerves and slides away. A perspiring local gentleman with a rotund stomach, who's dressed in a white shirt and a pair of flower-patterned knee-length shorts, welcomes us formally to Silversands.

'Welcomes gentlemens ... My name is Samuel. Welcomes to Silversands village for rest and recreation for Her Majesty's armed forces,' he says smiling.

We nod in response.

'Kitchen over there, sirs,' he says to the chefs. 'Door open, freezer switched on full.'

He turns to us four. 'Follow me please, gentlemens,' Samuel rotates a muscular arm and trudges away up a dusty red slope.

He stops partway up to enable us to catch up. 'I have special accommodation for you completely in best part of village.'

On the highest part of the complex overlooking deep green African savannah on three sides, we are offered a hut containing four bunks. Outside are trees with real oranges and lemons on them: unbelievable.

'Enjoy your stay with us, gentlemens. If you need anything you find me - OK I have spanking new wife so most times I can be found in our bed ... he he he heh!'

We all give him a knowing smile.

'Thank you, Samuel.'

'We understand, Sam. Thank you.'

Samuel continues to giggle as he adjusts himself before turning to skip away down the slope. By the time he disappears around a bend in the path his shorts are partway down.

Our two ship's chefs are unpacking food into majestic sized freezers alongside a couple of murmuring air conditioning units on the outside wall of a white painted building.

'You here for the next three days?' Mack asks them as we stroll past.

One of the chefs tosses a box full of frozen meat into the back of a freezer and wipes his nose on his forearm. 'Here for as long as the ship is here, mate. This is what happens when chefs request station leave.'

'You cooking for us then?' asks Burbs.

'No mate, we're here to do the ferkin gardening,' says a chef behind us, dragging a bag of potatoes through the red Silversands dust.

At relatively short notice, the chefs knock up a very acceptable beef stew for the evening meal. There is also some partially thawed ice cream for duff.

From somewhere Burbs has purchased a crate of Tusker beer.

'Is it any good?' asks Wheelie.

'I don't ferkin know, do I?'

With no thought of how we will be able to climb back to our hut after consuming a crate of Tusker we skip down the precipitous pathway to the beach. We each take our turn at carrying the Tusker.

We eventually come face to face with the gently rolling Indian Ocean. The only problem with the beer is that there isn't enough of it. None of us has bothered to do the maths: 24 divided by four equals six, and half a dozen cans certainly isn't a full evening's quota. We dig ourselves into the beach and drink our final can silently staring out over the placid, dark grey waters. Not for the first time I offer a silent thank you to the taxpayers of the United Kingdom.

'Fancy going back for another crate, Burbs?' asks Wheelie as he scrunches up his final can and tosses it in the general direction of India.

'You are ferkin joking.'

'It's a hell of a climb back up to the huts,' says Wheelie.

'So that's a 'no' then is it?' asks Mack.

'Correct.'

'You fancy a walk, Pete?'

'Nope.' I throw my empty can at the Indian Ocean and miss.

'Wonder what that glow is,' says Wheelie, pointing south.

About a mile distant, behind a gentle rise in a line of tall palm trees, is a faintly noticeable arc of yellowed light.

'Could be Mombasa ... the town,' says Burbs.

'Naah, it's too near,' I calculate.

'We'll have a wander tomorrow and find out what it is,' says Wheelie as he lights a cigarette

'Tomorrow then.'

'It's a hell of a walk back to the hut.'

'You can say that again.'

'It's a hell of a walk ba ...'

'We aint pissed, are we?' asks Mack as he stands up and stumbles arse over tit.

'We're not,' says Wheelie.

'So no hangover in the morning then,' I declare.

'That'll be a pity then,' says Burbs as he folds the empty cardboard crate into a manageable size.

On our journey back to the hut we all take the opportunity to irrigate the numerous exotic plants that we pass: hopefully they will all survive bladderised Tusker beer.

*

Breakfast is brilliant. *Gurkha*'s cooks have hot trays full of well-tanned sausages, crispy, curled bacon, fried eggs to order and baked beans for those who fancy taking a chance.

'You four look uncommonly fresh of face this morning,' says the chef we now know as Colin.

'Only had one crate of Tusker between us, didn't we?'

'Told ya,' says Colin. 'Ferkin told ya it wouldn't be sufficient.'

'That's a long word for a chef,' says Wheelie.

'What is?'

'Sufficient.'

Colin waves a grease-encrusted spatula at Wheelie. 'Do you want ferkin breakfast or not?'

We spend the rest of the afternoon lounging around in the shade of trees, smoking and breathing in the perfumed air of Silversands. We find a clutch of hammocks strung between strapping palm trees and spend some time falling out of them before mastering the swing and having an afternoon doze. We all buy some carved wooden animals from a number of local blokes who ply their wares throughout the camp. I buy a rather magnificently carved rhinoceros with an elongated front horn: somebody at home will love it. In a fit of unexplained madness, because my money is burning a hole in my pocket, I buy a locally made shirt of multiple colours with African wildlife peering through tropical vegetation on the front, back and from beneath both arm-pits.

The lemons growing on the trees outside our hut are very lemony; the oranges are bitter and awful.

One of the cleaners tells us that the glow to the south is the Nyali Beach Hotel, popular with international tourists. To us, who have just completed Beira Patrol, this screams women. So this evening we dress in what we consider will fit in with the Nyali Beach Hotel clientele.

'You're not wearing that shirt, Pete?' asks Mack.

'Why not?'

'It's naff.'

'It's new and it's … it's very Kenyan.'

The walk along the beach to the distant glow is longer than any of us realise. By the time we arrive my locally made shirt is a dripping rag; the bronze of a chimpanzee on my left sleeve is beginning to run into the rear end of a flag-eared elephant on my stomach.

Tables full of hotel guests stretch down to the beach from a patio area that surrounds the crystal clear waters of the hotel pool. Wheelie, who had once stayed in a hotel in Blackpool, spots an empty table and instructs us to sit down and act like we are residents. He clicks his fingers at a passing waiter dressed in a white uniform and swinging an empty tray, 'Four Tuskers please.'

'Your room number, sir?'

'Err ...' Wheelie is flustered. 'I need the heads.' He struts away.

'We'll pay cash,' I say.

'You from Silversands, sir?'

'Yes.'

'Four Tusker coming. Will cost you twelve shillings and eighty cent ... sir.'

'Bloody Nora,' says Burbs. 'Last night's crate cost less than that.'

'Still require four Tusker, sir?' the waiter asks.

'Yep,' says Burbs.

Wheelie returns from a visit to the heads with a spring in his step and a smirk on his face. 'The heads are ferkin brilliant. You've never seen anything like 'em. There's towels and soap and something nice smelling in a big glass jar thing.'

'Where are they?' I ask.

'Before you go,' says Wheelie with a wink, 'you'll never guess who I have seen in a secluded corner just on the other side of the pool.'

'John Lennon,' says Mack.

'Naah.'

'Sophia Loren,' I say. It's a long shot, but if you don't ask ...

'Naah,' says Wheelie. 'Sugar ... and you'll never guess who he's with.'

'Sophia Loren?'

'Naah ... but she's a woman in a bikini.'

'In a bikini?' blurts Burbs.

'A lime green bikini ... and she's got great legs, brown legs.'

'I've know Sugar for four years,' I say. 'I'm not surprised.'

'Some blokes just do it don't they?' says Wheelie.

'Shug does.'

Burbs claps his hands together. 'Joke ... I've got a joke.'

'Go on then.'

Burbs takes a deep breath. 'An old cowboy ambles to the bar and orders a drink. As he sits sipping his whisky a young lady sits next to him and asks him if he is a real cowboy. Well, he replies, I've spent my whole life on a ranch, herding horses, mending fences and branding cattle, so I guess I'm a real cowboy ... yep. "I'm a lesbian," says the young lady. "I spend my whole day thinking about women. As soon as I get up in the morning I think about women. When I shower I think about women. While I watch TV or even when I'm eating I think about women. Everything seems to make me think about women." The two sit drinking in silence. A short time later a man sits down on the other side of the old cowboy and asks him if he is a real cowboy. "I always thought I was," the cowboy replies, "but I've just learned that I'm a lesbian."'

I didn't expect that ending and splurt some of my Tusker into the ashtray.

*

As the following day is our last, we decide to catch a taxi and give the town of Mombasa the opportunity to entertain us.

'You're not wearing that shirt, Pete?'

'It's the only one I've got that has any character.'

In town we have a wander around the narrow streets bordering the popular Kilindini Bar area. Outside a neon-lit bar we are enticed into the darkened air-conditioned interior by good-looking young local ladies dressed in skimpy vests and short - very short - skirts.

'Don't the ladies have lovely backsides?' says Wheelie. He doesn't require, or expect, an answer.

The price of ice-cold Tuskers is substantially less than we paid at the Nyali Beach the previous night. The bar girls are overly friendly. Compared to the ladies of

Hong Kong and Singapore these are downright frantic. Before sitting down at our table all the girls hoist their vest to display their voluptuous and well-rounded breasts. Wheelie grabs the lady who is the proud owner of what must be the largest and most animated pair of breasts in the whole of Kenya. The young lady who homes in on me has triple tribal scars on both her cheeks and an enormous backside that quivers seductively whenever she moves. Mack is enveloped by a well-endowed lady with a large gold ring in her nose. Burbs has attracted a young lady who is almost as wide as she is tall, but very attractive in a strangely condensed way.

The ladies settle themselves down to drink exclusively with us. Occasionally, Burbs' little lady bounces away to fetch us more drinks.

What happens thereafter is a blur ...

The following morning I wake up slowly and with some difficulty. The first thing I notice is a small barred window set in a white-painted block wall. Alongside me is a naked lady with a head of curly black hair wedged under my right armpit. The shadow of the window bars arch over a well-rounded object alongside me. I slowly remove the sheet to reveal my bed-mate's gleaming backside. I pat it ever so gently; it ripples, but fortunately she doesn't wake. I decide that it's time to leave: I check with my tackle, and it agrees. I gently stroke a goodbye to my bed-mate's rear end.

Slowly, so as not to make a noise, I swing my legs out of bed. I find my shorts and check the contents of my wallet. I check that I have my ID card, my money, cigarettes and lighter before tip-toeing over to the metal door in the hope that it is unlocked and that I'm not in some sort of Kenyan prison cell. Thankfully the door opens without a sound. On the other side I close it with a surprising click. I tread on something sharp. I look down - I've forgotten my flip-flops. I try the door: it's locked. I hear a grunt and a cough from the inside and decide that my best option is to leave barefoot. I don't remember paying up-front and am determined to escape before my bed-mate realises that she has provided her services free of charge. Turning towards a pair of tall wooden doors in the wall opposite I stub my toe as I stride over the threshold into a side street which is clearly the toilet of choice for all of Mombasa's dogs. The noise of early morning traffic assaults me and I tip-toe in the direction of what I hope is the main road. I see the Mombasa tusks in the distance so I know that I am heading in the right general direction.

On the main street I flag down the first taxi I see. 'Silversands, please' I ask the elderly driver who is wearing a wide-brimmed dark blue hat on the back of his head.

He nods acceptance.

I settle myself in the back and check my monetary situation. I have a few cents more than four shillings. 'How much to Silversands?' I ask.

He shrugs his shoulders.

'I've got four shillings,' I explain.

He shrugs his shoulders again.

I relax. At least we both know where we stand. I light an early morning cigarette.

Thirty-five minutes later the driver pulls over to the side of the road and offers me his hand. 'This is four shilling.'

I look around. 'This isn't Silversands.'

'Correct, sir.'

'Where are we exactly?'

'Exact four shilling from pick up on Kilindini Road, sir.'

'So how far is it to Silversands?'

'By this road,' he scribes an arc in the air, 'bout thirty minute walk, sir.'

'But I haven't got anything on my feet.'

'One hour walk then, sir.'

I hand over four silver shillings. He waits for a tip but I don't give one. I slowly slither out of the car in the hope that the driver will take pity on my bare pink feet.

'You wearing shit terrible shirt, sir,' the driver says. Barely do my feet hit the warming road surface than the taxi screeches away.

'Bastard.' The road surface is already hot. I realise that I'm not going to make it back to Silversands without footwear. I look around me: the bordering African jungle grows to the side of the road so there is no option other than the road itself. Ten feet away is a large rock. I brush aside some powerful green stuff, perch myself on the rock and brush the debris from the underside of my feet. What to do?

I watch as a yellow striped snake, as long as my arm, wriggles out of the jungle and squirms across the road without any regards to the passing traffic.

I decide to thumb it. The road is reasonably busy and I have already attracted some interested glances from the drivers of passing vehicles. I don't suppose there are many white, barefoot young men perched on a roadside rock in Kenya this morning.

I'm not a natural 'thumber' and it takes me a while to co-ordinate my thumb and the speed of oncoming traffic as there is a blind bend to my right.

A truck growls to a halt some yards past me. I don't like the look of the truck, or the waving, muscular arm of the driver, so I pretend not to notice him. I light a cigarette.

As the truck pulls away a car brakes alongside me. 'Lost?' asks the driver.

'I've lost my shoes and need a lift to Silversands.' I hop off the rock and stand alongside the car.

The driver is a smartly dressed middle-aged bloke. 'Lucky you are, young man - that's where I go right now. Jump in.'

It's a fifteen-minute drive. My driver delivers for a

local brewery and has a boot full of Tusker. I tell him what a wonderful place Silversands, Mombasa and Kenya is.

'Good place for sailor to meet with women,' he says.

'Is it?' I ask.

'Oh yes. Bars down Kilindini Road full of available women ... all beautiful and reasonable price.'

'Really?'

'You can get lovely, clean woman for two shilling and sixpence average.'

'Really?'

We shake hands as he drops me off outside the main Silversands shop.

Nobody is in our hut. I wonder if Burbs, Wheelie or Mack have made it back from their respective cells yet.

I stroll over to the dining hall where all three are eating breakfast.

'Here he is ... the dirty stop-oot,' blurts Mack.

'Has anyone got a spare pair of flip-flops?' I ask.

Nobody says yes.

'Lost mine, didn't I?'

'Lost them where? Asks Burbs.

'In a place like a cell. Bars on the ferkin window. I legged it before paying. Couldn't get away quick enough. I'm out of money as well - the taxi from town dropped me off about a couple of hours' walk away.'

'Why did you stay in a cell?' asks Mack.

'That was where she took me.'

'Not the one with the tribal scars and the ginormous arse?' asks Wheelie.

'Yeah.'

'Whit was it like then?' asks Mack.

'Don't remember.'

'Good job it didn't cost you anything then.'

'I had four bob left to pay the taxi.'

'You had a few cents more than that after you paid for the last round last night.'

'So you had a free all-night-in then,' says Burbs.

'That's wasn't too bad then ... seeing as I don't remember anything,' I say.

'Good move.'

'Probably.'

'I ended up in a nightclub called The Casablanca and pulled a stripper frae Sevenoaks in Kent,' says Burbs.

'And lost his ID card and wallet,' adds Wheelie.

'You didn't?'

'Ferkin did.'

'Was she worth it?'

'I think so yes. I haven't got anything to compare her with.'

'Where did you end up?' I ask Wheelie.

'In an abandoned fishing boat on the beach.'

'Naah?'

'It was great, smelled a bit, but there was a large mattress and she had the most ginormous tits. Only cost me a little over two bob.'

'But he's got an itch already,' says Burbs, smirking.

'You haven't?' I look questioningly at Wheelie.

'It might just be my imagination,' declares Wheelie.

'Let's hope that's all it is.'

'Yeah,' says Wheelie.

'What about you Mack, what happened to you?'

'Nothing.'

'Nothing?'

'As a prospective man of the clo ...'

'Don't pull that one on us,' says Wheelie.

'I decided against it,' says Mack. 'It was the nose ring that put me off - covered in all sorts of strange deposits it was.'

'Has anyone got a spare pair of flip-flops?' I ask.

Nobody says yes.

Later in the afternoon, I manage to borrow a couple of shillings from Mack. It's quite an achievement as Mack is known to being as tight as a duck's arse.

I buy myself a new pair of flip-flops and a packet of local cigarettes.

We spend our last night at Silversands on the beach drinking Tusker, smoking and telling each other descriptive snippets of the previous night's amorous encounters: mine are all imaginary.

*

'UP SPIRITS.'

Jack tackles Sugar: 'Heard that you were spotted at the Nyali Beach Hotel with a bird, Shug - how the ferk do you do it?'

Sugar downs his tot in one, belches ever so politely and places his empty glass gently on the table in front of him.

'The lady you refer to as a 'bird', is my sister-in-law, married to my brother and out here working for the Kenyan Red Cross,' he says. 'She took a couple of days' leave when she knew that I was visiting.'

'So, you giving her one then?' asks Jack.

'She's my sister in law,' says Sugar indignantly.

'Did ya though? Give her one?'

'Don't be so crude,' replies Sugar.

'So that'll be a yes then?'

'I heard a strange dit from a couple of Stokers who went up to Nairobi by train,' says Chats. 'Looking for the heads, they had to fight their way through a large group of blokes surrounding the open door of the main carriage toilet. As the train stopped at a village one of the blokes dropped a handful of grain down the toilet pan that opened directly onto the track. Then a bloke with a looped wire waited with his arm partway down the bog. Then he tugged on the wire and pulled out a partially garrotted chicken. Another bloke strangled the chicken. Apparently the blokes performed the same trick at all the villages - sometimes they snared a chicken, sometimes not.'

'But they pulled it up through a bog ... a ferkin Kenyan bog.'

'Yeah,' says Chats.

'Ferkin Nora.'

'What's garrotted mean?' someone from the top of the mess asks.

Kit opens his mouth.

Mack silences Kit by holding a hand in front of his face.

'It means strangled,' whispers Mack.

'Don't ferkin believe him,' blurts Kit. 'It's a bright yellow vegetable normally eaten with poultry.'

'What's poultry?'

'Means small and insignificant,' says Kit. 'Now piss off for your dinner.'

Burbs finishes his tot and places his empty glass next to the rum fanny. 'I got something funny from my auntie the other day,' he says. He pulls a sheet of paper from his back pocket and unfolds it. 'I can't remember it, so I've got to read it: "The committee to clean up Soho's porn-infested areas continued its series of rallies recently. A huge, throbbing, pulsating crowd sprang erect from nowhere and forced its way into the steaming nether regions surrounding the glistening, sweaty intersection of Shaftsbury Avenue and Tottenham Court Road. Thrusting, driving and pushing its way ..."'

'Bloody hell, Burbs lad,' interrupts Kit. 'Remember those of us who haven't had a leg-over this year.'

Burbs snorts, takes a deep breath and continues. '"... Thrusting, driving and pushing its way into the usually receptive neighbourhood, the eager throng, now grown to five times its original size, rams itself again and again into the quivering, perspiring, musty, damp dankness."'

'Stop it, Burbs,' slobbers Kit, covering his ears.

'Carry on, Burbs ... quickly,' says Sugar.

'Yeah, quick as you like,' says Jan.

Burbs takes a sip of Queen's and exhales. '"Suddenly, the tumescent crowd are one heaving, turgid entity, ascending to heights never before experienced. Then ..."' Burbs sags and closes his eyes. '"Then with a gigantic, soul-searching heart-stopping series of eruptions, it's all over ..."'

'Thank goodness for that,' mumbles Kit, exhaling.

Burbs takes a deep breath and concludes. '"The crowd enjoy a fag and make their way home."'

'Brilliant ... ferkin brilliant,' says Sugar clapping.

'What does turgid mean?' asks Timber.

'It's a stringy form of vegetable,' explains Kit, pulling a disgusted expression. 'Not very appetising.'

Jack downs the last of the Queen's, collects the glasses and places them in the fanny. 'What's your auntie called, Burbs?'

'Leggy Peggy.'

'Leggy?'

'It's a nickname she got at school.'

'Why?'

'Apparently she had good long legs ... in her younger days.'

'Long legs and a sense of humour. Can I write to her?' asks Kit.

'No ... of course you can't. Anyway she's not fond of beards. Her fourth husband had a beard and she got rid of him within months.'

'Pity,' says Kit.

'Can I write to her then?' asks Sugar.

'You are ferkin joking,' splutters Burbs. 'You of all people. You said that you don't write letters.'

'You can do the writing on my behalf,' says Sugar with a grin.

'How many times has she been married then, your Auntie Peggy?' asks Jack.

'Five I think, but number five was getting on her nerves the last time I talked to her, so she could be up to six by now,' says Burbs.

'That's more than that film star ... what's her name ... Elizabeth Taylor.'

'Aunt Peggy is better looking than her,' says Burbs.

'Better looking than Elizabeth Taylor ... come on, Burbs, let me write to her,' pleads Jack.

'No chance.'

'Has anyone heard the result of the general election?' asks Jan.

Silence.

'Shit in it, Jan ... we're all still considering the possibilities of Peggy the Leggy.'

'Leggy Peggy,' corrects Burbs.

*

The plan is to depart Mombasa in the very early hours to avoid having to fire an expensive and unnecessary gun salute. We single-up but have to wait for some last-minute stores.

A Land Rover screeches to a halt at the bottom of the brow and the Buffers party skip over the brow to collect half a dozen large cardboard boxes. The eagle-eyed of those on the Quarterdeck spot that the boxes contain Izal toilet paper.

'That's bloody rubbish, that Izal stuff,' says Wheelie. 'We had it at St Vincent.'

'You had toilet paper at St Vincent?' I ask.

'Yeah ... of course.'

'At Ganges if you wanted to use the bog you had to submit a request form three days in advance. And you had to have a good reason to go.'

'Naah?' says Wheelie.

'Only joking,' I say.

'But you actually had toilet paper though ... didn't ya?'

'One sheet per visit,' I say. 'If we were lucky.'

There are no people on the jetty to wave us farewell. Mombasa slumbers as *HMS Gurkha* silently drifts away from the jetty and out into deep, turquoise waters of the Indian Ocean. Somewhere ashore is a lady with a voluptuous rear-end bemoaning the fact that the white boy she took to her cell a few days ago, left without paying.

We're all a little saddened at leaving Kenya. Particularly as we know that our next port of call is Aden.

*

Someone flashes a torch in my eyes and punches my exposed shoulder. 'Rise and shine, Pete. They want the RIB in the water in quarter of an hour.'

'Time ... what's the ferkin time?' It's acceptable to use colourful language when you're forcibly woken in the middle of the night ... and long before Charlie.

'Zero two ten. I'm shaking the RIB crew. Which is Mack's bunk? He's needed in the Ops Room.'

I wave a sleepy arm in Mack's direction. 'Over there ... bottom bunk.'

I light a cigarette to help calm myself, dress and slope up to the starboard accommodation ladder. All the upper deck lights are off, there is no moon and there is nobody else around. For a moment I'm convinced that this is a sick hoax to get me out of my bunk.

Major Munro leans over the guardrails on the deck directly above me. 'Have you got good eyesight, Able Seaman Broadbent?'

I rub my sleepy eyes. 'Average I suppose, sir.'

'Up here then.'

Major Munro is dressed in full combat gear. He hands me a pair of heavy, standard issue Admiralty binoculars. 'About green four five, tell me what you see.'

It takes me a while to focus the binoculars perfectly

in the dark. I position myself facing forty-five degrees from the bow, steadying myself on the starboard guardrail and scan.

'See anything?'

'Nothing yet, sir.'

'Keep looking.'

I see something silver after a minutes hectic scanning. 'I think I've got something sir, could be a small bow-wave.'

'Point.'

I reach out an arm.

'What range do you reckon?'

'Can't tell you exactly, sir - maybe three or four or even five miles ... or a bit more or less ... I'm guessing.'

At that moment Dodger and a small group of Marines appear dragging the bow rope of the RIB. Two members of the Watch on Deck start to wind the accommodation ladder outboard.

'Corporal, we have the target visual bearing green four five range approximately three to five miles,' says Major Munro.

As a Radar Plotter I can't help but inquire. 'Has the Ops Room got it on radar, sir?'

Major Munro sniffs. 'They didn't ten minutes ago.'

There is a break in the cloud cover. 'I can see it, sir,' whispers Dodger. 'Range about three to five miles.'

Major Munro grabs the binoculars, almost strangling me in the process. He refocuses. 'Looks like your average heap of shit. Range approximately three to five miles. Underway about four knots I reckon. Not towing anything. On a more or less parallel course.'

I cough.

'Don't just stand there, Broadbent - get down there and flash up the RIB.'

'Aye aye, sir.'

'On the RIB the first thing I check is the fuel.

Dodger parks himself alongside me. 'Bugger this for a

game of soldiers ... Oh two dubbs in the ferkin morning.'

'Do you know anything about this ferkin Dhow?' I ask.

'Only that it shouldn't be here - that's all I know. Obviously those on the Bridge have some intelligence otherwise they wouldn't have got us out of our stinking pits, would they?'

'I wouldn't be so sure.'

'Check your radio,' calls Major Munro. 'And check that you have an Aldis. Have you got my binoculars, coxswain?'

'No sir, you took them back.'

He finds them sitting on his chest. 'So you did, belay my last.'

I flash up the outboard. Once everybody is onboard I ask permission to cast off.

Major Munro holds up a waiting hand. 'The Ops Room confirm a range of three point four miles heading three five five magnetic.'

'Very good, sir.'

'How long for you to do three point four miles, coxswain?'

'Five to ten minutes depending upon sea state, sir.'

'On your way then. Chop chop.'

'Aye aye, sir.' I cast off and slew away.

Dodger gives the Marine with the radio a nudge. 'Have you checked comms?'

'Yes, Corp - clear as a bell.'

'Corporal.'

'Sorry ... Corporal.'

There is a slight swell running and we bounce along nicely. The bowman is continually pointing to the target Dhow.

Six minutes later we are circling the Dhow. Despite training the two Aldis lamps on the Dhow, we can't see anybody onboard.

'Put us alongside, Pete - we'll jump onboard and see

what the situation is,' says Dodger.

'Right.'

'Everybody,' yells Dodger, 'ready for boarding. Me first, then the radio, then those in turn from forward.'

Grunts of approval. Green berets shaped and secure.

I slide alongside the decaying hull. It's about five times our length. Dodger is up and onboard in a flash followed by the radio operator. Marine Browne is the final one to board.

I move the RIB further forward: I'm suspicious of the gaping, brown stained hole in the hull alongside me.

Eventually I hear the radio operator telling *Gurkha* that a preliminary search has revealed nothing suspicious. The crew consists of a young boy and his mother and the cargo appears to be bales of cloth and bundles of waste paper.

Gurkha tells us to return immediately.

Once the boat is stowed correctly I make my way back to the mess where everybody is still asleep. I grab my towel from my locker door and give the locker a kick to let my messmates know that I'm up and about, before shooting off to the bathroom where I enjoy an uninterrupted warm shower. Once back in my bunk it takes me ages to get back to sleep.

*

'UP SPIRITS.'

We are all sitting around the mess table waiting for Jack to arrive with the rum. The glasses are arranged neatly and the mess cloth is draped alongside ...

'ABLE SEAMAN BROADBENT AND ABLE SEAMAN McCUBBIN REPORT TO THE OPS ROOM.'

In the Ops Room Frothy is seated at the Helicopter

Controller's position as Mack and I arrive. He jumps up and points to a couple of swivel chairs nearest to the ladder leading to the Bridge. 'Take a seat each, young men - have I got a surprise for you!'

'It's tot-time, PO,' says Mack.

'Christ,' says Frothy looking at his watch. 'I didn't realise the time.'

'Our tot goes off, PO,' I say. 'Goes flat if it's left loafing for long.'

'Yeah I know and I need mine.' Frothy pulls an apologetic expression and jams my personal headphones on his head. 'Kate this is Mother, over.'

'Yes, over,' replies the unmistakeable exasperated voice of Pontius.

'We have a problem, sir,' says Frothy.

'What might that be?'

'It's tot-time, sir.'

'Can't they keep it?'

'Not on the lower deck sir - two-in-one goes flat after a while.'

'Two in what?'

'Two parts water to one part rum sir. Called grog ... named after an Admiral.'

'Admiral Grog?'

'Probably, sir.'

'Never heard of him.'

'It's a matter of naval record, sir.'

'So what shall we do? How long will tot-time take?'

Frothy looks inquiringly at me.

'Ten minutes tops.' I say.

'Fifteen minute delay, sir, over.'

'Let's do it then. I expect the first one of them down here in fifteen minutes.'

'Roger, sir. Will do, out.'

Frothy holds up a silencing hand. 'Before you ask, you've both been granted a flight in the Wasp. It's taken all morning to convince the Jimmy that the Helicopter

Controllers should take a short flight while things are quiet.'

'Right then.' I say.

'A ferkin flight?' asks Mack. There is a noticeable tremor in his voice.

'So back down the mess both of you, grab your tot and then you – Broadbent - come back here and you – McCubbin - report to the flight deck in full number 8s, not shorts, with shoes and socks ... not nylon socks or sandals. No cigarettes or lighter. OK?'

'Thanks, PO,' I say.

'I'm not too fond of heights,' splutters Mack.

'You'll be telling me next that you don't want to fly.'

'I don't, PO,' replies Mack.

Frothy exhales long and hard before clicking his headphones on. 'Kate, this is mother. Only one of the Controllers will be flying, sir, over.'

'Which one?'

'Broadbent, sir.'

'So the prospective Padre has chickened out then?'

'Yes, sir.'

Don't mention anything down the mess, Pete,' says Mack as we leave the Ops Room.

'Course not.'

'I really don't like flying and going up in something without doors on doesn't seem like fun to me.'

'What do you mean, without ferkin doors on?' I ask.

Down the mess Jack is dishing out the last of the rum. He hands me my tot.

'I need all of this today, Jack,' I say as I down my tot in one. I hand him my empty glass. 'I'm going up in the Wasp. Mack and I tossed for the trip and he lost.'

'I'm ferkin devastated,' says Mack. 'Been looking forward to a trip in the Wasp for yonks.'

'Pusser's socks don't have any nylon in them, do they?' I ask Chats.

'Don't think so.'

Duly decked-out in full-length No 8 trousers, shoes and full-length socks, I report to Pontius who is standing alongside the Wasp finger wiping some marks from the windscreen.

'Had your grog, Broadbent?'

'Yes, sir.'

'You looking forward to this?'

'After my tot ... I think so sir. Ready for anything.'

'In you get then. Put the helmet on and strap yourself in.'

I sit down on something less comfortable than your average car seat, with a single seat belt fastened diagonally across my chest. There are two gaping holes where the doors should be. Despite the intrepid properties of my tot, I am a little perturbed and asking myself what the ferk I'm doing.

'Why no doors, sir?'

'The weight saving gives us a little extra range in this part of the world.'

'Right then ... sir.'

'Golf Foxtrot Yankee Alpha this is X-ray Tango Four Three Four. Ready for takeoff, over.'

In my helmet earphones I can hear Frothy loud and clear.

'X-ray Tango Four Three Four this is Golf Foxtrot Yankee Alpha, roger.'

Pontius gives a thumbs-up signal to the Flight Deck Officer.

The engine starts, the Wasp shudders. There is a change in the rotor blade pitch. A couple of helmeted flight deck crew remove our holding-down straps and before I am sure what's happening, we are airborne. With a flick of the wrist Pontius spurts us up and over to the port side of *HMS Gurkha*.

'Golf Foxtrot Yankee Alpha this is X-ray Tango Four Three Four. Airborne. Permission to climb to altitude angels two. Request vector details, over.'

No sooner has Frothy given permission than Pontius points our bows skywards. I watch as *Gurkha* gradually shrinks. By the time we level off at two thousand feet my ship is a toy-sized vessel on a vast, relatively empty blue ocean.

'Kate, this is Mother, Squawk IFF for identification purposes, over.'

Pontius flicks a switch. 'This is going to be an informal flight then, Petty Officer Beer?'

'In a casual mood, sir,' says Frothy. 'Please retain your current height. Surrounding air space is clear. Look after my Controller, out.'

Pontius looks at me, winks and slews the Wasp over on her port side. With no door there is nothing more substantial than a single worn seat-belt strap between me and the Persian Gulf two thousand feet below. Instinctively my inboard right hand grabs the underside of my seat. I can feel what I hope is chewing gum.

'Let's go and find some fish,' says Pontius.

I nod as the Wasp slowly rights itself. Pontius is scanning the Persian Gulf. I am more than a little concerned that he is looking everywhere other than straight ahead.

'You feeling OK, Broadbent?'

'Yes, sir,' I lie.

'I see fish.'

Once again we are on our side, slewing around. 'Can you see them?'

'What, sir?'

'Fish.'

'No ... sir.'

'Missed the bastards,' spits Pontius. He swivels himself round. 'There they are ... the bastards.'

All I can see is distant blue water.

'I'm taking us down.'

All of a sudden the windscreen shows nothing but blue ocean.

'Kate, this is Mother. Have lost contact with you. Please confirm your altitude, over.'

Pontius points a finger at what I assume is the altimeter. 'It's in hundreds of feet.'

The needle is moving on the wrong side of 3. 'Three hundred feet is that, sir?'

Pontius spreads his arms, his joystick wavers uncontrolled. 'Just look at those bloody fish.'

I look in the direction indicated and can see a pod of about twenty large torpedo-shaped fish.

'If I'm not mistaken, Able Seaman Broadbent, that is a mob of sharks. Mob's not right ... what's the collective noun for a load of sharks?'

'A pod I think, sir.'

'That's it ... a pod ... a huge great pod. Just look at them. I'm going down closer.'

We drop like a stone, until we are skimming only feet above the surface. The sharks are far enough away to our starboard side not to be in helicopter-disturbed water. Only a few fins are visible.

'How many do you reckon?'

'Dunno, sir.'

'Let's log it as a hundred.'

'I don't think there are that many, sir.'

'We Fleet Air Arm gentlemen are prone to exaggeration.'

'If you say so, sir.'

'X-ray Tango Four Three Four this is Golf Foxtrot Yankee Alpha. Have lost contact with you. Please confirm your altitude, over.'

Pontius winks at me. 'Suppose we should put him out of his misery eh?' And with that we aim our bows at the stratosphere.

'X-ray Tango Four Three Four this is Golf Foxtrot Yankee Alpha. Have lost contact with you. Please confirm your altitude, over.'

'Going up to angels two,' says Pontius.

'Thank you Kate,' says Frothy. 'Now I've got you ... I think. Squawk IFF for identification purposes, over.'

Pontius flicks a switch.

'Got you. Thank you, Kate.'

I am beginning to relax a little, although I do need the heads.

'Landing back onboard is a bit hit and miss,' smiles Pontius. 'Wonder how it's going to be today? Ready to go back home?'

'Yes, sir ... if you say so, sir.' All of a sudden I'm apprehensive again.

'Mother, this is Kate, over.'

'Kate, this is Mother, over.'

'Ready to return to Mother. Request vector, over.'

'Roger. Course to steer 270 magnetic, range 22 miles, over.'

'Roger. 270 magnetic range 22 miles. ETA ... shortly, out.'

We are on our beam ends and spinning. I'm looking at rotating blue water.

'Enjoy that, Able Seaman Broadbent?'

'Yes, sir,' I lie.

Soon I spot a toy frigate in the distance. Our bows dip and slowly, ever so slowly ... a full size *Gurkha* materialises.

We hover off the port beam opposite the flight deck.

Once the flight deck crew have our holding-down straps sorted I watch the guy with the table-tennis bats as he waves us back onboard.

To say it's nice to see the flight deck below me again is an understatement. We hit the deck, the rotor pitch changes and our straps are attached. The engine is cut and I'm back onboard, safe and sound. My heart rate settles to a little less than alarming.

'Kate, this is Mother, send Able Seaman Broadbent to the Ops Room, over.'

'This is Kate. Who? Did I have a Helicopter Controller

with me? He must have fallen out somewhere.' Pontius can't suppress a giggle.

'Send him up to the Ops Room please, sir.'

'Roger, will do, out.'

I walk off on wobbly legs.

In the Ops Room, Frothy and Mack are waiting for me.

'Whit was it like then, Pete?' asks Mack.

'Ferkin brilliant. Wouldn't have missed it for the world.'

*

This morning the winder of my wristwatch comes away in my hand. I try to put it back in but can't. I suppose I'm asking too much of a cockie watch I bought for less than ten dollars during my last days in Singapore, well over a year ago. 'Shit.'

Jan, who has a large diving watch which I've always admired, looks balefully at my watch as he takes a seat opposite me in the dining hall. 'Get yourself a proper watch, Pete,' he says, tapping the face of his watch.

'What is it?'

'Submariner ... Rolex Submariner.'

'I can't afford a Rolex.'

'You got your LOA for Beira, didn't ya?'

'Yep.'

'And we're going back to Aden, aren't we?'

'Yep.'

'The Brits are moving out so there could be some bargains to be had in those shops that do business with NAAFI. Go and organise one of those Credit Sales Agreements with the NAAFI Damager.'

'I had one of those when I bought my camera in Singers.'

'Right then, see how much you can borrow. Use some of your LOA money to put a reasonable deposit down and go and buy yourself a decent watch.'

'A Rolex.' I was getting excited. I munched on my last slice of crispy bacon. 'Me, buy a Rolex?'

'Why not? Doesn't have to be a Submariner, there are other models ... but buy an Oyster.'

'An Oyster?'

'They're the waterproof ones.'

'Right then.' I'm excited. I've known about Rolex watches ever since I'd seen them advertised in the National Geographic magazines borrowed at school.

'James Bond wears one,' says Jan.

'Does he?'

'Yep.'

'Have you seen Goldfinger?' I ask.

'No, not yet,' says Jan.

'I was far more interested in the gold-painted Shirley Eaton than the watch he was wearing,' I explain, smiling.

Jan smiles. 'I've seen the adverts.'

'I might go for it then.'

'After all, you're a ferkin Helicopter Controller, aren't ya?'

'I am.'

'You need a good watch doing that job, don't ya?'

*

It's the back end of April when, once again, we berth on Aden's well-protected Admiralty jetty.

'ALL SHIP'S DIVERS REPORT TO THE GANGWAY.'

'That's another ferkin bottom search,' says Jan.

'Bottoms is all you think about ... you divers,' quips Chats.

I track the NAAFI Damager down and get directions to the best place in town to buy a watch through the NAAFI.

'Beware the local currency - there are two currencies in common use in Aden,' he says. 'The East African shilling is the same as an English shilling and the new South Arabian Dinar is the same as an English Pound and divided into a hundred fils.'

'Fills?'

'Fils.'

Mack decides to join me in my watch-hunting spree. He says he's also interested in buying himself a Rolex, but I doubt he's serious. The confusion about the local currency has made him suspicious about parting with any of his money.

Jan says he will help me pick the right watch, but he and Sharky Ward are busy this afternoon co-ordinating the bottom search along with some fledgling divers from the 1st Battalion The Argyll and Sutherland Highlanders.

'THE INFORMATION OFFICER SPEAKING. THE SITUATION ASHORE REMAINS SERIOUS. WHILST SHORE LEAVE IS GRANTED, IT IS RECOMMENDED THAT YOU GO ASHORE IN GROUPS AND REMAIN ALERT AT ALL TIMES. ALL LEAVE EXPIRES AT 18:00 FOR JUNIOR RATES AND 18:30 FOR SENIOR RATES. IT IS IMPORTANT THAT WHEN ASHORE YOU AVOID LARGE GATHERINGS OF LOCALS. THAT IS ALL.'

Jan and I exchange troubled glances. Personally I am on the verge of cancelling the whole 'watch buying' episode when ...

'ABLE SEAMAN BROADBENT REPORT TO THE NAAFI MANAGER IN THE SENIOR RATES MESS.'

What the hell is that for?'

I knock on the Senior Rates mess door and ask for the NAAFI Manager.

'You still wanting to buy a decent wristwatch?'

'Yep.'

'One of the Marines is also wanting to buy a watch, so it may be a good idea for you to go ashore together.'

'Yeah, great idea. What's his name?'

'Ransom ... Larry.'

'Thanks.'

'He's planning on going tomorrow.'

'Perfect.'

'Don't forget to negotiate a price.'

'Negotiate?'

'Haggle.'

'Right then ... will do, thanks.'

Down the mess I break the news to Mack. 'Cracked it, mate ... we've only got our very own bodyguard for our watch-buying run tomorrow, haven't we?'

'Have we?'

'Bootneck.'

'Great. Will he be armed?'

'Dunno.'

'Promise you won't wear your Mombasa shirt though, Pete.'

*

I spend most of the following morning doing some work on the RIB. There are outboard areas that were damaged by those mail pods. I have all the stuff to stick neoprene reinforcing patches at the same place on both sides.

Jan spends the morning charging dive bottles, checking equipment and arranging the dive schedule for the afternoon's bottom search.

About twenty soldiers from the 1st Battalion The Argyll and Sutherland Highlanders patrol the jetty, which is kept clear of anyone remotely local. Timber, who is duty, is one of a team of youngsters told to patrol the outboard side of the upper deck. In order to put the shits up the local insurgents he has been kitted out in the standard Royal Naval riot control gear: a steel hat, a metal tipped wooden night-stick, a pair of green gaiters and a matching belt. He looks every bit the scary sailor.

'What you looking for then, Timber?' Mack asks as we are waiting at the top of the gangway for our Royal Marine escort to appear.

'Surgeons, I think.'

'You mean insurgents.'

'Yeah ... them as well.'

'Must be something serious or else they wouldn't have issued you with a stick of wood,' I say.

'I know,' says Timber as he whacks the stick in the palm of his hand. He winces.

'And a steel hat,' adds Mack.

At exactly 14:00 Larry Ransom, Royal Marines, appears at the top of the brow ... unarmed.

'So you're after a watch, Larry?' I ask.

'Yeah. I was thinking about an Omega but I also collect old watches. Just wanted to see what's available before our lads pull out for the last time. Might be able to bag a bargain.'

'That's what we thought,' says Mack.

We give young Timber a farewell wave as we leave.

The atmosphere ashore is quite different from four months ago. Apparently there has been a second grenade attack on the High Commissioner's office and our forces are currently on a war footing. Certainly the look and attitude of the people we pass is bordering on hostile. Larry suggests that we divert our eyes.

Fortunately the NAAFI-approved shop is on a main road with lots of open space on all sides. There isn't a vast range of watches but enough to keep us occupied. Larry doesn't find anything in the Omega range that suits him and instead concentrates on an unused 1950s Hopalong Cassidy watch strapped around a small, plastic saddle. He explains that they are collectable and that he could sell it for three times today's asking price. He

Aden's finest ...

haggles the price down by fifty Fils.

I fancy a black-faced Rolex Oysterdate which I fondle at great length while I make up my mind ... its price is thirty-two Arabian Dinars, equivalent to thirty-two English quid. Mack has decided to go for something slightly less expensive and plumps for an all black Mido which the shop owner assures him is one hundred percent watertight to a maximum of ten English feet.

I ask the shopkeeper if he will accept thirty Dinars. He looks at me, sighs apologetically and explains that unfortunately the Rolex office in Switzerland won't allow any price negotiations. He's an Arab with a curved dagger in a scabbard, so he has the negotiating edge.

Within the hour Mack and I have signed the appropriate NAAFI paperwork, paid our deposits and obtained stamped receipts. It is agreed that our watches will be supplied to the NAAFI onboard tomorrow. Larry pays in sterling for his Hopalong Cassidy watch. The shopkeeper holds each of the bank notes up to the light to check that they are genuine. He gives us all a wide, grey-toothed grin as we leave.

Back onboard, Timber is lounging on a washdeck locker with his cap off, his night-stick dangling between his legs, and is staring outboard at nothing in particular.

'Everything secure ,Timber?' I ask. 'Can we rest peaceful in our bunks?'

'Yep,' replies Timber without averting his eyes from whatever he is looking at.

Down the mess I tell Jan that I'd got myself a Rolex Oysterdate for thirty-two quid.

Jan jabs me in the rib. 'That's a good price ... if it's genuine of course.'

'Wha?'

'There are fakes about.'

'Naah.'

'Have you got it yet?'

'No.'

'I'll have a look at it when you get your hands on it. It's easy to spot the fakes.'

The following day Jan and I collect my brand new Rolex from the NAAFI. Jan assures me that I have a 'genuine Bedouin' Rolex. I sign the appropriate sheet of paper and am contractually bound to pay the NAAFI three quid a month for the next ten months. If I miss a payment I will be flogged around the fleet, hung, drawn and quartered before being black-listed for life by the Navy, Army and Air Force Institution.

Jan helps me adjust the metal strap and to set the time accurately. After a few tries we get it perfect. I lay on my bunk looking at my Rolex ... I've made it.

Mack flashes his Mido around the mess. For a relatively inexpensive eleven-dinars-fifty-fils watch it gets a number of admiring comments.

*

As is *Gurkha*'s habit we depart Aden very early the next morning. The Gunnery branch are convinced that we do this to avoid the expense of firing saluting rounds and of getting the Gunnery Officer out of his comfortable bed before the morning stand-easy.

It's another cloudless day and the waters are a placid blue. The fresh air is a welcome change from the dust and heat of Aden.

The Navigator's Yeoman says that the logged midday temperature yesterday was 129 degrees Fahrenheit. The highest so far this trip.

11

An 'explosive' intercept

I AM halfway to the bathroom dressed in flip-flops and towel.

'FLYING STATIONS.'

By the time I make it to the Ops room Frothy is already sitting at the controllers' PPI talking to Pontius. He looks quizzically at me.

'I was on my way to the bathroom, PO ... sorry.'

'We've got a suspicious vessel on radar. Bogey Charlie.'

'Oh great.'

'We've darkened ship and the Wasp is ready to go.' He hands me the headphones.

'Where have you been, Broadbent?' asks Pontius.

'I was in the bathroom, sir.'

'Bathroom?'

'Yes, sir. That's where we shower, shave and do our dhobying.'

'Don't be sarcastic with me, young man ... just because you've been up in my contraption. Ready to go, over.'

'This is Golf Foxtrot Yankee Alpha, roger.'

Frothy leans over. 'Get him to steer 340. Bogey Charlie is about four miles distant.'

'X-ray Tango Four Three Four this is Golf Foxtrot Yankee Alpha. When airborne vector 340. Bogey Charlie range approximately four miles, over.'

'Roger. Vector 340 range four miles, out.'

I track the Wasp and report her position to the surface plotting team who confirm she is on the correct heading and closing Bogey Charlie.

'AWAY DHOW BOARDING PARTY. MUSTER ON THE QUARTERDECK.'

That's me. I wave at Frothy. 'That's me, PO. I'm boarding party coxswain ... the RIB.'

'Leave it with me. I'll take over.'

I hand him my headphones.

As I scramble through the door I can hear Frothy: 'X-ray Tango Four Three Four this is Golf Foxtrot Yankee Alpha. A change of controller. Not even Able Seaman Broadbent can manage to be in two places at the same time.'

I'm almost on the Quarterdeck when ...

'BELAY MY LAST. DHOW BOARDING PARTY MUSTER BY THE STARBOARD ACCOMMODATION LADDER.'

I screech to a halt, do an about-turn and scamper up the ladder to the starboard waste.

Sergeant Lecky and his band of armed Royal Marines

are waiting for me. The RIB is in the water and being pulled up to the bottom platform of the ladder. *Gurkha* has switched all her upper deck lighting off. It's ink black dark.

'I was controlling the Wasp,' I say to Sergeant Lecky.

'A likely story,' he glares at me.

Someone throws me a lifejacket.

From the deck overhead someone shouts, 'Chop chop there, we have Bogey Charlie visible from up here. She is towing something suspicious.'

'Down you go.' Sergeant Lecky waves a hand at me.

I bound down the ladder, plonk myself at the back of the RIB, make all my pre take-off checks and start the outboard in neutral. Sergeant Lecky standing alongside me waves us away from the ladder as the final Royal Marine boards.

The Marine with the radio makes contact with *Gurkha*'s bridge. 'Bogey Charlie bears 340 range exactly four point three miles, Sergeant.'

'Very good,' says Sergeant Lecky as he adjusts his beret.

The RIB doesn't have a built in compass. Sergeant Lecky has a hand compass and he directs me until I am heading 340. Almost as soon as I settle my course the Marine in the bow reports that he has Bogey Charlie visible at two o'clock.

I throttle back slightly.

The Wasp is hovering high above the Dhow's port quarter.

One of the Marines coughs.

'Silence in the boat,' shouts Sergeant Lecky.

The Marine on the radio whispers something to Sergeant Lecky.

Sergeant Lecky whispers, 'The Wasp pilot says that Bogey Charlie is towing a flat contraption. We will approach from astern. No lights and little throttle. Who has the Aldis?'

'I have, Sergeant,' Someone up forward whispers.

'Have it ready when I say.'

'Roger.'

'Sssshhhh.'

There are no lights onboard Bogey Charlie. The Wasp has gone. I can clearly see the disturbed water made by whatever is being towed. I throttle back and approach from directly astern. It's a raft about the same size as the RIB and sitting about a foot out of the water. On it are what looks like wooden boxes or crates. The tow-line to the Dhow dips.

'The Dhow has stopped or he's reversing or he's dropped the tow,' whispers Sergeant Lecky.

A face appears at the stern of the Dhow. It quickly drops below the stern rail. The end of the tow-rope slips into the water.

Sergeant Lecky says to the radio man: 'Tell the ship that the Dhow has abandoned the tow. Ask them if we should take the raft in tow or board the Dhow.'

The guy with the radio whispers to the ship and listens to the reply. 'Take the raft in tow, Sergeant ... on a long tow if it is considered safe to do so.'

'Bridge speak,' mumbles Sergeant Lecky. 'Right then. Get a line on the raft.'

I push the bows against the raft. I'm concentrating on keeping my stern away from the abandoned tow-line.

'You, up forward, grab that tow-line! Whoever has the Aldis let's have a look at the Dhow,' whispers Sergeant Lecky.

There is no sign of activity onboard the Dhow, which is making about five knots directly away from us.

'Tell the ship that we have the raft tow-line and the Dhow is opening on a heading of ...' he looks at his compass, 'about magnetic north.'

Sergeant Lecky is suddenly suspicious about the raft. 'Back off, coxswain - gently. Put some distance between ourselves and the raft.'

I back off. A Marine in the bow has the tow-rope in hand and is paying it out. The moon appears from behind a long thin cloud and I spot *Gurkha* in the distance.

'I think I know what's in those boxes, Sergeant.' says one of the Marines.

'They smell familiar,' says Sergeant Lecky. 'I want at least a tow-line distance away from the raft, coxswain - there is definitely something nasty onboard.'

One of the Marines volunteers to board the raft.

'You done your last will and testicle then?' someone asks.

'Once we have some more distance between us, empty a magazine into that pile of boxes. That should tell us if there is anything explosive onboard,' says Sergeant Lecky. 'Who is the best shot?'

'I am, Sergeant,' says someone.

'Who's that?' asks Sergeant Lecky.

'Marine Browne ... Browne with an 'e', Sergeant.'

'You can have the pleasure.' He turns to the radio man. 'Tell the ship what we are doing and why.'

'Why are we doing it?' asks the radio man.

'Because it smells suspicious.'

'Roger.' The bloke with the radio talks into the microphone.

We all watch as the distance between ourself and the raft increases.

'Right then, Marine Browne with an 'e'.' Sergeant Lecky claps his hands. 'Take aim and empty a magazine into that pile of boxes.'

Marine Brown rests himself on the gunwale and settles himself.

'Nobody move,' says Sergeant Lecky.

'Can we smoke, Sergeant?' someone asks.

'Don't be so ferkin stupid.'

I search for *Gurkha* in the gloom. She's visible only because she is stowing the Wasp away in the hangar and the hangar lights are on.

The radio crackles. 'Mother is waiting for a progress report, Sergeant.'

'Tell mother to ferkin wait one.'

'Shall I actually say ferkin, Sergeant?'

'Of course not.'

We wallow in almost total silence.

Marine Brown sprays the now-distant raft with a five-second burst.

Nothing.

'Give it another burst, Marine Browne,' says Sergeant Lecky.

The click of another magazine being installed is audible. 'Can I fire at will, Sergeant?'

'No, Will's done nothing wrong ... fire at the ferkin raft.'

Giggles from up forward.

'That's enough,' says Sergeant Lecky.

'It should have gone bang by now shouldn't it?' someone asks.

Sergeant Lecky turns to the nearest Marine. 'Is Marine Browne definitely our best shot?'

'I think so, Sergeant.'

'Who said he definitely was?'

'Marine Browne, Sergeant.'

Sergeant Lecky cups his hands. 'Fire at the raft, Marine Browne. Try not to miss.'

'OK, Sarge.' He fires a short burst and the raft explodes in a ball of bright orange flame.

'Shit,' yells Sergeant Lecky. 'And don't call me "Sarge"!'

'What shall I tell the ship, Sergeant?' asks the Marine with the radio.

'That the explosion they have no doubt witnessed was the raft.'

'Roger.'

'Suppose we could have a cigarette break for those of you who smoke,' says Sergeant Lecky.

I tap my pockets. I've left mine in the Ops Room. 'Can I cadge a fag?' I ask the Marine with the radio.

We all finish our cigarettes at much the same time and flick them into the Gulf of Aden.

'The ship wants to know what is going on, Sergeant,' the Marine with the radio asks.

'Tell them we are on our way back. I think there will be a long night of report-writing ahead of us.' He removes his beret and wipes the top of his head with the sleeve of his jacket. 'That could have been a total ferkin disaster if we hadn't backed off when we did.'

'Who writes the reports, Sergeant?' I ask.

'I suppose it will be down to me and Marine Browne ... and probably the Radio Operator.'

'Not me then?' I ask.

'Doubt it.'

'That's OK then.'

I put us alongside the Accommodation ladder and Sergeant Lecky is the first one to bound up it. The rest of the boarding party follow. At the top of the ladder Sergeant Lecky is explaining things to Major Munro. I sprawl on a washdeck locker, scrounge a cigarette from one of the Marines and smoke it hurriedly. What a ferkin evening.

In the Operations Room, Mack is putting his gear away. 'Chopper is in the hangar,' he says.

'The ferkin raft was packed full of explosives. It ferkin exploded ... ginormous explosion ... bits all over the place,' I explain.

Nobody appears that interested.

The surface plotting team have been told to track Bogey Charlie until it has been decided what to do about it.

Frothy asks the Bridge where we are exactly.

'Ops Room, this is Bridge. We are currently opposite a place called Ras Fartak. Continue to track Bogey Charlie. We are attempting to make contact with the authorities in Bahrain to clarify what action we should take.'

'Very good sir.'

I cup my ear. 'I think I can hear a can of beer calling me.'

'Me too,' says Mack.

*

The following morning while I am enjoying a plateful of bacon, eggs, deep-fried white bread and hot tomatoes ...

'FLYING STATIONS.'

I wrap my rashers of bacon in a couple of slices of bread and leg it up to the Ops Room.

I'm the first arrive. One of the surface plotting team says, 'I think they're going to helicopter a boarding party to Bogey Charlie.'

Frothy arrives, a little out of breath. 'I was in the middle of shaving,' he says.

'I was just about to attack a slice of crispy fried bread,' I reply, waving my bacon butty 'Apparently, according to the surface team, we're going to fly a boarding party to the Dhow.'

'At this time of the day? Put your headphones on, see if you can raise Pontius.'

'X-ray Tango Four Three Four this is Golf Foxtrot Yankee Alpha, over.'

'Yes, I'm all present and correct. Looks like I'm the taxi driver this morning. Three passengers - Major Munro plus two armed Bootnecks ... sorry, Royal Marines.'

'Roger.'

'Ops Room this is Bridge. Is the helicopter control team closed up?'

'Yes, sir.'

'This is the Officer of the Watch speaking. The

situation is as follows. We will not take Bogey Charlie in tow. There is nowhere on the mainland where we can take the Dhow. We have requested advice from the Ministry of Defence but have not yet received a meaningful response. We are therefore going to board Bogey Charlie, issue the crew with an official Royal Naval bollocking and send it on its way.'

'Roger, sir. Are we transporting the entire boarding party by air?'

'Under discussion.'

'STAND DOWN FROM FLYING STATIONS.'

'Right then - I'm back to the dining hall to finish my fried bread,' I say as I remove my headphones.

'AWAY DHOW BOARDING PARTY. MUSTER AT THE STARBOARD ACCOMMODATION LADDER.'

I toss my headphones to the side. 'Never ferkin rains but it ferkin pours.'

Within ten minutes I'm skimming the RIB away with five armed Marines onboard plus Major Munro. Bogey Charlie is about five cables ahead. In the morning light, she has a weathered green-blue hull.

Major Munro shuffles himself to a position alongside me. 'I want you to put us parallel to the Dhow at a distance of about fifteen yards on her port beam so that I can communicate with the captain prior to boarding.'

'Aye aye, sir.'

Five minutes later I am positioned as requested. There is nobody visible onboard the Dhow.

Major Munro cups his hands. 'Ahoy there. Major Munro Royal Marines speaking. Can I speak with your captain .... over?'

Up close the Dhow looks like it had been around for some time: unpainted hull and a couple of stumpy masts.

Atop the hull is a single square structure at the stern with bare openings on both sides. The engine exhaust splutters thick grey smoke from a hole in the starboard quarter.

Nobody responds to Major Munro's request.

Major Munro re-cups his hands. 'Ahoy there. Major

Bogey Charlie

Munro Royal Marines speaking. Can I speak with your captain .... over?'

A young boy, no older than twelve or thirteen, leans his shoulders on the hull top and stares at us. He is wearing a white turban with the ends draped over his skinny shoulders.

'Can I speak to your captain?'

The young boy points to his bare chest.

'I would like to speak to your Captain.'

Once again the young boy pokes his chest.

'Are ... you ... the ... captain?'

No response.

'Capitan?'

The young boy smiles and nods.

'A knowledge of the local lingo generally helps,' Major Munro says to himself.

I watch in silence as he cups his hands and points them at the young boy. 'Do you have any objection to my coming onboard, Capitan?'

The young boy shakes his head, indicating that he doesn't understand.

'Do ... you ... have ... any ... objection ... to ... my ... coming ... onboard?'

The young boy disappears.

'I don't think he understands sir,' says one of the Royal Marines.

'Of course he does,' mumbles Major Munro. 'When it comes to the crunch they understand English perfectly well.' He claps his hands. 'Prepare for boarding. Put us alongside, coxswain - avoid that exhaust.'

I skim up to a position on the port beam.

'After me, men,' shouts Major Munro as he grabs hold of the gunwale top and hoists himself up and over. The five Royal Marines follow. Once all my passengers are safely onboard I slew myself away to a position about ten yards distant. I feel exposed, all by myself, no radio or anything ... and I'm not too sure how much fuel I have.

Within minutes one of the Royal Marines leans over the Dhow's gunwale and beckons me nearer. He cups his hands. 'The youngster is the only person onboard,' he shouts. 'Doesn't speak a word of English. The Major is trying to find out how old he is.'

Major Munro appears at the transom. 'Do you have a radio, coxswain?'

'No, sir. The radio man is onboard with you.'

'Of course he is ... I know that. Everybody back onboard the RIB!'

The Dhow's exhaust splutters.

Once everybody is onboard I'm instructed to return to *Gurkha*.

'That young lad is eleven at best - he's never been anywhere near a razor blade. Captain of a Dhow at the age of eleven, would you believe it?' says Major Munro to himself.

'Today sir, I would believe absolutely anything,' I say.

'Towing a barge full of explosives at his age.'

Back onboard *Gurkha*, Major Munro disappears up to the Bridge. I check the RIB's fuel. I've been running on fresh air and the priming can is empty.

In the dining hall all the warm, deep-fried bread has gone.

I give myself the rest of the morning off and I hope an unofficial afternoon make & mend.

That evening I come across Marine Browne, sitting on one of the Quarterdeck's washdeck lockers smoking.

'How are ya?' I ask.

'OK.'

'The raft was a banger, wasn't it?' I ask.

'I knew exactly what was going to happen, I've smelled that stuff before - and so had Lecky. Peculiar smell.'

'Really?' I don't have a clue what he's on about.

'Tomorrow's tot is yours, Pete. Just pop down our grot at the appropriate time.' He flicks his cigarette end over the side. 'To be honest I don't like the stuff much myself.'

'I'll see you then.'

'Lost my beret over the side of the RIB. Pissed off about that. Had it since I finished my initial training.'

'What a bastard!' I exclaim.

*

The following day at Tot-Time I present myself, a touch apprehensively, in the Royal Marines' mess.

'Peter, young man, take a seat, welcome to the mess,' says Marine Browne as he pours his own tot out from the unattended rum fanny. He hands his tot to me. 'Thanks for your driving the other day.'

I have to uphold the reputation of the forward Seamen's mess, so I down Marine Browne's tot in one.

I leave half an hour later, having downed a number of tots. I don't remember the stagger back to my mess, or clambering into my bunk.

My own tot is waiting for me.

I awake a few minutes before midnight. The mess is in total darkness; everyone is asleep. I have one hell of a headache and I want to be sick. I make it as far as the mess gash bucket.

'I put your tot in with Queen's,' says Jack.

I couldn't be less interested.

The remainder of the day is a blur.

*

As we wallow off the Mina Sulman Jetty, we request permission to berth alongside *USS New*, using her as a rather expensive and friendly fender. But she emphatically refuses: so much for Anglo-American relations. We berth at the far end of the jetty where the overflowing waste bins are located.

As soon as our brows are in place a delegation from *USS New* appears at the bottom of the brow. With respectful deference, a sharply uniformed group ceremonially returns our name-plate and ask Midshipman Bellringer, as Officer-of-the-Day, if the return of the undamaged name-plate would signify a truce between our two ships. The Midshipman makes a couple of telephone calls and on behalf of the entire crew declares a peace agreement.

Down the Seamen's mess we are formulating a plan to recapture their eagle.

'Distract the blokes at the top of their brow and ...'

'You mean those cowboys with six-guns on their hips?' I ask.

'They've got six-guns?' asks Mack. 'Loaded?'

'Probably.'

'So the distraction will have to be a clever one then?' says Jan.

'It will, yeah. If we have Kit with us, with the Land Rover, we can quickly flip their eagle onto the back seat and away.'

'What if it's bolted down?' asks Jan.

'Then we'll need a Stoker with a spanner ... an adjustable one.'

'An adjustable Stoker?'

'Why not?'

'That'll slow things doon,' says Mack.

'Shall we scrub round the whole idea then?'

'Yeah,' says Jan.

'Suppose so, yeah.'

'Lets go down to the Jufair Canteen and get pissed.'

'OK.'

'Lead on MacDuff.'

'MAIL IS NOW READY FOR COLLECTION.'

I receive a reply to my letter from Margaret, who lives in East Ardsley, near Wakefield in Yorkshire with her mum, dad and brother. She has sent me a couple of photographs: she's a good-looking girl and in one of the pictures she's sitting at the wheel of a car. She's twenty years old and has access to a car. I write her another letter and enclose a picture of myself in my jungle greens taken at Kota Tinggi a couple of years ago - that'll impress her.

*

'UP SPIRITS.'

The mess telephone rings. Burbs, who is nearest, picks up the receiver and almost drops it again.

'The Institute of Higher Education, Professor Mackintosh speaking.' He listens intently. 'Pete, the Bootnecks' mess want to see you.'

I hand my tot back to Jack. 'Put that with the Queen's,' I tell him.

Margaret Mary Lamin

'Sounds like I have to help the Marines cope with their rum issue ... once again.'

Jack ceremoniously pours my tot back into the fanny.

Down the Bootnecks' mess, Lance Corporal Dodger Long asks me if I want a coffee.

'No thanks.' I look around. The rum fanny is empty and all the tot glasses are stowed away.

'Have you been told to clean the RIB or help with the stripping of the outboards?' asks Dodger.

'Nope.' I say, more than a little disappointed.

'So it's just the Marines doing the crappy jobs again is it?'

'Dunno.'

Marine Browne waves a welcoming arm at me. 'Hiya Pete. If you'd been here five minutes ago you could have had my Tot.'

'Sorry,' I say. I really mean it. My tot will have been offered around by the time I get back to my mess.

'I'm going to see Lecky about this cleaning business,' says Dodger.

I can only offer one simple explanation. 'Maybe it's because I'm one of only two Helicopter Controllers onboard.'

Dodger spreads his arms wide. 'Maybe that's why then. OK then, Pete, see you when we next do battle with a suspicious Dhow.'

'OK, thanks.'

Back down the mess our tot glasses and rum fanny are stowed away and everybody has gone for dinner.

'WILL THOSE RESPONSIBLE FOR THE REMOVAL OF USS NEW'S EAGLE REPORT TO THE GANGWAY.'

'It must be the ferkin Stokers,' says Mack.

'Must be, yeah.' I agree.

'Thieving bastards.'

The following day the Buffer is beside himself at both watches. 'If any of you know who is responsible for nicking that blasted Eagle, I want to know,' he says.

'UP SPIRITS.'

Mack's been telling us that his Mido is waterproof,' says Jan. 'I think he should prove it.'

'How do I do that then?' asks Mack.

'Put it in your tot.'

'Whaaa?'

'Put it in yer tot. If it's waterproof it'll be OK.'

'I'll do it if Pete puts his in.'

I look at my tot and my watch. I've showered in it every day since I bought it - it's still working perfectly and Jan assures me it's genuine. 'You're on, mate.' I say.

'Contest!' Chats claps his hands. 'Contest!'

'You dunk yours first, Pete,' says Jan. 'Yours will be no problem.'

'I know.' I remove my watch and drop it confidently into my tot. Mack, Jan and Chats peer intently at my Rolex immersed fully in the amber liquid. The second hand ticks away. 'How long do I leave it?'

'About a minute?' asks Chats.

Jan nods agreement. He's a diver and knows about such things.

After a minute or so I remove my watch.

'Can I lick it dry for you?' asks Kit.

'Gerraway.' I lick it and wipe it on my shorts.

'Your turn now, Mack ... drop yewer watch in yer tot,' says Jan.

Mack slowly unbuckles his watch and hangs it tentatively over his glass.

'Gerritin,' says Kit.

'Give me a minute,' says Mack. 'This is an eleven-and-a-half Dinar ferkin watch this is.'

'Gerritin.'

Partially submerged, the first bubble escapes from the Mido. Mack misses it but Jan doesn't. 'All the way in, Mack - submerge the bugger.'

Mack grimaces and drops the watch. The bubbles escape in earnest.

'Looks like a glass of fizzy piss to me.'

The second hand stops.

'The bloke in the shop told me it was waterproof down to ten feet,' says Mack.

'But it's not tot-proof,' says Jan, grinning.

'I'll lick it dry for ya, Mack mate,' says Kit.

'On yer bike.'

'Worth asking,' says Kit, shrugging his shoulders.

Mack removes his dripping watch and drinks his tot.

Kit wipes his finger in the Mido's puddle, licks his finger and quickly scoops up the dregs.

'I've seen everything now,' says Chats.

We are all drinking our tots in contemplative silence when Sharky Ward slides down the mess ladder. 'If you want to see something unbelievable,' he says, 'take a butchers at what's going on, on the jetty.'

Along with Chats and Sugar, I scramble to the upper deck. At the end of the brow is a group of young Stokers dressed in their best suits with white webbing, caps with chin-stays down, and Lee Enfield rifles on their shoulders. Between the two ranks is a trolley on which is *USS New*'s Eagle. In charge of the squad is a very, very annoyed looking Petty Officer Stoker.

'Well, well, well,' says Chats.

'Indeed,' I say.

Midshipman Bellringer, dressed in his best suit and carrying a ceremonial sword, marches over the brow. 'Bring them to attention, Petty Officer!' he yells.

The Petty Officer Stoker shakes himself, pulls his shoulders back and coughs. 'Sqwadda ... Sqwadda ... Hay ... Ten ... shunna.'

The young Stokers are not prepared and come to something resembling 'attention' at very different times.

'Do that again, Petty Officer.'

The Petty Officer Stoker says something to his squad and tries again.

'March them off, Petty Officer.'

'Sqwadda ... Sqwadda ... By The Right ... Qwicka March.'

The two leading Stokers, who are not armed, each grab a handle of the trolley and the entire squad march semi-smartly down the jetty towards *USS New*.

'No bayonets then,' says Chats.

'Fixed bayonets would really put the shits up our American cousins,' replies Sugar.

'Must have been the Stokers who nicked the Eagle then,' I say.

Down the mess Mack gives the Mido a vigorous shake and watches while the second hand moves sluggishly for about ten seconds before stopping - for ever.

'Heap of shit ... one hundred percent knackered.'

'Tell the NAAFI Damager that the bloke in the shop

said it was waterproof,' I suggest.

'I ferkin well will.'

After dinner I'm near to the gangway enjoying a slice of afternoon sunshine when ...

'DUTY LAND ROVER DRIVER REPORT TO THE GANGWAY.'

Kit arrives, fresh from a shower, swinging the Land Rover keys from his index finger. 'I'm the duty Land Rover driver sir,' he says, brushing a lock of wet hair from his face. 'You caught me in the middle of a shower.'

The Officer-of-the-Day tells him to go and collect Midshipman Bellringer from *USS New*.

'Can't he walk half the length of the jetty then, sir?'

'It's what is known as looking after our crew members, Able Seaman Carson. Away you go - chop chop.'

'Very good, sir. Shall I run a shuttle service to collect all the Stokers as well?'

'That won't be necessary.'

'Aye aye, sir.' Kit tosses the Land Rover keys in the air and catches them before skipping over the brow.

Later this evening most of the mess are in the *Jufair* Canteen working on yet another Bahrain hangover. There's a large group of Americans in the far corner of the bar near to the door. A couple of Americans I recognise walk over flanking one of the largest blokes I have ever seen.

'Hello Buick, hello Merle,' I say.

'Hi,' says Buick rather frostily. What is it about our Eagle?'

'Dunno. You got it back I believe,' I say, half expecting a smile and a laugh.

'That is the second time that Jelly here has had to bolt the eagle back on the ceremonial plinth,' says Merle nodding at the big bloke.

Jelly nods and takes a large breath. 'I've been

instructed to use tamper-proof locking nuts this time,' he drawls.

'Would you like a beer?' asks Chats.

Sugar reaches up, taps Jelly on the shoulder and nods towards an empty table in the corner.

We buy beers that are nicely warm.

The bloke behind the bar shrugs his shoulders, 'If you want cold beer then we'll have to switch the fans off.'

'Then switch the ferkin fans off,' says Jan.

'When does *Gurkha* sail?' asks Merle.

'Tomorrow morning,' I say.

'Bound for where?'

'Ferk knows.'

'Don't take anything of ours, will ya? We're on our way back to the States at the end of the month.'

'We promise. You don't have anything of ours, do you?' Chats asks.

'Not as far as I know,' says Merle.

'So everything is where it should be then?'

'Yeah.'

Kit arrives, has a beer and offers Sugar, Chats and me a lift back to the ship.

Sugar asks Kit if he has room for his new friend Jelly.

Kit takes stock of Jelly's dimensions and pulls a doubtful face.

Jelly is silently pleading.

'I'll go on the roof if it helps,' I offer.

'That'll probably do it,' says Kit.

Outside we offer Jelly up to a short-base British Land Rover. He crawls onto the back seat and lies down, unable to manoeuvre himself into a sitting position.

'You going to sit on mi knee then?' Chats asks Sugar.

'I'll go on the roof with Pete.'

So it is that Kit drives the ship's Land Rover back along the Mina Sulman jetty with me and Sugar hanging onto the roof rack for dear life.

We stop opposite *USS New*. Extracting Jelly from the

back seat proves to be more difficult than installing him. It takes Sugar and Chats pulling from one side and Kit and I pushing from the other to get him onto the jetty in one piece.

In a surprisingly squeaky drawl Jelly thanks us for the ride and bounces up his ship's gangway without a backward glance. His trousers are all skew-whiff.

Chats and I stand and salute the Eagle before jumping in the Land Rover and screeching off to the top of the jetty ... and relative safety.

*

We leave Bahrain early the following morning, avoiding the ceremonial firing of any salutes. Having a reasonably fresh flow of wind across the ship is refreshing.

'Yesterday's noon temperature was logged at 124 degrees Fahrenheit,' says Jack for no apparent reason.

Down the mess is a pile of 'Crossing the Line' certificates, a pretty amateurish attempt in black and white. We each pick one. I write my name and rank in the appropriate place and toss it into my locker.

How many of these have you got, Pete?' asks Kit.

'A couple.'

'Only two?'

'Yep. How many you got then?'

'At least half a dozen.' He counts six using the fingers of both hands.

I am curled up in my bunk later that evening looking forward to half an hour or so with a crumpled, well thumbed copy of December 1963's edition of *Playboy* magazine when ...

'FLYING STATIONS. DHOW BOARDING PARTY MUSTER BY THE STARBOARD ACCOMMODATION LADDER.'

'Time to split yourself in two again, Pete,' says Jan from the bunk opposite.

I stuff the *Playboy* under my pillow. 'Yeah. Don't let anybody snaffle mi mag. I haven't got further than the first ferkin page.' I wriggle into my shorts, grab my steaming boots, my shirt and my cape.

I get to the accommodation ladder before the RIB. I look around for Sergeant Lecky. Marine Browne drapes an arm over my shoulder. 'The Sergeant has pulled a muscle,' he says.

I smile, expecting a humorous explanation.

'Seriously, he's pulled a major stomach muscle doing sit-ups and is incapacitated ... on light duties. Munro is really pissed off.'

'I bet he is.'

'Dodger is in charge today - he's helping to bring the RIB up.'

The RIB arrives as Major Munro appears. 'Coxswain. You have a dedicated radio operator with you this evening and Corporal Long is in charge of the Boarding Party.'

'Aye aye, sir.'

I hear the Wasp engine start up.

'Coxswain,' Major Munro continues, 'the Wasp is being scrambled to investigate a Dhow to the south of us. The Wasp should be in direct communication with your radio operator. Water conditions are good so I would expect you to reach the target Dhow in approximately fifteen minutes by which time the Wasp will have made a low pass and assessed how many crew are aboard. This is an intelligence-led boarding - that's as much as I can tell you.'

'RIB's at the ladder, coxswain, ready to board,' says someone.

In the RIB I quickly check the fuel situation.

Someone slaps me on the shoulder. It's Dodger - he of the massive hands. 'Here we go again, young Pete.'

Once everyone is onboard, Dodger sits the bloke with the radio down aft within shouting distance. We have an armed party of four Royal Marines including Marine Browne.

'When you're ready, Pete, let's go.' Dodger claps his hands together enthusiastically.

I open her up and slew away. 'Anybody got a compass?' I ask.

'I've got the Wasp visual,' says someone.

'That'll do me then,' I say and head in the direction of the Marine's pointed finger.

The water conditions according to those onboard *Gurkha* may be classified as 'good' but at sea level the water makes us bounce alarmingly at full throttle. I back it off a little until I regain full control.

'The Wasp has the Dhow visible and is doing a low pass, Corporal,' says the radio operator.

Dodger nods. He'd recently been soaked by a rogue goffer and is in silent, soaking-wet mode.

Marine Browne looks at me, points to his beret and mouths: 'New one.'

I give him a thumbs-up.

'The Wasp reports two crew visible, Corporal.'

'Thanks.' Dodger addresses his team. 'We'll adopt a normal boarding procedure - me first, radio man brings up the rear. No pissing about. I want this vessel secure within minutes.'

Within spitting distance the Dhow looks like it was thrown together from the remains of scrap vessels. It's stationary and wallowing on a bumpy sea. The Wasp hovers a good distance away to starboard. I put the RIB alongside the port side. Dodger is the first up and onboard followed by three others. By the time Marine Browne climbs onboard a Marine leans over the side and gives me a thumbs-up signal. I hear the radio man telling *Gurkha* that the target vessel is secure with a crew of three, one of whom is a young girl.

Dodger leans over the gunwale. 'Stay where you are, Pete,' he says. 'All is well and calm onboard. I'll whistle you in when we decide what to do.'

I can hear the radio man asking *Gurkha* for guidance as the only cargo they can find are cages full of birds ... live birds.

Gurkha asks: 'What kind of birds ... over?'

There is a pause. The radio man says, 'Nobody onboard speaks English and we don't have a bird expert in the Boarding Party ... sir, over.'

Gurkha replies: 'We shall close you. The Stores Officer claims to be a "twitcher" and can probably help in identifying the birds. Are they all the same or different?'

'All the same, sir ... I believe.'

'Retain command of the vessel until told otherwise.'

'Roger, sir.'

Eventually someone is told 'otherwise' and we have permission to return to mother - but to bring one of the birds with us.'

Dodger leans over the gunwale. 'We've got a bird Pete,' he says. 'We thought we'd take the most attractive one back to *Gurkha*.'

I throw a line to one of the Marines who takes a turn around something or other.

Marine Browne appears holding a large bamboo cage. I can't see what is inside from where I am.

'Do you want a bird, Pete?'

'Please ... but not the kind you've got in that ferkin cage.'

'It's a good-looking bird.'

'I'll take your word for it.'

One of the Marines clambers down into the RIB and carefully manhandles the cage. The bird wobbling inside has one heck of a beak. Its beady eyes stare at me, threatening me to make any sort of move.

'It can shit for England, this one,' says the Marine.

'But we're not anywhere near England.' I explain.

'You've got a good point there, young Pete. It can shit for the Middle East then.'

Dodger is the last one to clamber back onboard.

We wallow a couple of cables off *Gurkha*'s stern while the Wasp is recovered.

I secure the RIB to the bottom of the accommodation ladder and the bird cage is handed to an Officer who whisks it away to the Wardroom.

'It will probably take a while for the Wardroom to consult their I-Spy book of birds,' explains Dodger.

Eventually Major Munro appears at the top of the accommodation ladder and proclaims: 'The bird has been identified as a Saker Falcon, a rare species that is protected. The Dhow may not be running contraband but it looks like it could be trafficking rare birds. We are communicating with the relevant authorities in Bahrain and are waiting for a reply.'

'It's Friday, sir,' says Dodger.

'Friday?'

'Yes, sir. Doubt if you will receive an answer, sir.'

'Wait one,' and Major Munro scuttles up the ladder to the bridge.

'Can we have a smoke, Corporal?' someone asks.

'Negative ... oh sod it ... smoke if you want.'

A quarter of an hour later Major Munro re-appears. 'No reply from the Bahrain authorities. We have decided to let the Dhow proceed. Nothing is officially logged.'

'What shall we do with the bird we have onboard, sir?'

'The Stores Officer has agreed to look after it until we can hand it over to the relevant authorities.'

'Very good, sir.'

I leave the RIB for the Marines to put back on the Quarterdeck.

Down the mess I'm cross-examined by Sugar.

'What was the girl like?'

'Dunno.'

'What do ya mean ... you don't know?'

'I didn't see her.'

'Kids these days ... no ferkin initiative.'

The following day we pass through Elphinstone Creek once again. Our passage across the Persian Gulf is uneventful and we launch the Wasp once we are within range of Bahrain. Pontius says he has to have some technical servicing done at *RAF Muharraq*. We reckon that it's not the Wasp that's due a service and that he has an eye on one of the WRAFS.

The Mina Sulman jetty is empty apart from a couple of our Minesweepers.

'Could be because it's Ramadan,' says Chats. 'The month of fasting, religious contemplation and no smoking during daylight hours.'

'No ferkin smoking?'

'Who says that?' I ask.

'Nobody said anything to us about stopping smoking,' says Kit.

'You're having us on, Chats?'

'I'm not. Muslims aren't allowed to eat, drink or smoke during daylight hours during the holy month of Ramadan.'

'It doesn't apply to us though, does it?'

'Not really,' says Chats. 'But common sense dictates that you have to be careful when out and about during Ramadan. Openly smoking could be offensive to some, as could drinking anything ... and eating.'

'Blimey.'

We have to berth ourself, as the Minesweeper's crew are employed elsewhere: *HMS Jufair* canteen probably.

'MAIL IS NOW READY FOR COLLECTION. UP SPIRITS.'

A few of the lads receive letters from Leeds. One of the Communicators in the mess opposite has been writing to a girl called Pauline, who claims to be a management trainee and is writing a letter every day. She hasn't yet sent a photograph and he is getting a little worried as she says she plans to be in Rosyth when we return to the UK ... and he already has a so-called fiancée in Queensferry.

'What can I do, Pete?' He offers me a pile of unopened letters.

'I dunno. I only wrote to Moorhouse's - doesn't make me a relationship expert.'

'I know but ...'

'Not my problem - you're the Communicator, mate. Tell her that we are coming back to Plymouth instead of Rosyth ... she'll get the message when she's waiting for us to appear in Guz.'

'That's a good idea, thanks.'

'You going to tell her then?'

'Naah ... I'm not going to write to her anymore.'

'That poses an additional problem then.'

I have a letter from Wakefield. Margaret thanks me for the photograph I had sent and includes a couple more of herself: she's still an attractive girl. She explains that her car is a company car. She's twenty years old and has a company ruddy car. I ask her if we can meet when I come to Wakefield on leave sometime in early August. Fingers crossed.

The dinner-time chicken is pleasantly different.

'Chicken's good today,' declares Cliff.

'Something different,' declares Chats: our acclaimed scran expert. 'Different in a strange way ... but nice.'

'Must be the spices,' says Cliff.

'You're probably right, Cliff lad.'

Sugar joins us, places his plate full of minced beef on the table. 'One of the chefs was trying to tempt me with poultry,' he says. 'He told me that the young Chinese chef did something special with it today. Told him I don't like eating birds - never have.'

'Don't know what he's done with it, but it's brilliant,' says Chats. 'Succulent and spicy. I'll have a word with the duty chef before I leave. He can pass on our compliments to the Chinese Chef.'

*

In order to avoid upsetting those observing the holy month of Ramadan, we depart Bahrain and join a flotilla of craft anchored some distance away from peering eyes, where we can eat, smoke and drink unobserved for the remainder of the holy month. We pootle around the western Gulf for a few days until we convince Pontius that he should unravel himself from whatever comforts he is enjoying at *RAF Muharraq* and make his way back to mother with 'due dispatch'.

At dinner time we have a stew, dished out and knocked up by the smiling Chinese chef.

'What meat is it, chef?' asks Cliff.

'Same as yesser-dayah.'

'Yesterday's chicken was brilliant.'

'Than yew.'

Both Cliff and Wheelie grab a bowl and watch in silence as the smiling chef ladles them both a steaming measure of stew.

I opt for a couple of large, nicely browned Cumberland sausages, mashed potatoes and baked beans. I'm in an adventurous mood.

Both Cliff and Wheelie are halfway through their stew when ...

'DO YOU HEAR THERE, THE STORES OFFICER SPEAKING. WOULD ANYBODY KNOWING THE WHEREABOUTS OF A LARGE CAGED BIRD, KNOWN AS A SAKER FALCON, PLEASE CONTACT THE OFFICER OF THE DAY. IT WAS LAST SEEN, IN ITS CAGE, OUTSIDE MY CABIN THAT IS OPPOSITE THE WARDROOM PANTRY, YESTERDAY MORNING.'

Sugar and Kit join us. 'There's a rumour going around that the young Chinese chef had something to do with its disappearance,' says Kit pointing at the Tannoy.

'Whaa?' yells Cliff who throws his spoon onto the table and leans back in his chair. 'You're not telling me ...

'It's only a rumour,' says Sugar.

'You know what the Chinese are like ... they'll eat anything,' I add.

'Even falcon?' asks Wheelie as he tosses his empty spoon into his bowl with a clatter.

'You did say that the chicken tasted different yesterday, Cliff,' says Sugar.

'And the falcon's been missing since yesterday morning ... from outside the wardroom pantry,' says Kit.

Cliff jabs a finger at the remains of his stew. 'That tastes the same as yesterday's chicken. That could be ferkin falcon.'

'Falcon stew,' says Sugar, smiling. 'Duty Chef said poultry... not chicken.'

'That's it then, isn't it?' spurts Wheelie before taking a long swig of water. 'We've been eating ferkin falcon.'

'I knew there was something different about it,' says Cliff.

Kit slowly gets to his feet. 'I'll go and see the killick chef, clear this up.'

We all sit in silence and watch Sugar dig in to his sausages.

Kit returns. 'The Chinese chef is being cross-examined by the PO chef. Someone from the Stoker's table found a curly claw in his stew.'

'Shit.' Wheelie pushes his bowl away. 'Shit.'

'How are your bangers Shug?' I ask.

'Brilliant, Pete mate ... brilliant. How are yours?'

'Fabulous ... fabulous, thank you for asking, Shug.'

*

'FLYING STATIONS.'

It's my turn. Pontius is very chatty as he skims his machine towards us at five hundred feet. He reports that he only has official mail onboard.

'He's had more than his flying machine serviced,' says Frothy who has sneaked alongside me and is putting Mack's headphones on. 'You can tell by the tone of his voice.'

'Can ya?'

'Yeah ... like someone who has recently had a good overhaul.'

Once Pontius and his machine are safely back onboard, I wander down the Quarterdeck where I help with the cleaning and servicing of the RIB.

Dodger tells me that some of his lads were detailed off this morning to do sentry for a chef who's in the forward cell.

'That could be the chef who cooked up the falcon we took from the Dhow the other day,' I say.

'He what?'

'Cooked that falcon we took from the Dhow.'

'Chinese eh? They'll eat anything, won't they?'

'A couple of our lads said it was nice ... succulent in fact.'

*

We are cruising the south coast of Arabia, off a place called Taqah, when ...

'THE INFORMATION OFFICER SPEAKING. WE HAVE RECEIVED A SIGNAL INSTRUCTING US TO PROCEED TO THE SEYCHELLES WITH ALL HASTE TO HELP QUELL CIVIL UNREST. OUR ETA IS EARLY THURSDAY 30TH JUNE.'

'Anybody been to the Seychelles before?'

'I have,' says Chats.

'And?' asks Sugar.

'Brilliant place. Lots of dusky women.'

'Geographically what's it like?' asks Wheelie.

'You are taking the piss, Wheelie ... I was talking about dusky women.'

'Sorry.'

'More info about these dusky women then, Chats?' says Timber.

'There's a French influence, some people still speak French despite it being very English in some parts. It's a bit run-down but the people are friendly enough. The dusky women in particular.'

'Waah hey!'

'Shower time.'

'Get the foo-foo out, lads.'

One of the Communicators from the opposite mess tells us the officially logged midday temperature today was 113 degrees Fahrenheit. It's getting cooler.

Two and a half days later we are 125 miles to the north, and within Wasp range of the Seychelles.

In the Ops Room, Frothy explains that we are to shuttle our Royal Marines into the town of Victoria to support the local authorities; three fully kitted and armed Marines each trip.

'Careful with the first trip, Broadbent - the Sergeant and Major Munro will be onboard,' says Frothy.

After the first trip Pontius informs us that there is a Royal Navy frigate anchored off the harbour flying a yellow flag.

'A yellow flag means the ship is medically quarantined,' I say to Frothy, remembering it from my Leading Seaman's examination.

I control a couple more trips and am relieved by Mack who takes control for the last couple of trips.

We establish contact with *HMS Carysfort* who

explains that she has an outbreak of something really infectious onboard. She is in quarantine and all leave has been cancelled. She can't help us with quelling any civil unrest.

'THE STORES OFFICER SPEAKING. THE WHERABOUTS OF THE MISSING SAKER FALCON ... AN ENDANGERED SPECIES ... HAS BEEN ESTABLISHED. IT IS OFFICIALLY BROWN-BREAD. A SEARCH IS NO LONGER NECESSARY. THAT IS ALL. AYO GURKHA.'

Down the mess Cliff looks at Wheelie. Wheelie looks at Cliff.

'Not only have we eaten falcon ... but it was a dangerous one,' says Cliff.

'He said endangered ... not dangerous,' corrects Chats from behind his book.

Wheelie takes a deep breath. 'We survived though, didn't we mate?'

'What's endangered mean?' asks Cliff.

'Means it was rare,' says Chats.

'Looked well done to me,' says Sugar.

'The Chinese chef is in the cell apparently,' I say.

'Bastard!' says Cliff.

'At least you didn't get a claw,' says Sugar, smirking.

'That's OK then,' says Cliff before shooting off up the mess ladder.

'You've upset him now,' explains Wheelie.

We wallow off the port of Victoria waiting for a report from Major Munro. Eventually we are assured by Sergeant Lecky that all is quiet ashore and that the island authorities have officially declared that the civil unrest has been quelled. Our Royal Marines are currently deployed at the bottom of the jetty alongside a landmark clock called 'Little Ben' and are awaiting further instructions.

We lower the whaler. The Jimmy, the Buffer and a

couple of experienced Seamen are sent to survey the wooden jetty to ascertain if we can berth alongside. They return with the news that the jetty is in danger of imminent collapse and suggest that we anchor off.

'FORECASTLE PART OF SHIP SEAMEN AND CHIEF SHIPWRIGHT MUSTER ON THE FORECASTLE. 'UP SPIRITS.'

Gurkha anchors within spitting distance of Victoria's rickety wooden jetty.

'Are we going to be allowed ashore?' asks Jack while dishing out the first of the tots.

'Dunno.'

'Wonder what type of infection Carysfort has then?'

'I don't ferkin know, do I?' says Kit.

'Your sippers are bordering on wets, Jack.'

'Sorry.'

'There are dusky women ashore waiting for us ... apparently,' says Jack.

'He-he.'

'THE INFORMATION OFFICER SPEAKING. ON THE ADVICE OF THE ONSHORE HEALTH AUTHORITIES WE CAN ONLY GRANT SHORE LEAVE TO THOSE WHO HAVE BEEN VACCINATED AGAINST HEPATITIS B. VACCINATIONS WILL BE ADMINISTERED BY LOCAL STAFF AND WILL TAKE PLACE IN THE JUNIOR RATES DINING HALL AS SOON AS SUPPLIES OF THE VACCINE ARE RECEIVED ONBOARD. AYO GURKHALI.'

'Must be Hepatitis Bravo then,' says Kit.

'Nothing gets passed you, does it mate?' says Chats.

'Lets go and get in the queue,' says Sugar.

'The prospect of dusky women has got Shug all wound up,' explains Mack.

'Did you tackle the NAAFI Damager about your Mido?' I ask Mack.

'Yeah. He said take it up with the shopkeeper in Aden.'

'That's easier said than done then. Are you still paying your monthly instalment?'

'Aye.'

In the canteen there are two queues for vaccines. The longer one for those wishing to be jabbed by the little male nurse snakes around the canteen bulkheads. The other, much shorter queue, is for jabbing by an attractive middle-aged female nurse who has noticeable shakes and is wearing thick-lens spectacles.

Sugar and I decide to join the shorter queue as we will get ashore quicker. Ahead of me Sugar is jabbed by the middle-aged nurse who giggles and smiles coyly at something he says. Unbelievably, after jabbing him, she gives him a kiss on the cheek as she helps him pull the sleeve of his shirt down. She stamps his hand with an indelible blue stamp. Unsmiling, she calls me forward. She waggles her fingers at Sugar as he departs. She jabs and stamps me. I don't get a kiss and I have to unroll my own sleeve.

'Let's get amongst it then, lads,' Sugar says down the mess.

Cliff and Mack are detailed off as boats' crew for the evening. I decide to accept Sugar's invitation and go ashore with him: after all, what better run-ashore oppo could I have than Shug, who has already made an impression on one of the Seychelles ladies ... without setting a foot ashore?

A member of the local Police Force checks our blue stamp before we are allowed into the whaler.

'Don't drink the local water whatever you do,' says the Officer-of-the-Day. 'The local authorities have yet to identify the source of the infection.'

'Do we have any Pusser's johnnies?' Cliff asks the Quartermaster.

'Not today, Cliff lad. Maybe tomorrow ... so keep it in your pants.'

'Bugger!'

The whaler drops us at the bottom of a badly rusted vertical ladder on the side of the frail wooden jetty. Sugar and I wipe our hands on a coir boat fender as we crest the ladder. It's a busy, working jetty awash with nets, fenders and other associated fishing equipment. Men in thin, colourful shirts, sarongs or shorts, lounge around. They acknowledge our greeting. I half expect a female member of the island's medical staff with an attractive, dusky companion to be waiting for us, but unfortunately not.

It takes us about ten minutes to walk down the jetty. At the base of the jetty where it joins the Island proper is a tower that looks strangely familiar.

'What does that look like?' I ask Sugar.

'Looks like a miniature version of Big Ben.'

Then it clicks. 'That could be what the Booties called Little Ben this morning.'

'Probably,' says Sugar ,rubbing his hands together. Now all we have to do is find a place called the Blue Cross Bar.'

'How do you know about ... where to go?'

'You don't honestly think I was chatting up the lady nurse who jabbed me for nothing, do ya?'

'I did wonder.'

'I have it on good authority that the town's nurses congregate at the Blue Cross Bar.' He checks the time on my Rolex. 'Around about now.'

'But she kissed you, Shug.'

'That was because I didn't cry or faint when she jabbed me.'

'You don't normally faint when you're jabbed, do you?'

Little Ben

'No ... but she didn't know that. I mentioned that the nurses in England gave us boys a kiss if we don't cry after being jabbed.'

'And she believed you?'

'Must have. I'm a well practised bullshitter.'

I stare at the cloudless blue sky. 'You can say that again.'

He taps my shoulder. 'It's a God-given gift I have, Pete lad.'

Between us we manage to ask a local policeman where the Blue Cross Bar is and we are directed, by a series of sweeping arm gestures, to a back street.

I am pleased to see a pair of large air conditioning thingies on the outside wall.

Inside we battle our way through a crowd of blokes in nurses' uniform at the bar. Eventually we manage to order a couple of John Collins.

'Ice with that sir?' asks the barman.

'Yes please.'

We settle ourselves in a corner of what we quickly realise is a male-dominated bar.

'Do you see any women?' I ask.

'I think,' says Sugar, his eyes scanning the joint, 'we've been sold a bummer.'

'Don't say that too loud, Shug.'

We both laugh briefly, until we attract the attention of a couple of large bearded nurses.

'We had ice in our drinks,' says Sugar.

'Aaarrgh ... so we did.' I reply.

'How stupid are we?'

'And here we are in a bar full of men.'

'Drink up, let's get out of here.'

After a few more failed attempts to find a bar containing anything but men we ask an English barmen where all the women are

'Là où tous Officers sont? ... where are all our Officers?'

'Grand Hotel ...piscine peut-être.'

'Grand Hotel around the pool maybe,' I translate.

We get reasonably accurate directions to the Grand Hotel from two over-friendly nurses.

After a few false alarms we find ourselves a vacant table on the Grand Hotel's veranda overlooking the pool area. There are no women.

A couple of our ship's Officers are sitting at a table opposite. One was the guy who told me to get my hair cut some months ago: he doesn't recognise me. They try hard to ignore us but have to return a rather embarrassed wave eventually. A very attractive, willowy lady serves our table. Sugar tries all his best chat-up lines but to no avail.

'Lesbian,' declares Sugar as she departs out of earshot

'Not necessarily,' I reply.

'Bet you I'm right.'

Sugar initiates me into the delights of neat Macallans

whisky for which I will be forever grateful.

The last boat back to the ship is 01:00. Thanks to the relaxing properties of Macallans, we catch it by the skin of our teeth. Cliff is the stern-sheetsman.

'How did Sugar get on?' he asks me.

'He didn't,' I reply. 'Must be the Hepatitis scare that has kept the women away from us.'

'No?'

'Could be,' I say.

'Ferk me,' exclaims Cliff.

'Don't bend over, Cliff lad ... or Sugar probably will.'

*

'MAIL IS NOW READY FOR COLLECTION.'

In principle I've got a confirmed date with Margaret Mary Lamin from East Ardsley. If everything goes according to plan I should have the first weekend off after arriving in Rosyth as I'd volunteered for second summer leave. I write suggesting that we meet outside the Wakefield Mecca at 3pm on Saturday 6th August.

12
Abandon ship!

THE ROYAL Marines execute an orderly dawn withdrawal from Victoria town. We shuttle them back onboard using the whaler.

'FORECASTLE SEAMEN AND CHIEF SHIPWRIGHT MUSTER ON THE FORECASTLE. SPECIAL SEA DUTYMEN WILL CLOSE UP AT 07:45. HANDS OUT OF THE RIG OF THE DAY CLEAR OFF THE UPPER DECK. CLOSE ALL UPPER DECK SCREEN DOORS AND HATCHES. STOW ALL BOOMS AND LADDERS.'

We haul in our anchor, which comes up surprisingly clean. As we fall-in for leaving harbour a few of us notice a pair of willowy, dusky ladies on the far end of the jetty both waving something lacy. They certainly aren't waving at any of us from the Seamen's mess ... unless someone was being uncharacteristically tight-lipped.

'Anybody know who they are?' asks Sugar.

Silence.

'They don't look like anything the Stokers would attract.'

'Quiet in the ranks,' someone orders.

We gaze in silence as we drift away from the Seychelles. Personally I don't think our visit was long enough to find the heart - and the affection of the people - notably the dusky ladies.

Later down the mess ...

'Did anyone have a sexual encounter of any description while visiting the Seychelles?'

'Somebody did. Did you see that couple of duskies on the end of the jetty?' asks Sugar.

'It's the first time I've ever seen anybody wave farewell knickers in the air,' says Cliff.

'They weren't really waving their knickers, were they?' I ask.

'Not sure,' says a grinning Cliff. 'Good story though, isn't it?'

'UP SPIRITS.'

As Jack passes Chats his tot he asks if anyone has the result of England's opening match of the World Cup.

'I'll call the Communicators mess,' says Jan. He checks the number in our latest revision of the Ship's Internal Telephone Directory and dials it. 'Is that the Communications mess? This is Able Seaman Fletcher from the University of Seamanship. Can you tell me the result of England's opening match of the World Cup ... if it's not too much trouble?' He pulls a surprised expression. 'Thank you. You're not taking the piss, are ya?' he asks whoever is on the other end of the telephone.

'Well?' asks Chats.

Jan replaces the handset. 'Nil nil draw with Uruguay.'

'At least we didn't lose,' says Chats.

'You offered me sippers yesterday,' Mack says to Jan.
'Did I. Why?'
'As a sign of friendship.'
'That's ferkin bollocks.'
'Naah, you promised.'
'Bollocks.'
'So, no sippers then.'
Jan downs his tot in one and waves his empty glass in front of Mack.
'Definitely not - have a snifters if you want.'
'You're a tryer, Mack, I'll give you that,' says Chats.

*

We head north, bound for the delights of Aden. A few of the lads who are still writing to Moorhouse girls are beginning to think about going to Leeds when they are next on leave. I keep my arrangements to myself.

I am awakened by ...

'ABANDON SHIP. CLEAR LOWER DECK. MUSTER AT YOUR ABANDON SHIP STATIONS. THIS IS NOT AN EXERCISE. I REPEAT THIS NOT AN EXERCISE. CLEAR LOWER DECK. MUSTER AT YOUR ABANDON SHIP STATIONS.'

'Shit.' It's exactly one thirty-three in the morning.
'What the ferk is going on?'
'Get out of your stinkin' pit!' yells Chats.
'Where is my abandon ship station?'
'Just get up top. Don't sit there putting your ferkin shoes on ... get out of here,' shouts Chats.

There scrambling bodies everywhere. Everybody is trying to get dressed at the same time: it's panic.

In the passageway above the mess it's obvious that something is wrong: there is a burning smell coming from aft. Blokes in fire-fighting suits are dragging hoses and fire extinguishers aft. There is a scramble up the ladder to the upper deck.

Gurkha is stopped and wallowing. I think my abandon ship station is on the starboard side of 01 deck forward of the starboard whaler. I amble about, not knowing exactly what to do. This is one exercise that we have never practised before ... and this is not an exercise.

Sparks are coming out of the forward funnel and the area surrounding both funnels is out-of-bounds and already roped off.

'It's an engine-room fire. The automatic steam drenching system is activated,' someone says.

'And boundary cooling on the forward bulkhead because that's a magazine,' says someone else.

'What prick designed it that way then?'

'I've left my fags down below.'

'Me too.'

'I've left my watch by my bunk,' I say.

'Are there any sharks in this ocean?'

'Loads.'

'Who's got fags?'

'I've got some.'

'Gerrem out then.'

'Where are the ferkin lifejackets?'

'Buffer's Store.'

'It'll be ferkin locked.'

'Stay together. Do not wander around,' someone in authority shouts.

There is nobody on the Bridge wing.

The waters of the Indian Ocean look uninviting and dangerous all of a sudden.

'ALL HANDS ARE TO REMAIN AT THEIR ABANDON SHIP STATION. THE ENGINE ROOM FIRE IS UNDER CONTROL. YOU WILL BE INFORMED WHEN IT IS SAFE TO RETURN TO YOUR MESSES. REMAIN AT YOUR ABANDON SHIP STATION.'

'I've got the morning watch.'

'I'm going down the mess to get my watch,' I say.

'Don't be a ferkin idiot. You're staying here,' says Chats.

'I'm still paying for it,' I whisper.

The night chill slowly gets to all of us and for a couple of hours we sit huddled in a morose, silent heap out of the wind.

Eventually we get the order to return to our mess and I'm glad to find that my watch, my fags and my lighter are exactly where I'd left them.

A small bunch of us make a wet, light up and muster around the mess table getting our nicotine levels back to something like normal and discussing what an engine room fire means.

'Could mean a loss of electrical power.'

'Water rationing.'

'Lights are still on though,' says Jan.

'Hope nobody was hurt. Stokers I mean.'

'Never thought of that.'

Eventually, unlike those unfortunate enough to have the morning watch, I crawl back into my bunk, give my watch a welcome tap and sleep rather fitfully until the morning.

The following day, more fire information becomes available. The engine room is badly damaged. The automatic steam drenching system worked perfectly and minimised equipment damage. Thankfully, there are no casualties as nobody was in the engine room at the time. The exact cause has yet to be established and teams of experts from the Portsmouth and Rosyth Fleet Maintenance Units are on their way to Aden. We are making-way slowly on our auxiliary engine but have insufficient fuel to reach Aden. It is rumoured that we probably won't be allowed through the Suez without main engines and will have to return home via the Cape of Good Hope. That could significantly delay the time we arrive back in Rosyth and jeopardise my date with Margaret from Wakefield.

'WE HAVE ARRANGED FOR AN RFA TO RENDEZVOUS WITH US TO SUPPLY ADDITIONAL FUEL. THE FRESH WATER SITUATION WILL BECOME SERIOUS AS FROM THE FIRST DOG WATCH TODAY. FRESH WATER IS TO BE CONSERVED.'

'What did I ferkin tell ya?' says Kit.

'You'll be OK. You can officially scrub round your monthly shower,' says Jan.

'The great toilet roll shortage, almost having to abandon ship in shark-infested waters and now a shortage of water,' mumbles Kit. 'Life's a bitch.'

'Shortage of water should be no trouble to you, Kit. The only time your towel gets wet is every two months when it finds its own way to the laundry.'

'On yer bike.'

*

For the next three days we slowly push our way north. Our fresh water tanks are empty and we can't replenish them. Against the oncoming tide we are just losing and getting pushed further away from Aden.

We rendezvous with a Royal Fleet Auxiliary who gives us enough fuel to get us to Aden. The situation in the main engine room varies depending on who you speak to. A young Stoker, who works in the Senior Rates pantry, tells me that the engine room is a total 'write off'. Someone else, with a two-star Stokers' badge on his arm, tells me that there is only slight damage and that it's repairable.

Whatever the truth, we seamen are only interested in whether *Gurkha* will be allowed through the Suez Canal and that we will be home on time.

HMS Londonderry appears over the horizon. As she closes she sends a message, 'What can we smell?'

I don't know what our official response is.

'THE PERSONAL HYGIENE OFFICER SPEAKING. WE WILL BE RUNNING A SHUTTLE SERVICE TO AND FROM HMS LONDONDERRY SO THAT OUR FIRE FIGHTING AND DAMAGE CONTROL TEAMS CAN SHOWER FIRST. OTHERS REQUIRING A SHOWER WILL FORM AN ORDERLY QUEUE AT THE STARBOARD ACCOMMODATION LADDER. AWAY SEABOATS CREW.'

Nobody in our mess was actively involved in fighting the fire or damage control.

'Have you seen the bathrooms on that class of boats?' says Chats. 'She's a Rothesay Type anti-sub Frigate and the bathrooms are crap.'

'A rub-down with the mess cloth and an oily rag should do it,' says Kit.

An hour later Bagsy and Wheelie, both whaler's crew, come down the mess soaked through.

'The ferkin wind has got up,' explains Bagsy.

'Londonderry is a heap of shit ... rust bucket,' says Wheelie.

'We only had five for showers,' says Bagsy vigorously wiping his hair with his towel. 'Sergeant Lecky, two marines, the number one Chinese laundry man, who was part of the damage control team apparently, and ... I can't remember the other one.'

'NAAFI Manager,' says Wheelie.

'That was him ... yeah.'

'He likes his showers, does the NAAFI Manager,' says Jan.

*

If anything, Aden looks less inviting than before. An un-quarantined *HMS Carysfort* is berthed on the far end of Admiralty Jetty. No sooner have we found a spare section of the same jetty large enough to accommodate us than ...

'THE DIVING OFFICER AND ALL SHIP'S DIVERS MUSTER ON THE QUARTERDECK. ALL SHIP'S DIVERS.'

'Here we go again,' says Jan.

The Army are much in evidence, armed and dangerous, protecting access to the jetty, *HMS Carysfort* and us.

The Fleet Maintenance Unit personnel from Portsmouth and Rosyth are waiting in an organised heap on the jetty. Behind them are numerous crates of guarded equipment and a long-armed crane.

As soon as the brows are rigged, overalled engineers scramble onboard and the crane plonks all the equipment crates on our quarterdeck. *Gurkha* has a bit of a rake on.

'MAIL IS NOW READY FOR COLLECTION.'

There are few 'Dear Johns' from the Moorhouse girls.

'How dare she!' says Cliff as he waves a sheet of blue airmail paper.

'What's she done?'

'Refused to come over to Otley when I'm on leave.'

'Where's ferkin Otley?' asks Kit.

'Yorkshire. Just north of Leeds.'

'Why don't you go to Leeds then?' I ask.

'Don't want to appear too keen, do I?'

'Stalemate then.'

'Mine's a definite 'Dear John',' says Stormy.

'What does she say?'

'Told me to ferk off.'

'That's not the kind of language I would expect from a lady who works in Leeds,' I say.

'She's only four foot eight tall. Coupled with her foul ferkin mouth it wouldn't have been much of a match.'

'Why's she told you to ferk off then?' asks Jan.

'Dunno.'

'She must have had a reason.'

'I sent her a photograph.'

'That'll be why then,' says Jan.

'It was a picture of you I sent,' says Stormy.

'THE INFORMATION OFFICER SPEAKING. THE POLITICAL SITUATION IN ADEN HAS DETERIORATED SIGNIFICANTLY SINCE OUR LAST VISIT. UNTIL WE CAN ACCURATELY ASSESS THE SITUATION WE WILL NOT BE GRANTING SHORE LEAVE. OUR RELIEF HMS NUBIAN IS SCHEDULED TO BYPASS ADEN WITHIN THE NEXT FEW DAYS ON HER WAY TO BAHRAIN. WE ARE ASSURED THAT OUR PLACE IN THE NORTH BOUND SUEZ CANAL CONVOY IS CONFIRMED DESPITE THE DAMAGE TO OUR MAIN ENGINES. AT THE MOMENT OUR SCHEDULED ROSYTH ARRIVAL DATE REMAINS UNCHANGED.'

Eventually, having re-assessed the Middle East situation, shore leave is granted for a few hours to the none duty part of the watch. Mack and I go ashore with Chats to tackle the bloke who sold Mack the Mido. The shop where we bought our watches no longer exists. Mack and I know that it was next door to a place that sold hubbly-bubbly pipes and we find that easily enough. Next door is now boarded up and has no roof: distinctly derelict.

'Sod's, law Mack,' says Chats.

'Shit,' says Mack.

*

Towards the middle of July the last of the Fleet Maintenance Units packs up and departs. According to the Stokers, the important bits and pieces in the main engine room have been repaired or replaced and there is no reason why we shouldn't make it back to Rosyth on time.

'Wonder whether the fresh water situation will get back to normal?' asks Kit.

'Why would that interest you?'

'Cheeky sod.'

'England beat Mexico two nil,' says Chats as he places the bulkhead telephone back on its cradle.

'Who scored?'

'Bobby Charlton in the first half and Hunt in the second. And Uruguay beat the Frogs 2-1 yesterday.'

'So will we go top of our group if we beat the French then?' asks Wheelie who has been calculating the group positions. In real life, he's a Portsmouth supporter.

'Suppose so.'

'Why aren't any of our Scottish colleagues joining in the World Cup discussions?'

'They didn't qualify,' says Chats.

'Didn't they indeed?' says Jan, grinning.

'Piss off,' says Mack.

'Still planning on being a man of the cloth, Mack?'

'Of course.'

'You'll have to learn to control your temper and your ferkin language then.'

'THE ENGINEERING OFFICER SPEAKING. OUR BASIN TRAILS HAVE BEEN SUCCESSFULLY COMPLETED. OUR CONGRATULATIONS TO THE MARINE ENGINEERING DEPARTMENT FOR THEIR UNSTINTING EFFORTS IN GETTING GURKHA READY FOR SEA IN SUCH A SHORT TIME ... WITH THE SUPPORT OF THE FMU TEAMS FROM PORTSMOUTH AND ROSYTH. UP SPIRITS. AYO GURK ...'

'And Ayo Gurk to you, pal.'

'Did you offer me sippers?' Cliff asks Jack.

Jack ponders a moment. 'Of all the people onboard this war canoe you'd be the last to get even a snifter. I'd rather give a snifter to a Stoker ...'

'Surely not.'

'Why not?' asks Jack. 'At least they're going to get us back to bonny Scotland on time.'

'THE INFORMATION OFFICER SPEAKING. WE SHALL BE SAILING AT 05:45 TOMORROW MORNING. MAIL WILL CLOSE ONBOARD AT 23:30 FOR JUNIOR RATES AND 23:59 FOR SENIOR RATES AND THE WARDROOM.'

Chats finishes his tot. 'That's probably because we can write quicker than they can.'

'So that's it! I thought they were discriminating unnecessarily,' says Kit, tapping his teeth with a pencil.

'Where did you drag that one up from?'

'He'll be in the Wardroom before long with bullshit statements like that,' says Chats.

'Bollocks,' says Kit.

'Belay my last ... no he won't. CW papers immediately withdrawn due to an outburst of bad language,' says Chats.

*

It's no effort at all for me to drag my body out of my bunk at some ungodly hour the following day. Like everybody else I'm pleased to be leaving Aden and the Middle East behind and to be heading north to the ever-so-slightly more stimulating shores of Fife.

We slip away from Aden's Admiralty Jetty for the last time as the sun casts its long early-morning shadows. Quietly and without fuss or salutes, with only Seamen on the upper deck, we leave Aden's charms behind.

It's a morning of lounging around on the upper deck, soaking up the Red Sea sun as we pass the Island of Mayyun to starboard and trundle our way north. All we upper deck Seamen have deeply weathered tans that will distinguish us as travellers back home.

'UP SPIRITS.'

'So that's it then, lads. What did you think of the Middle East?' asks Chats.

'Different.'

'Absolutely rubbish.'

'Culture shock then?'

'Sure was.'

'Looking forward to getting back home then ... Rosyth?'

'Yeah,' says Mack.

'There speaks a Scotsman.'

'Rosyth ... twinned with Abadan.'

Everybody, except Mack and Burbs, finds that hilarious.

*

Chats, Wheelie and I are lounging on a couple of washdeck lockers in the port waste, enjoying the fresh air, smoking, drinking our allotted two cans of evening beer and flicking our dog ends into the Red Sea. Exactly the same as we did eight months ago on our way south.

'Roll on the Med,' says Wheelie.

'Can't wait,' I say.

'We beat the Frogs two nil,' says Chats as he lights a cigarette.

'So how are we placed in the group now?' I ask.

'Top,' says Wheelie, confidently.

'Who scored?'

'Dunno.'

'What was the high point of your eight months in the Middle East then, Pete?' asks Chats.

It takes me a couple of seconds to come up with it. 'The backside ... the stern of the free girl in Mombasa.'

'Good answer - but I meant what was the high point of your trip ... culturally?'

'Told ya - the rear end of the girl in Mombasa.' I hand my cigarette packet to Wheelie.

'See if I can get some sense out of you, Wheelie. What was the high point of the last eight months for you?'

Wheelie inhales deeply, closes his eyes and slowly lets the smoke drift out of his nose. 'Having given your question some thought ... I think I haven't got one.'

Chats flicks his half-smoked cigarette into the Red Sea and storms off.

'What was your high point then, Chats?' I ask before he reaches the ladder.

'I kept it in my trousers so I haven't got one either,' he says with a smirk and disappears.

'I'm looking forward to getting back to civilisation though, aren't you?' asks Wheelie.

'Sure am.'

'Pity we're going to Rosyth then.'

*

'UP SPIRITS.'

We have been devoid of female company for too long and the tot-time discussions are becoming more sexual by the day. Today's subject of conversation is women's underwear.

It's a surprise to learn that Jack's favourite colour of female underwear is brown.

'I always check the label on the back of bra's ... so I know what I'm dealing with,' says Kit, smirking.

'It's a good bet that at that stage, you're dealing with tits,' says Jack.

'We had a locker full of knickers on Bermuda ... women's knickers,' I say as my contribution to today's discussion.

'Wha?' asks Jack.

I take a deep breath. 'Locker sixty-six ... full of knicks. Some freely given, most of them nicked ... so I was told.'

'Nicked knickers?'

'Most of them yeah.'

'A locker full ... never.'

Sugar bounds down the ladder and without saying a word holds his hand out for his tot.

Jack pours it, takes his sip but doesn't hand it over. 'Young Pete here reckons there was a locker full of nicked knickers on Bermuda. Correct or not, Shug? ... yours and Pete's tot depend on your honest response.'

'We did yeah ... Bermuda's messdeck locker number sixty-six.'

'Ferkin told ya ... ferkin told ya,' I say, grabbing the tot from Jack's hand, downing it in one, burping loudly and folding my arms.

'That was Sugar's tot,' says Jack.

'He can have mine,' I say.

Jack hands Sugar the next tot. Sugar knocks back half of it and exhales in a satisfied way. 'It was a unique collection,' he says. 'I myself donated a number of items.'

'Nicked or freely given?' asks Mack.

'Freely donated of course,' replies Sugar, staring lovingly at the remainder of his tot.

'Weird ship, Bermuda,' says Chats.

'Great ship,' I say indignantly.

Sugar finishes the other half of his tot. 'Locker sixty-six contained items going back to the nineteen forties apparently. It was a museum of female underwear.'

'Washed and clean?'

'Of course not.'

Sniggers all round.

'What happened to the contents of the locker when Bermuda went for scrap?' asks Kit.

'Got scrapped along with the rest of the ship I suppose,' says Sugar.

'Did you ever do a detailed itinerary of the contents, Shug?'

'Naah.'

'Any gentlemen's underpants in there?' asks Jan.

'We had some strange messdeck characters - so I suppose it was possible.'

'We kept our champion cockroach in locker sixty-six. Lived in there quite happily,' I say, in an attempt to elevate the subject above groin level.

'Ferk off,' says Jan.

'Now you really are pulling our plonkers,' says Burbs.

'It's true isn't it, Shug?' I ask.

'Yep. It had a little harness and every day its trainer would take Roger for a stroll around the Quarterdeck,' explains Sugar.

'Naah?'

'I know about cruisers' Quarterdecks,' Kit says, tapping his chest. 'The Quarterdeck was for Officers only.'

'And cockroaches under training ... we negotiated special permission,' says Sugar.

'Now you really are taking the piss,' says Burbs.

'Tell 'em, Pete,' says Sugar.

'Absolutely true.'

'You said a champion cockroach.'

'Correct,' I reply.

'And it had a trainer?'

'Of course - every successful cockie has to have a trainer. To keep it in pick fitness.'

'Peak, not pick,' whispers Sugar.

'Sorry ... peak fitness.'

'Bollocks,' says Jan.

'Roger was an athlete,' I add.

Jan holds his head in his hands and rolls backwards on his chair, almost falling over. 'Why Roger?'

'Roger Bannister of course.'

'You're a bullshitting pair of bastards.'

Sugar leans close to me. 'Don't tell them about the assault course we had rigged on the flag deck, Pete ... don't tell 'em.'

I look around at all the watching faces. 'No, I think we've said enough.'

'Why did you need a trained cockroach anyway - trained for what?' asks Kit.

'Because we had races,' I say.

'What kind of races?'

'Cocky races in the mess.'

'Ferk off.'

'We did,' says Sugar.

'Ferk off.'

'The Stokers' mess on Bermadoo collected women's shoes.'

'Aaarrggh,' Kit holds his head in his hands and bangs his fists on the tabletop in frustration.

'Stokers' mess locker number twenty-two ... all the twos, full of shoes.'

'That's bollocks that is - must be!' yells Kit.

'You Bermuda bastards are bullshit artists, weird bullshit artists,' says Burbs.

Everybody else, apart from me and Sugar, nods in agreement.

Nobody speaks to either of us for the rest of the day.

*

Our Suez Canal convoy leaves at midnight and consists of six other ships. Ahead of us is a small Italian ship that looks like a floating pile of rusting scrap metal. Behind us is a Turkish frigate. There is nothing like the *Arabian Enchantment* anywhere.

We steam through the Bitter Lakes and by noon the following day we enter the Mediterranean. We hear that England have beaten Argentina in the Quarter Final by a single goal scored by Geoff Hurst.

'Breath that air,' says Sugar, inflating his lungs on the back end of the Quarterdeck. 'Sand-free air.'

'Almost,' I say.

'Europe, where the women don't look like walking, no-talking Coca-Cola bottles.'

'Yeah.'

'You got a draught yet, Pete?'

'Yeah. Back to Dryad.'

'For what?'

'A ferkin RP1s course.'

'You?'

'Yeah ... would you Adam and ferkin Eve it?'

'Must be getting desperate.'

'You can say that again,' I mumble.

'Has anybody spoken to you today?' I ask.

'Yeah. Jack spoke to me after I gave him a wet of mi tot.'

'What did he say?'

'He said "Thanks, Sugar".'

'Nobody has spoken to me at all ... all day,' I say.

'It won't last - never does.'

*

It was programmed that we would make a 24-hour stop in Malta in order to collect mail, check our engine room repairs and give Lieutenant Margolis the opportunity to give his young Maltese wife of thirteen months a good 'seeing to'. But when England trounce Portugal 2-1 in the World Cup semi-final the Captain decides to steam directly to Gibraltar in time for the Final scheduled for 30th July.

'Who do we play in the final then?' asks Mack.

'What do you mean ... we? You're not in the ferkin final,' says Kit.

'You know what I mean,' says Mack, 'and watch your language. Remember who you're talking to - a future member of the effin clergy.'

Kit falls off his chair laughing.

'England play West Germany in the final. The Gerries beat the Ruskies yesterday,' says Wheelie.

'It's at Wembley. We'll smash 'em, says Kit.

Sugar slides down the mess ladder, stands in the mess square and opens his arms wide. 'Are Pete and I still in Coventry?'

'Naah.'

'No you're here - you're in the ferkin mess, aren't ya?'

'No, you were never officially in Coventry,' says Chats.

'I'll tell ya then,' says Sugar. 'We must be passing Malta because I've just seen a tearful Margolis staring out to sea with steam coming out of the bottom of his shorts.'

'With a big bulge in his trews no doubt,' Mack adds.

'That's not a clergy-like observation, young man,' says Kit.

Mack mouths 'sorry'.

'You got any contacts in Malta, Shug?'

'None that I care to own up to.'

13

England 4 - West Germany only 2

WE ARE within range of Gibraltar. The Captain has decided to send the Wasp in to collect mail instead of waiting until we dock tomorrow, as we will be arriving during the Cup Final.

'FLYING STATIONS.'

I look at Mack. Mack looks at me. We hadn't expected this and neither of us know who is duty controller.

'I'll do it,' I say. 'We English chaps have to stick together.'

'Sassenach,' splutters Mack, tapping me on the shoulder and scooting away.

I stumble up to the Ops Room. Frothy is busy talking with Pontius when I arrive.

'Golf Foxtrot Yankee Alpha this is X-Ray Tango 434, over.'

'This is Golf Foxtrot Yankee Alpha, over,' says Frothy.

'Pre flight check complete,' says Pontius. 'Ready for take-off. If you unexpectedly lose contact with me I may divert to Malaga for a night out.'

'Roger.'

'Only joking of course.'

'This is Golf Foxtrot Yankee Alpha. Understood, over.'

The Wasp returns within the hour with a couple of bags of mail. Pontius also claims to have onboard a couple of bottles of up-market alcohol to boost the Wardroom's depleted coffers.

'MAIL IS NOW READY FOR COLLECTION.'

I have a letter from Margaret who tells me how much she is looking forward to meeting me. She confirms our date outside the Wakefield Mecca on 6th August; she won't work that weekend. It looks like the letters from the other Moorhouse girls have dried up. Maybe they've chickened out now that *HMS Gurkha*'s finest and fittest are within striking distance of the UK.

Mack has a letter from home saying that his family will be in the dockyard to welcome him home. His younger sister wants to know if he has bought her any presents.

'Well, have ya?' asks Kit.

'Of course not.'

'You Scotsmen don't buy family members pressies then?'

'Never thought about it much,' says Mack.

Most of us nod understandingly.

'I did buy mysel' a pair of desert boots, yae ken,' says Mack.

'So you did,' says Kit.

'Do they know about your plans for the future ... you know, the clergy stuff?' asks Chats.

'Not yet ... no.'

'That should make a good pressie then.'

'THE INFORMATION OFFICER SPEAKING. TROPICAL WORKING ROUTINE IS NOW CANCELLED. TO MAKE US ALL FEEL AT HOME WE SHALL ADJUST GURKHA'S TIME TO BRITISH SUMMER TIME. THIS IS THE LAST TIME WE SHALL ADJUST GURKHA TIME AS SCOTLAND IS ALSO ON BRITISH SUMMER TIME. GURKHA TIME, GIVE OR TAKE A MINUTE, IS NOW ELEVEN FORTY-FIVE. UP SPIRITS AND AYO GURKHALI.'

'Total ferkin confusion with the dishing out of the rum today,' says Jack. 'Jack Dusty claims he didn't hear the pipe about tropical routine being cancelled ... and the clocks.'
'Bless the S&S department.'
'What time are they patching the game through?'

'THE SPORTS OFFICER SPEAKING. WE NOW HAVE A CLEAR CONNECTION WITH THE BBC WORLD SERVICE AND WILL BE PIPING THROUGH THE WORLD CUP FINAL AS FROM 15:40 GURKHA TIME. WE AIM TO BERTH ALONGSIDE AT HALF-TIME TO AVOID ANY CONFLICT WITH LOCAL DOCKYARD STAFF. SPECIAL SEA DUTYMEN CLOSE UP AT 15:20 GURKHA TIME. AYO WHATSIT.'

'Getting a bit bored with this 'Ayo Gurkhali' stuff,' says Kit as Jack is organising the glasses.
'You can tell it's getting close to getting home, can't ya?' says Cliff.
'Who is the ferkin Sports Officer anyway?'
'The one who most recently upset the Jimmy probably,' explains Chats. 'Let's clear up one thing now. We don't have any German supporters, do we?'
Silence.
'We've gorra beat the Gerries this time,' says Cliff.
'Yeah.'

'Ferkin right,' says our prospective 'man-of-the-cloth'.

The Skipper times everything to perfection. We berth alongside at exactly 15:40 *Gurkha* time. The score, with only five minutes to play of the first half of the 1966 World Cup Final, is England 1 West Germany 1.

The upper deck Tannoy system is broadcasting the match so we take our time tidying up. I get back down the mess to a rousing cheer. It isn't my arrival that everybody is celebrating, but Martin Peters' seventy-eighth minute goal. England have the lead and there is only twelve minutes to go until full time.

Convinced that we have the World Cup in the bag, I decide to go for a shower in preparation for a celebratory pub-crawl down Main Street this evening. We have loads of shoreside fresh water and the bathroom is steaming when someone flings open the door. 'The bastards have scored. The ferkin Gerries have equalised!'

'Wha?

'The bastards.'

'Ferkin bastards.'

'A German bloke called Weber scored.'

'The German bastard,' whoever is in the next shower cubicle shouts.

We all wrap our towels around us, collect our washing gear and flip-flop it back to our respective messes.

I plonk myself down on a spare bit of a bottom bunk near to the Tannoy.

'Fifteen minutes each way extra time,' explains Chats.

'The German bastards!' exclaims Burbs.

'Yeah, Burbs, we've done all that,' says Chats.

'Sorry.'

A dozen cigarettes are lit as the whistle blows to signal the start of the first period of extra time.

Eleven minutes later Geoff Hurst scores for us. Another dozen cigarettes are lit. The score is now England 3 West Germany 2.

'The bastards will equalise again ... you wait,' says Burbs.

'Think positive,' says Wheelie.

'There speaks one of the half-dozen Pompey supporters worldwide.'

At half-time Chats declares only fifteen minutes to go.

'Anything can happen in fifteen minutes,' says Mack.

'You can slope off up top if that's all you've got to contribute,' says Chats. 'Go on.'

Mack pretends to skulk away up the ladder as the whistle blows for the start of the second part of extra time. He returns to his seat alongside me and jabs me in the ribs and smiles. 'Today I'm an honorary England supporter.'

'I know you are, mate ... your holiness,' I say.

The game is sounding a bit scrappy and the commentator is getting on our nerves repeating the fact that England are on the verge of winning the World Cup for the very first time.

I'm not the only one who lights a cigarette from the stub of my previous one. The mess ashtrays are overflowing. My bum is itching because I'm sitting on a damp towel.

Then: goal of goals. Geoff Hurst scores again with only seconds to go. England have won the 1966 World Cup final by four goals to two.

'Up the West Germans.'

'Yeah ... right up the West Germans.'

'It'll be a great night down Main Street tonight,' says Chats.

In the distance we can hear fireworks and car horns blasting away.

'Two days' tot for anyone who will do my duty tonight,' says Kit.

'Ferk off.'

'No way.'

'Three days then,' says Kit.

'A week's tot and I'll consider it,' says Sugar.

'OK then, a week's tot.' Kit holds his hand out.

Sugar pretends to take Kit's hand. 'We'll be in Scotland in four days' time and you're going on draft the day we get in ... leaving the ship.'

'Didn't think you'd work it out.'

'It's me you're dealing with. I didn't come in on the last banana boat you know.'

We are the only ship in Gibraltar and have the pick of the bars: Main Street is awash with dancing, drunken *Gurkha* crew members, Union flags are everywhere. The Troc is bursting with *Gurkhas* who are encouraging a couple of girls serving behind the bar to 'Get your top off to celebrate winning the World Cup.'

The Wren from Pontefract says confidently that she's heard it all before and that if she was to show us anything it would be a knuckle sandwich.

The other girl, the flat-chested one with a noticeable Fu Manchu moustache, unbuttons her blouse and struts up and down in the hope that she might excite someone ... but she doesn't.

Goodness knows what time it is when we all stagger back onboard with a bilge full of local beer 'free surfacing' around our stomachs.

*

The following morning we are once again swamped by two Fleet Maintenance teams who scurry around everywhere checking the engine room.

'DO YOU HEAR THERE. THE SHIP IS UNDER SAILING ORDERS. IN ORDER TO MEET OUR ETA ROSYTH WE SHALL BE SAILING AT 14:00 THIS AFTERNOON. THE CAPTAIN HAS DECLARED TODAY A GURKHA HOLIDAY TO CELEBRATE ENGLAND'S WORLD CUP VICTORY. LEAVE IS GRANTED UNTIL

13:00 FOR JUNIOR RATES AND 13:30 FOR SENIOR RATES. YOU ARE REMINDED THAT LEAVE BREAKING WHILE THE SHIP IS UNDER SAILING ORDERS IS A SERIOUSLY PUNISHABLE OFFENCE ... DESPITE IT BEING A HOLIDAY. THE JOHN WAYNE FILM 'THE SEARCHERS' WILL BE SHOWN IN THE JUNIOR RATES DINING HALL IN 15 MINUTES. AYO GURKHALI.'

I agree to do the last couple of hours of Timber's forenoon watch on the gangway so that he can go ashore and get some restorative work done on his tattoo.

Chats is the relief Quartermaster. We both look at each other as a beat-up yellow van splutters to a halt at the bottom of the brow. A monster of a bloke rolls out of the driver's seat and tucks his threadbare T-shirt into his shorts as he stands and stares at us. He has an enormous stomach which he scratches as he stumbles up the brow, tripping up more than once over the raised tread-strips.

Chats positions himself at the top of the brow and waits.

Our large visitor stops at the top of the brow and looks down at Chats. There are beads of sweat on his forehead. He removes his cap, wipes his face and scratches the top of his head. 'Her Majesty Ship Gurkha?' he asks.

'Yes sir,' says Chats.

'Help me find bad man please?' he asks. He is not smiling.

'Help you find a bad man?'

I stay in the background, coiled like a rusty spring, ready to help if anything untoward should happen.

Our visitor hands Chats a slip of paper as the Officer-of-the-Day appears. 'Everything OK, Quartermaster?' he asks.

Chats waves our visitor onboard. 'Everything is in hand, sir,' he says as he unfolds the slip of paper, reads it and signals our visitor to stand away from the top of the brow. 'This gentleman says he wants to find a bad man.' He waves the slip of paper in front of the Officer-of-the-Day. 'He has given me this chit with Able Seaman Kayne's name on it.'

'Leave this with me,' says the Officer-of-the-Day.

'Aye aye, sir,' says Chats as he takes a few steps backwards.

The Officer-of-the Day walks over to where our visitor is patiently waiting. Our visitor is well over six feet tall with shoulders like an all-in wrestler. In contrast, our Officer-of-the Day is a wisp of a man with no shoulders to speak of. 'You wish to see a man called Able Seaman Kayne.'

'Yes ... I do, sir.'

'May I ask why you would like to see Able Seaman Kayne?'

'Private matter, sir.'

'I'm afraid, my good man, I need to have more information before I will see if we have an Able Seaman Kayne onboard this ship.'

'Able Seaman Kayne from Her Majesty's Ship Gurkha has dishonoured my family.'

'In what way, my good man?'

'He has ... err ... he has pregnated my daughter.'

'Pregnated your daughter?'

'Yes.' Our visitor inhales deeply, his enormous nipples protruding threateningly through the stretched fabric of his T-shirt.

The Officer-of-the-Day signals our visitor to stay where he is. He strolls over to our desk. 'We do have an Able Seaman Kayne onboard, Quartermaster, don't we?'

'Officially or unofficially, sir?' asks Chats.

'Pardon?'

'The Royal Navy doesn't normally comply with requests such as this, sir.'

'But we do have an Able Seaman Kayne onboard don't we, Quartermaster?'

'Unofficially we do, sir.'

'Pipe for Able Seaman Kayne to report to the brow then,' he says to me.

I grab the microphone.

Chats cups the microphone and swerves it away from me. 'If we do that, sir, our visitor will know that Shug ... that we have an Able Seaman Kayne onboard.'

'And?'

'It is not Royal Naval policy, sir ... to place a crew member in a sensitive situation without having heard his side of the story first.'

'Get me Able Seaman Kayne.'

'I'll go and have a look for him ... unofficially,' I say and slope away.

I know that Sugar will be in the dining hall because they are showing his favourite film yet again.

In the dining hall a bearded communicator is threading the second reel of the film through the complicated projector mechanism. Sugar is sitting in the centre of the front row.

I tap him on the shoulder. 'There's a big Gibraltarian bloke on the gangway asking to see you.'

'What?'

'A big bloke with an enormous stomach ... and threatening nipples.'

'Shit.'

'He's on the gangway and the Officer-of-the-Day wants to hand you over to him.'

'Oh no ... bugger.'

'The big bloke says you have ... pregnated his daughter.'

'Pregnated ... ferkin pregnated?'

Yeah ... that's what he said.'

'If it's who I think it is, we both enjoyed each other - she was more than a willing participant.'

'That'll probably make everything OK then.'

'It was a Europa Point job. On a gently sloping plot of

land with unrestricted views across the Mediterranean to North Africa.' He waves an arm. 'With the Trinity House lighthouse to the left of us. A memorable and romantic early evening, if I remember correctly.'

'I don't need a ferkin picture, Shug. This could be serious - her Dad looks like an all-in wrestler.'

'He is.'

'He's what?'

'Champion wrestler of Gibraltar. His daughter was also something of grappler.' Sugar forces a smile. 'Pregnated doesn't necessarily mean pregnant, does it?'

'I don't ferkin know, Shug.'

'Tell him that I'm not onboard. Great film this is, you know.'

The lights are switched off and almost immediately switched back on again. 'Will Able Seaman Kayne make himself known?' says a voice from the back of the room. It's the Officer-of-the Day, officially wearing his cap.

Sugar ducks and lies flat on the deck.

I walk up to the Officer-of-the-Day. 'I can't find anybody to confirm that Able Seaman Kayne is onboard, sir.'

'I've looked, Broadbent, I've looked. There is an Able Seaman Kayne on the Watch and Station Bill ... and he's duty watch.'

'He may have got a sub and gone ashore, sir.'

The Officer-of-the-Day stares at the blank white screen. 'Is there an Able Seaman Kayne here?'

Silence.

'For the last time, is there an Able Seaman Kayne here?'

Silence.

The Officer-of-the-Day waits for a while before stomping away.

Back at the gangway our visitor is still waiting, his muscular arms folded across the top of his bloated belly. The Officer-of-the Day grabs the Tannoy microphone.

'Able Seaman Kayne, report to the Officer-of-the-Day on the gangway immediately.'

It is ten minutes before the Officer-of-the-Day accepts the fact that Sugar isn't going to present himself.

'I am sorry, sir,' the Officer-of-the Day explains to Gibraltar's champion wrestler. 'It looks like our Able Seaman Kayne is not currently onboard.'

The big fellow scratches the waistband of his shorts and says that he is going home but will return later to see the Capitan.

The Officer-of-the-Day makes a note.

'What is the normal procedure in cases like this, Quartermaster?' he asks Chats as our visitor mooches over the brow and away towards his van.

'We don't hand our crew members over to irate fathers ... or mothers, sisters, brothers, boyfriends, husbands or casual acquaintances, sir.'

'Is that official Royal Naval policy?'

'I understand that it is, sir. If we hand over every crew member who had ... err ... pregnated a young lady ashore, sir, we would have nobody left onboard.'

'I'm sure that we would have a few. I'll be in the Wardroom if you need me.'

'Very good, sir.'

We watch as the Officer-of-the-Day struts away.

'Looks like Sugar's enviable reputation has caught up with him this time,' says Chats.

'I know.'

'Her old man is a bit of a bruiser, isn't he?'

'According to Sugar, he's a champion wrestler.'

'Oh shit.'

'UP SPIRITS.'

'Her old man is coming back later to see the Skipper,' Chats says to Sugar who is cracking a can of beer open.

'Good job we're sailing at 14:00 then,' he says.

'You are a jammy bastard.'

Sugar smirks. 'There is a God then.'

'I hope the wrestler's daughter was worth it.'

'Yeah,' says Sugar. 'A bit inexperienced if I recall - a little raw around the edges but overflowing with enthusiasm. We were at Europa Point with unrestricted views of North Af...'

'You're unbelievable, you are,' interrupts Chats.

'How can a woman be overflowing?' asks Bagsy.

'Patience, young Baker - you have that wonderful experience to look forward to,' says Sugar.

I down my tot.

'I wonder if pregnated actually mean pregnant?' Sugar asks nobody in particular.

Silence.

I look questioningly at Kit, supposedly the fountain of all knowledge.

'That's a tricky one,' says Kit. 'When applied to us lesser mortals I would say no ... but as it's Sugar I would say yes.'

'THE FIRST LIEUTENANT SPEAKING. PRESIDENTS AND LEADING HANDS OF MESSES ARE TO REPORT MESS MEMBERS WHO ARE ASHORE TO THE REGULATING OFFICER.'

Timber is unaccounted for.

'FALL IN SPECIAL SEA DUTYMEN, HANDS OUT OF THE RIG OF THE DAY CLEAR OFF THE UPPER DECK. CLOSE ALL UPPER DECK SCREEN DOORS AND HATCHES.'

A blue Naval patrol Tilly screams to a halt at the bottom of the gangway and Timber is escorted up the gangway by a couple of Naval Patrol personnel. It's exactly 13:30.

The Officer-of-the-Day nods understandingly and the Naval Patrol skip back over the brow. The Quartermaster hands Timber his station card - jammy bastard.

In the mess Timber explains, 'I was next in the queue when some arsehole from HMS Rooke dressed in Naval Patrol gear came and dragged me out. So I never got my tattoo finished.'

'You'll have to wait until the next time you're in Gib.'

'That could be years - or never.'

At exactly 13:55 we unberth. Sugar and I are hauling in the after spring as a yellow van screeches to a halt on the jetty.

Gurkha's bow drifts slowly away from the jetty as the corpulent figure of Gibraltar's champion wrestler rolls out of the driver's side.

Sugar ducks down. 'Shit.'

'He's a big bugger, isn't he?' I say.

'He is, yeah.'

From the passenger side of the van a young lady with waist-length glistening black hair and a noticeably 'pregnated' stomach emerges.

'Is that the daughter?' I ask.

Sugar raises his head a little, 'No, it's the Virgin Mary. Course it is - well and truly pregnated eh? Europa Point has got a lot to answer for. I bet she ...'

'It's a ferkin Sugar lump!' I declare. 'How long since we were last in Gib?'

'I worked it out. Two hundred and fifty-eight days since Europa Point.'

'And what's the average length of a female pregnancy?'

'Nine months isn't it?' says Sugar.

'That's three quarters of a year then.'

'Err, that'll be right,' says Sugar. 'I like the bit about the Sugar lump - that's funny.'

'So if I divide three hundred and sixty-five by four and then multiply by three I'll get the number of days for a Gibraltarian pregnancy.'

'If you say so.'

I poke my chest. 'Mental arithmetic, Shugs - simple mental arithmetic.' I write my sum in the air. 'Three-six-five divided by four is ninety-one and a bit. Ninety-one multiplied by three is exactly two hundred and fifty-eight. How many days did you say since you and the champion wrestler's daughter played hide-the-sausage at Europa Point?'

'Two hundred and fifty-eight days. Oowaahhh shit!'

'Shugs, we've gotta get away from Gib ... it's due today.'

The stern rope is removed from the shoreside bollard and our stern drifts slowly away from the jetty.

Sugar's suntan is fading.

'Only joking, Shugs,' I say. 'Ninety-one multiplied by three is two hundred and seventy-three. You've got fifteen days yet.'

'You bastard.'

'Sorry, mate.'

'Are you positive that you're the one responsible for her lump?'

'Pretty confident ... I'm a walking, talking, champion sperm bank you know.'

'Crikey, Shug - that's a declaration and a half. You reckon that your sperm is something special then?'

'Always active ... always ready to go.' Sugar disappears inside a screen door.

The lady with the bump gives *Gurkha* a two-arm wave before her father grabs her arm and pushes her back into the van.

Sugar re-emerges once we are clear of the jetty and the yellow van has departed.

'I hope it grows up to be a staunch Gibraltarian,' says Sugar with a strange, reflective expression on his face. 'Male or female. It could be a girl, you know.'

'Suppose,' I say.

'Yeah .. could be a girl.'

'Hope her mum teaches her to keep her knickers on then, when the Navy's visiting Gib in sixteen years' time.'

'Sixteen years and fifteen days,' says Sugar. 'Course if it's a boy, he'll inherit some of my ... err attributes, won't he?'

*

Gurkha 'puts her foot down' and by the morning of the following day we are clear of the north-west corner of the Iberian Peninsula and ready to do battle with the Bay of Biscay. Leave request forms for the forthcoming weekend have been signed and distributed. I am pleased that mine has been granted without any problems. By hook or by crook I will now be able to make it to Wakefield this coming Saturday.

We transit the Bay of Biscuit without problems. According to those who know about such things, the normally feral waters in the emotionally challenged bight south of the Brest peninsular, take a break at this time of year and are reasonably calm.

'FLYING STATIONS.'

Once again Mack and I don't know whose turn it is and we arrive in the Ops Room together. Frothy is sitting in our chair.

'I'll do the last one, lads,' he says.

So Mack and I find seats and watch and listen as Frothy controls the Wasp to the mainland and to the Royal Naval Air Station *Yeovilton*. Lots of hackneyed pleasantries are exchanged between himself and Pontius. Mack and I don't get a mention.

Once Pontius is under the control of *Yeovilton*, Frothy hangs up his headphones. 'Pete, you're going on to Dryad to do an RP1s course. Maybe I'll see you there: I'm joining the instructional staff later on this month.'

'Be weird if you end up being my course instructor.'

'Wouldn't it? Best of luck anyway, Able Seaman Broadbent, you've done OK onboard Gurkha.'

'Thanks, PO.' We shake hands.

'And you too, Able Seaman McCubbin. You're going to HMS Cochrane for a while I believe.'

'Aye, PO.'

'Gone all Scottish already eh?'

'Och aye.'

'I understand that your plan is to purchase your discharge and train for the clergy?'

'It is, PO.'

'So you've heard the call,' says Frothy looking at the Ops Room deckhead. 'From the big fella, from the man in charge?'

'I have ... aye.'

'I can't change your mind, Able Seaman McCubbin ... can I?'

'Sorry, PO.'

'So when you're on the altar doing baptisms or conducting a wedding or a funeral will you spare a thought for your days onboard HMS Gurkha?'

'I doubt it very much. I'll probably have more important things on my mind.'

'Blimey Mack, that's very profound,' I say.

Frothy holds his hands out. 'Thanks for all your efforts, lads. It's been a pleasure working with you. The best of luck with whatever you both choose to do in the future. Say a prayer for me, Able Seaman McCubbin.'

'Of course I will, PO,' says Mack.

*

Wednesday 3rd August 1966. The sun has long since set as *Gurkha* enters the Firth of Forth. The islands we pass are black and lifeless. A yellow-windowed train trundles across the Forth Railway Bridge as we lay out our berthing ropes and wires. We don't expect the Rosyth Dockyard staff to be here to welcome us home. Throughout the ship the Scots are talking to each other in strange, high-pitched, excitable 'tongues'.

We slide past a hardy bunch of local dockies with their hands stuffed firmly in their pockets: they don't look as though they are interested in taking our lines. Sugar throws a perfect heaving line towards them just in case. It arches skywards and is stopped from snaking back into the waters of the Forth by one of the bunch, who traps it with a booted foot. A group of three haul over our head rope.

A small local welcoming party, some waving the Saltire, appear from around the corner of one of the sheds and trudge towards us.

Once the brow is rigged, a lengthy line of our Scottish crew hurtle ashore. Some are greeted by members of the welcoming party. Others skulk quietly away towards the unlit Dockyard Gate. There are lots of Scottish-sounding expletives in the Rosyth dockyard air.

Mack McCubbin, whose family live in Edinburgh, is resplendent in his best civilian suit and well-shined shoes as I get back down the mess.

'That's the quickest I've seen you change, Mack,' I say.

'I'm on leave and draft, Pete. If I don't see yae again, all the best.' He holds out his hand and smiles.

'Good on ya, Mack.'

'Have a good leave, Pete. Thanks for all your help.'

Kit gives us a farewell wave as he brandishes his leave pass. 'Goodbye Gurkha, Hello HMS Excellent and good old Pompey.'

We shake hands and exchange some disparaging remarks before he drags his bulging kit bag up the mess ladder and away.

There is a definite change in the messdeck atmosphere once it is Scot free.

'I'll miss their dour sense of humour,' I say.

'Pardon?' says Jan.

'I'll miss their dour sense of humour.'

'We can be a bunch of sarcastic bastards, can't we?' exclaims Jan, stifling a giggle.

'We English?' I ask.

'Yeah.'

'You going to the Dockyard Canteen tomorrow, Shug?' I ask. 'To let Sorcha welcome you home in the time-honoured fashion?'

'It's difficult to say no,' says Sugar.

'You could be a Dad by now, Shug ... in Gib,' says Jan.

'I reckon you've got some time to go yet, Shug,' I do a quick mental calculation. 'You might be a walking, talking, champion sperm bank, but nature will take its course I should imagine.'

'I know,' whispers Sugar. 'Makes you think about things in a different, more mature way though, doesn't it?'

'So you going to see Sorcha or not?' I ask.

'I might pop in for a wet or two sometime tomorrow.'

The mess telephone rings. Jan answers it 'University of Seamanship, Principle Lecturer speaking.' He listens for a while. 'Sugar, it's for you.'

Sugar slowly strolls down the mess.

'It's Sorcha,' whispers Jan as he covers the wrong end of the phone.

Sugar hesitates and takes a deep breath before taking the offered telephone.

'How does he ferkin do it?' Jan asks me.

I shrug my shoulders.

Sugar whispers something into the telephone before placing it back onto its cradle. 'Can you do the rest of my duty, Pete? The insatiable Sorcha needs some four-letter attention.'

'What an inconvenience,' says Chats without raising his eyes from the book he's reading.

'When duty calls,' says Sugar as he flings open his locker.

'Hang about - I haven't agreed to do the rest of your duty yet, mate.' I say.

'Tomorrow's tot?' says Sugar as he extracts a shirt from his locker and gives it an enthusiastic waft.

'That'll do nicely,' I say. 'Give Sorcha one for me.'

'If I can slip it in to a busy schedule,' says Sugar as he buttons his shirt.

Later in the evening I get a shore telephone call from Lorna. She says that she is calling to welcome me back to Scotland and to check that I'm OK. I say that I'm well and ask how her family is. Regretfully she reports that they are all in good health. We wish each other a fond farewell ... and that's it. I was ready to say I was duty but I never got the chance. A part of me was really cheesed-off that she didn't ask to see me.

The following day Sugar is typically tight-lipped about his night with Sorcha. We ask him - no, we beseech him - for details but he doesn't divulge much.

'Did you manage to give her one for me?' I ask.

'I think I did yeah,' says Sugar, looking at the deckhead for inspiration. 'But I don't remember exactly which one it was.'

'Pass your tot over then.'

Sugar's tot is definitely the best I've ever had. I only drink half of it and hand him his glass.

He looks longingly at the remaining half. 'You're a real mate, Pete.'

'I know I am.'

*

It's Friday 5th July and I'm on a long weekend. The weather improves dramatically as the train sweeps through the Scotland-England border. In the outskirts of Newcastle a sliver of sunlight manages to streak through the cloud canopy for a while.

As the train slows to a stop at Newcastle's main station, the two Geordie greenies sharing my carriage bid me farewell in true Naval fashion: 'Hope you get stacks, Pete.'

'And you both,' I reply.

The remainder of the journey to Pudsey is uneventful.

At home my brother Tony says, 'Bloody hell, you're tanned.'

'That's the Persian Gulf for ya,' I explain.

What shall I wear for my date tomorrow? Mum says that we can expect rain in the afternoon and she's not often wrong.

Saturday dinnertime. I select the one and only suit that fits me: the dark blue mohair jobby, made for me by Sew-sew onboard *HMS Lincoln* a couple of years ago. It requires a brush and a little fresh air to put it into impressive order. To complement my suit I have a white shirt, a dark tie and well-polished shoes. I decide to drape my raincoat over my arm ... just in case Mum is right and Wakefield rains on me.

So it is that on Saturday 6th August 1966, I catch a bus into Wakefield from my home in Newton Hill. I leave myself plenty of time so that I can stroll contemplatively from the bus station to the Mecca. What is Margaret going to be like? Despite what they say, photographs can lie. What if she's sent me pictures of a friend and she's like the 'back end of a bus'? What if she didn't like my photographs? What if she has decided not to bother? What if she has had a better offer?

In her letter Margret said that she will be driving a red Mini. I pace the pavement outside the Mecca; the traffic is one-way so I only have to concentrate on one direction. There are a good number of red Minis on the Wakefield roads today.

At 15:00 exactly a red Mini pulls up and a lady leans

over to open the passenger door. I bend down and mouth 'Margaret?'

She nods.

I get in the car and shake hands with the gorgeous Margaret Mary Lamin. In those opening seconds I see a beautiful young lady who is giving me the most wonderful welcoming smile. She is wearing an exquisitely cut, cream Jaeger suit and has long, shapely nyloned legs and high-heeled shoes. I take it all in. It's a meeting that changes my life forever.

It begins to rain and one of Margaret's well-manicured fingers flicks the windscreen wiper toggle switch.

Off we go.

******

PS: Eleven months later the delectable Margaret Mary Lamin and the very average Peter Nigel Broadbent are married. Forty-eight years on, we have two wonderful children (Paul and Helen), three fabulous grandchildren (James, Oscar and Star) and a whole stack of fantastic memories. Unfortunately the Jaeger suit, along with the red Mini, have long gone.

Lightning Source UK Ltd.
Milton Keynes UK
UKHW020850051021
391705UK00013B/765

9 781911 105404